Introduction to Mortgages & Mortgage Backed Securities

Introduction to Mortgages & Mortgage Backed Securities

Richard Green
Lusk Chair in Real Estate,
University of Southern California,
Los Angeles, CA, USA

AMSTERDAM • BOSTON • HEIDELBERG • LONDON
NEW YORK • OXFORD • PARIS • SAN DIEGO
SAN FRANCISCO • SINGAPORE • SYDNEY • TOKYO

Academic Press is an imprint of Elsevier

Academic Press is an imprint of Elsevier
The Boulevard, Langford Lane, Kidlington, Oxford OX5 1GB, UK
225 Wyman Street, Waltham, MA 02451, USA
Radarweg 29, PO Box 211, 1000 AE Amsterdam, The Netherlands
525 B Street, Suite 1800, San Diego, CA 92101-4495, USA

Notice
No responsibility is assumed by the publisher for any injury and/or damage to persons or
property as a matter of products liability, negligence or otherwise, or from any use or operation
of any methods, products, instructions or ideas contained in the material herein. Because of rapid
advances in the medical sciences, in particular, independent verification of diagnoses and drug
dosages should be made

British Library Cataloguing in Publication Data
A catalogue record for this book is available from the British Library

Library of Congress Catalog Number
A catalog record for this book is available from the Library of Congress

ISBN–13: 978-0-12-401743-6

For information on all Academic Press publications visit
our website at http://store.elsevier.com/

Printed and bound in the United States of America

14 15 16 17 18   10 9 8 7 6 5 4 3 2 1

Working together
to grow libraries in
developing countries

www.elsevier.com • www.bookaid.org

Contents

11. The Yield Curve, Monte Carlo Methods, and the Option-Adjusted Spread

12. A Brief Discussion of Duration and Convexity

13. The Rise and Fall of Fannie Mae and Freddie Mac: Lessons Learned and Options for Reform

Companion Website for this Book:
http://booksite.elsevier.com/9780124017436/

Contributors and Acknowledgments

Vanessa G. Perry The GW School of Business, Washington, DC, USA
Anne B. Schnare AB Schnare Associates LLC, Washington, DC, USA

Hannah Green, Morgan Green and Elizabeth Reynolds for reading the draft.
Paul Carrillo for providing the appraisal data.

A Brief History of Mortgages

Mortgages have been around for nearly 1000 years, if not longer. James Kent's Commentaries of American Law, Volume 4, notes:

The English law of mortgages appears to have been borrowed in a great degree from the civil law; and the Roman hypotheca corresponded very closely with the description of a mortgage in our law. The land was retained by the debtor, and the creditor was entitled to his action hypothecaria (obtain the surrender of the thing mortgaged), to obtain possession of the pledge, when the debtor was in default; and the debtor had his action to regain possession, when the debt was paid, or satisfied out of the profits, and he might redeem at any time before a sale.

We can find references to mortgages in the United States stretching back at least as far as 1766, when the first mortgage was issued in St. Louis. The instrument has been around for a long time.

For the purposes of this book, however, our discussion will begin with the nineteenth century. Two things important for the development of mortgages in the United States occurred during this time: the development of legal recourse for lenders when borrowers failed to repay their mortgages, and the development of primary and secondary channels for financing mortgages.

Let us begin with the definition of a mortgage: it is a loan that is secured by real property. The word has its roots in French, where its literal meaning is dead (*mort*) pledge (*gage*). The pledge part of the word is straightforward, but the meaning of death is not. One interpretation is as follows:[1]

---

1. See www.thefreedictionary.com/mortgage

Introduction to Mortgages & Mortgage Backed Securities.
http://dx.doi.org/10.1016/B978-0-12-401743-6.00001-9

The great jurist Sir Edward Coke, who lived from 1552 to 1634, has explained why the term mortgage comes from the Old French words mort, *"dead," and* gage, *"pledge." It seemed to him that it had to do with the doubtfulness of whether or not the mortgagor will pay the debt. If the mortgagor does not, then the land pledged to the mortgagee as security for the debt is taken from him for ever, and so dead to him upon condition, &c. And if he doth pay the money, then the pledge is dead as to the [mortgagee].*

Modern Americans might assume that death refers to the self-amortization feature of mortgages, but the fact is that mortgages generally did not amortize (there were exceptions) until the 1930s, in the overall scheme of things. Mortgages also tended to have short lives: Snowden (1987) showed that the average life of a mortgage ranged from 1.92 to 5.99 years, depending on region of the country. Rose and Snowden (2013) describe the typical method of mortgage finance for a good part of the nineteenth century:

The share accumulation plan was the contractual foundation of the building and loan movement in the U.S. In the earliest B&Ls, all members joined in order to eventually become borrowers. From the outset each member would commit to accumulate shares of the size he needed to pay for a home, through the payment of compulsory monthly dues. For example, if a member desired to accumulate $1000 for a house, he would subscribe for five shares with maturity value of $200 each. Members would then take turns in borrowing from the pot of money created by these dues. By the time it was a member's turn to borrow, he would have already accumulated part of his shares (and retained dividends) that would eventually be used to pay off the loan in full.

Share accumulation loans were straight, balloon loans that also required the creation of a sinking fund in the form of shares to repay the loan at maturity. Thus, they were quite different than balloon loans offered by other lenders that did little to require borrowers plan for repayment. Of course, the B&L loan required not just monthly dues but also interest payments, on the full amount of the loan since that amount remained outstanding until the shares matured and the loan was cancelled. However, as a borrower's sinking fund grew, it would accumulate retained dividends that in some sense offset the interest payments. The pace of these retained dividends would determine the maturity of the loan, which was indefinite.

Rose and Snowden go on to show that while mortgage amortization started to become a feature of some loans by 1893, it was still a fairly unusual phenomenon. Their best estimate of the share of direct reduction, or amortizing loans, just before the introduction of New Deal programs was about 20 percent, meaning that it had become an important but by no means ubiquitous method of mortgage finance. This would change with the introduction of New Deal programs.

Before moving on, it is important to recognize that mortgage laws developed quite differently across states, particularly with respect to the issue of foreclosure. Andra Ghent provides an excellent treatment of the development of mortgage law across the various states in the United States. We will discuss the issues of judicial and nonjudicial foreclosure as well as recourse and nonrecourse lending elsewhere in this book.

THE GREAT DEPRESSION, THE NEW DEAL, AND THE TRANSFORMATION OF THE AMERICAN MORTGAGE MARKET

Five New Deal era programs provided the foundation for the modern US mortgage system. Four of these programs were specifically related to housing finance, and one restored confidence in the US banking system as a whole. The four programs related to housing finance were the Federal Housing Administration (FHA), the Home Owners' Loan Corporation (HOLC), the Federal Home Loan Bank System, and the Federal National Mortgage Association. The program related to banking was the Federal Deposit Insurance Corporation (FDIC). We will discuss each in turn, except for the Federal Home Loan Bank System, which we will discuss when recounting the Savings-and-Loan era of home lending.

In 1933, many American banks were insolvent. The insolvency arose from many defaulted mortgages on bank balance sheets. Many of these defaults were maturity defaults. That is to say, borrowers made the payments required of them until their loans came due, but the same borrowers were unable to make the final balloon payment that was ultimately required of them.

In response to this, the Roosevelt administration was able to get Congress to authorize the HOLC. The HOLC got into the business of buying defaulted loans from banks using funds from the US Treasury. The government floated bonds for the purpose of raising money to purchase the defaulted mortgages. The HOLC bought loans at a discount—not so large that it threatened banks with insolvency, but large enough that the HOLC could offer principal reduction to borrowers. Rose (2011) shows that the HOLC used the mechanism of generous appraisals to make terms attractive to lenders. The HOLC "discovered" more value in houses than perhaps was warranted by market conditions, which gave it the fig leaf it needed to offer generous prices to banks for the mortgages it purchased.

The most important thing that the HOLC did to provide relief to borrowers, however, was to convert the mortgages from short-term loans with large balloon payments into self amortizing 15-year fixed payment mortgages. Although fixed payment mortgages existed before the New Deal, they were not ubiquitous, and usually had terms of less than 15 years.

The HOLC bought and reconstituted loans for four years, 1933 through 1936. After that, the mortgage finance system was considerably more stable and the HOLC no longer found it necessary to purchase loans. It stayed in business for another 15 years until the loans it had on the books were paid off and then in 1952 it put itself out of business. It was thus a rare example of a government agency that came into existence to solve the crisis, and then went out of business when the crisis was over. As we shall see one scene later, another example of such an agency, the Resolution Trust Corporation, was also put in business to solve a mortgage-related crisis, and again put itself out of business when the crisis was resolved. Courtemanche and Snowden (2011) and Crossney and Bartelt (2005) show that the HOLC was valuable to restoring macroeconomic stability.

The second important entity that arose from New Deal mortgage policy was the FHA, which was authorized in 1934. Lenders were wary of lending to borrowers who did not make large down payments. This prevented many Americans from acquiring a mortgage, which meant that it prevented many Americans from becoming homeowners. The FHA was created to insure loans that had relatively low down payments. Specifically, the government would collect insurance premiums that would go into a fund to ensure that lenders would not bear losses on defaulted loans. Beyond that, the federal government would put its full faith and credit behind the loans.

The first FHA loans required down payments of 25 percent. Seventy-five percent loan-to-value ratio loans were considered risky at the time. By allowing Americans to buy houses with a 25 percent down payment, the FHA program helped stabilize the housing market.

Finally, with respect to new mortgage institutions, Congress authorized the establishment of the Federal National Mortgage Association in 1938. The Federal National Mortgage Association, which would come to be known as Fannie Mae, was initially a government agency. Its purpose was to raise money through capital markets (with government backing), and then distribute mortgage funds throughout the country. Fannie Mae remained a very small entity for several decades, but would become considerably more important in the 1970s and especially in the 1980s.

Even though it was not invented specifically for this purpose, perhaps the most important institution for stabilizing housing finance was the FDIC. This entity, which was funded by bank fees and guaranteed by the federal government, assured depositors that their money was safe up to a certain limit. The initial limit was $2500.

The bank panic scene in *It's a Wonderful Life* is among the most iconic scenes in film. The lesson of the scene was that even sound financial institutions can be ruined through depositor panic. Loans, even when sound, are not liquid. This means that if all depositors want their money back at one time, the bank will be unable to produce the cash necessary to fill its obligations.

The only reason however, that all depositors might want their money at once is a collapse in confidence. The invention of the FDIC allowed depositors to be confident about their ability to recover their money at any time from their federally chartered financial institutions; one of the remarkable things about the recent financial crisis was the absence of bank runs. Incidentally, the current ceiling on deposits insured by the FDIC is now $500,000 per depositor per institution.

These institutions evolved after World War II through mechanisms we will talk about next, and they became the backbone of housing finance for many years thereafter.

THE POST WORLD WAR II ERA

In the aftermath of the invention of New Deal programs, housing markets stabilized. Prices, which had fallen 30 percent from peak to trough, started rising again. Even though housing markets did stabilize, they were hardly reignited. New construction remained at low levels in the late 1930s as the Great Depression lingered, and in the early 1940s, as materials were reserved for the war effort instead of consumer goods such as housing.

Housing did reignite immediately after World War II. The country faced a housing shortage, as very little had been built for 16 years. The condition of the country's housing stock was also poor; for example, only around 60 percent of housing units had indoor plumbing (Census of Population and Housing 1940). At the same time, American incomes recovered robustly during World War II, but Americans spent relatively little on consumer goods because of rationing. Consequently, families demanded housing and had large amounts of savings with which to purchase it.

Simultaneously, Congress passed a law that came to be known as the GI Bill of Rights (the formal name of this law was the Servicemen's Readjustment Act of 1944). Among other things, the GI Bill established the Veterans Administration (VA) loan program. The VA program was very much like the FHA program; it was an insurance program that allowed borrowers to get loans with small down payments because the loans were backed by the full faith and credit of the US government.

The VA program, however, went a step further than the FHA program in that it allowed veterans to buy houses with very low down-payment loans. In fact, veterans could buy homes with down payments as small as $150. Thus the program did two things; it allowed millions of veterans returning home from Europe and the Pacific to purchase a new home, and it provided an experiment for the success of very low down-payment loans. As it happened, the default rate on VA loans in the 1950s was too high to have been sustained by a private sector entity required to return profits to its owners, but not so high as to be ruinous. It is important to remember that the VA program was more than a housing program; it was also a subsidy to compensate veterans for their service.

The combination of a decade and a half of little housing construction, higher incomes, high levels of saving, and the VA and FHA programs led to a boom in housing construction from 1945 into the 1950s. At the same time, the home-ownership rate rose sharply, from 43.6 percent in 1940, to 55 percent in 1950, to 61.9 percent in 1960 (Census of Population and Housing 1940, 1950, 1960).

Some scholars argue that federal programs not only allowed for a rapid increase in the demand for housing and a rapid increase in the homeownership rate, but also changed the composition of housing in the United States.

In particular, they argue that housing finance encouraged movement from the cities to the suburbs. A few also argue that housing finance encouraged developers to move away from mixed-use development to court single-use development. These statements are somewhat controversial, but certain elements of the FHA and VA programs are consistent with them.

First, the appraisal guidelines for the HOLC, the FHA program, and the VA program all contained neighborhood grading schemes where grades were tied to race and ethnicity. For example, the map of Philadelphia (Figure 1.1)

FIGURE 1.1   Philadelphia map. *Source: National Archives and Records Administration.*

has red- and green-shaded areas. The areas shaded in red had a large African American population and were thus deemed by the government as being less desirable neighborhoods than those with smaller African American populations. Federal program documents encouraged appraisers to downgrade values in neighborhoods that were shaded in red. This discouraged capital from flowing into these neighborhoods. At the same time, suburban neighborhoods were shaded in green, reflecting the government's perception that the neighborhoods were desirable, principally because of their ethnic makeup. Because suburban neighborhoods had small African American populations, in part because of the deplorable existence of restricted deed covenants, capital flowed easily to them.

So at the margin, there is no doubt that the FHA and VA programs encouraged migration from central cities to suburbs. It is difficult, however, to evaluate the magnitude of this capital market effect. In other countries—countries that never had FHA or VA type programs—we have also seen substantial suburbanization in the post-World War II era. For example, the population of the city of Paris has shrunk since 1950, while the population of metropolitan Paris has nearly doubled since then.[2]

As for the issue of mixed use versus single use, it is true that FHA loans have only financed housing. This has generally been true of Fannie Mae loans as well. Some urbanists have argued that this led to the deteriorating market share of mixed-use development since World War II. However, the postwar era has seen Euclidean zoning become ubiquitous. Such zoning, which separates uses, is more likely the source of the decline of mixed-use development than are financing arrangements.

Between the end of World War II and the 1960s, housing finance in the United States worked quite well. Most housing finance came from depository institutions. Among depositories, the most important for housing finance were Savings and Loans (S&Ls). As Figure 1.2 shows, in 1970, more than 70 percent of all mortgages were held by depositories.

S&Ls were highly specialized institutions. They had certain limits placed upon them. For example, they were local institutions, and were not permitted to lend beyond a certain radius, although the radius got larger with time. They also were required to specialize in home lending. In exchange for these requirements, S&Ls got access to capital through the Federal Home Loan Bank system, were permitted to pay their depositors slightly higher interest rates than banks, and received certain tax benefits. It's worth taking a little time to discuss each of these features.

The Federal Home Loan Bank system was organized as a cooperative system by the Hoover administration in 1932. The system created 12 banks whose function was to lend to lenders. It was essentially the first housing-related government-sponsored enterprise.

---

2. www.un.org/esa/population/publications/wup2001/WUP2001_CH6.pdf

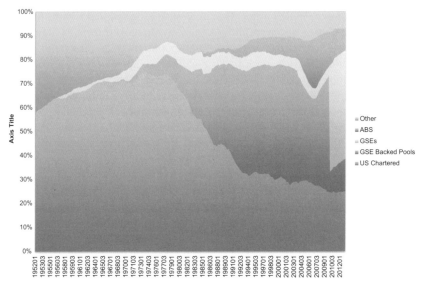

FIGURE 1.2 Market share of mortgage debt outstanding by holder *Source: Flow of Funds Data Table L.218 and Author Calculations.*

Each Federal Home Loan Bank has shareholders, which are the financial institutions that borrow money from the bank. Total liabilities of any one of the Federal Home Loan Banks are also the liabilities of the other banks; this is what it means to be a co-op. The Federal Home Loan Banks borrow money in capital markets, and then use that money to make advances to depositories that can be used to finance mortgages. The fact that the Federal Home Loan Bank system is jointly and severally liable for the debts of any one bank may explain why its creditors look so favorably upon it. However, as with other government-sponsored enterprises, the capital markets presume that the Federal Home Loan Bank system carries an implicit guarantee from the federal government and consequently issues very low-risk securities.

The ability of S&Ls to access capital through advances from Federal Home Loan Banks gave them a cost advantage relative to other financial institutions with respect to funding mortgages. This in part explains how they came to dominate the mortgage market for more than 20 years.

Beyond Federal Home Loan Bank advances, S&Ls use deposits to fund mortgages. From 1933 until 1986, the Glass-Steagall act, in particular, regulation Q—one of the regulations that implemented that act—prohibited depositories from paying depositors more than a ceiling amount of interest on savings accounts. S&Ls, however, were permitted to pay 50 basis points more in interest than banks. This allowed S&Ls, also known as thrift institutions, to attract capital they otherwise might not have.

Finally, thrift institutions were permitted to deduct potential mortgage losses against profits for tax purposes. Although this was entirely reasonable in

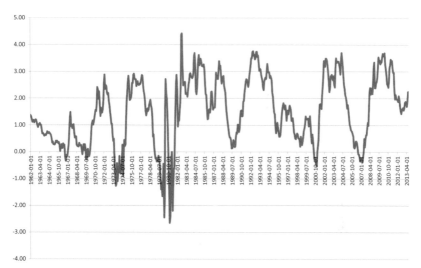

FIGURE 1.3   10 year constant maturity treasury rate - 3 Month CMT. *Source: St. Louis Fed.*

principle, the amount of losses they were allowed to deduct was typically much higher than default losses they might have actually expected. As such, thrifts had a substantial tax advantage over banks.

So for many years, S&Ls constituted boring business. The old joke was that it was the 3–6–3 business: pay depositors 3 percent interest, collect 6 percent interest from borrowers, and be on the golf course at three in the afternoon. S&Ls were small, local, monoline, profitable institutions.

The 1960s changed all of this for a simple reason; for the first time since World War II, short-term interest rates rose sharply, whereas long-term rates rose at a slower pace. This created a duration mismatch problem for S&Ls. The year 1966 was particularly noteworthy as the first year in which S&Ls faced major liquidity problems since the Great Depression (Walter 2006).

As Figure 1.3 shows, the yield curve in 1966 turned negative. The yield curve is the difference between long-term interest rates and short-term interest rates. Most of the time, long-term interest rates are higher than short-term interest rates. S&Ls borrowing started short and went long. Now think about the problem facing S&Ls when short-term interest rates rose. They had many long-term mortgages (the typical fixed rate mortgage in 1966 had a 20-year term) on their balance sheet paying interest rates of between 4.5 and 5.5 percent. When short-term interest rates rose past 4 percent, S&Ls margins disappeared. What was once a profitable business became at best a break-even business and in some cases a losing business.

Regulation Q made things even worse. Because S&Ls were forbidden from paying depositors rates that were better than treasury rates, money flowed out of S&Ls deposits and into US treasuries. This led S&Ls to become insolvent.

It is perhaps not a coincidence that the source of higher interest rates was the large deficit the US government began to run to finance the Vietnam War and the War on Poverty. The Johnson administration, as a result, began to look for ways to make the federal deficit appear smaller. One of the mechanisms the administration used for doing this was the privatization of Fannie Mae. Fannie Mae debt moved in 1968 from the balance sheet of the federal government to the private sector. The federal government invented Ginnie Mae to finance FHA and VA loans, but Fannie Mae was permitted to finance purely private-sector business.

S&Ls were unhappy with the development of Fannie Mae as an entity that could provide mortgage finance in the private sector. In particular, the S&Ls consider themselves at a disadvantage because they were local institutions and were competing against mortgage bankers who could raise money nationally, or even internationally, through Fannie Mae. S&Ls quite correctly noted that Fannie Mae could provide investors with the advantage of geographical diversification in a way that they themselves could not.

In response to the concerns of S&Ls, Congress created Freddie Mac. Freddie Mac's purpose was to allow S&Ls to sell their mortgages to investors throughout the country. As we shall see, Fannie Mae and Freddie Mac evolved to become very similar types of institutions, but at their origins, they were actually different from one another. Fannie Mae was known as the S&Ls for mortgage bankers, while Freddie Mac was known as the mortgage banker for S&Ls. The difference in character between the two institutions is revealed by their balance sheets 20 years after Freddie Mac's creation. At this time, Fannie Mae had 114 billion dollars of mortgages on its balance sheet, while Freddie Mac owned a tiny share of that at 21 billion dollars.[3] The reason for the difference is that Freddie Mac was not in the portfolio mortgage business, but rather the mortgage guaranty business.

To understand how the mortgage guaranty business works, we need to go back to 1968, which was the year that Ginnie Mae was created and issued its first mortgage-backed security.

The first mortgage-backed securities were simple pass-through entities. Ginnie Mae gathered together FHA and VA mortgages and bundled them into securities that would then be sold to investors. Each investor received a pro rata share of the cash flows going into the security for mortgage borrowers. So if a particular investor owned 1/30 of the interest in the Ginnie Mae security, the investor would receive 1/30 of the principal and interest payments paid on the specified pool of mortgages in a particular month. Note that all loans within a Ginnie Mae security were backed by the full faith and credit of the US government. Hence Ginnie Mae carried no default risk.

---

3. Balance sheet information comes from the Federal Housing Finance Agency's Annual Report. www.fhfa.gov/webfiles/25320/FHFA2012_AnnualReport-508.pdf

Yet, as Susan Woodward has shown, the interest rates on FHA and VA loans dropped quickly after the invention of the Ginnie Mae mortgage-backed security (United States Senate Banking Committee 2013). Woodward argues that the reason for the drop in interest rates was the introduction of liquidity into the mortgage market. When individual S&Ls owned FHA mortgages, they could not easily sell these mortgages in order to improve their capital position when necessary. With the introduction of Ginnie Maes, anyone holding FHA mortgages could easily sell those mortgages to willing borrowers. Because buyers and sellers of mortgages could now more easily find each other, effective bid-ask spreads for mortgages declined, mortgage markets became more liquid, and spreads between mortgage rates and treasury rates narrowed.

The newly invented Freddie Mac took a lesson from the experience of Ginnie Mae. Freddie Mac decided that the best way to bring liquidity to the private mortgage market was to package private mortgages into mortgage-backed securities and then guaranty timely payment of principal and interest to the buyers of those securities. Freddie Mac issued its first mortgage-backed security, which was known as a participation certificate (PC) in 1971. The use of mortgage-backed securities would change the US mortgage market forever.

It would take a while, however, before mortgage-backed securities would dominate the mortgage market. Financial conditions calmed down during the 1970s. In particular, the yield curve turned sharply positive, and as a consequence deposit-lenders could earn money on spreads between what they charged long-term mortgage borrowers in interest and what they had to pay short-term lenders (depositors). At the same time, the country was experiencing the twentieth century's worst bout of inflation: house prices were rising (in nominal if not in real terms), giving homeowners with fixed-rate mortgages rapid equity buildup. This meant that the default rate on a majority of fixed-rate mortgages was quite low, and so the mortgage business was once again highly profitable.

The late 1970s changed this. First, the late 1970s to early 1980s was a period of substantial economic dislocation. In particular, the rust belt—Ohio, Michigan, and Indiana—lost hundreds of thousands of manufacturing jobs and experienced unemployment rates in excess of 20 percent. This led to a collapse in housing markets in the upper Midwest. Note that prices did not fall because they pricked the bubble, but rather because economic fundamentals turned so sour. The combination of falling house prices and high unemployment meant that people with negative equity in their houses were unable to make their mortgage payments. This led to a steep rise in defaults, particularly in Michigan and Ohio.

At the same time, the yield curve became more steeply negative than at any other time in the twentieth century (see Figure 1.3). The combination of high rates of default and the steep negative yield curve rendered many S&Ls insolvent. The S&Ls were losing money on default because the amount they needed to pay depositors to stay solvent was much higher than the amount they were earning on current mortgages.

To illustrate the problem, consider a simple balance sheet of a simple S&L. The assets of the S&Ls are mortgages. The liabilities are deposits. The balance of assets and liabilities is retained capital. S&Ls typically had capital of 10 percent.

Now suppose a S&L in Ohio saw defaults of 10 percent. Also assume that the cost of a defaulted loan to a S&L was 30 percent. Hence defaults caused the capital position of our example S&L to deteriorate by 30 percent.

Although this was a serious problem, the more serious problem was that the present value of the S&Ls assets fell with the increase in short-term interest rates. Consider a loan paying 6 percent interest annually that had a remaining life of 25 years. Suppose the S&L in our example now needs to pay depositors an interest rate of 12 percent. This would cause the value of the typical loan to fall by nearly 39 percent, essentially wiping out the capital position of the S&L and more.

At this point the US housing finance system was broken. There were few sources of funding for home mortgages; indeed, seller financing or land contracts became a common method of housing finance. This method was of little help to cash-strapped sellers. And so it was that we saw a decline in housing sales from 3.8 million in 1978 to 2.9 million in 1980.[4]

This crisis led to two major changes in the US housing finance system. First, Congress permitted adjustable-rate mortgages, which removed the interest rate risk from lenders and distributed it to borrowers. Peek (1990) shows that the market share of adjustable rate mortgages rose from almost nothing to nearly 70 percent in 1984, and again in 1988.

A really revolutionary thing that happened to the American finance system was the rise of mortgage-backed securities in government-sponsored enterprises. In 1980, the government-sponsored enterprises (GSE) Fannie Mae and Freddie Mac had a very small share of the mortgage market. By the end of the 1980s, the market share of GSE-backed mortgage-backed securities had increased to 50 percent. The United States had moved from a housing finance system that relied principally on deposit to one that relied principally on capital markets.

The GSE system worked quite well between 1980 and 1997 to 1998. Indeed, Americans rightfully considered their mortgage system the envy of the world, and other countries looked at the United States as a country they wished to emulate in this regard.

But something changed in 1997. The charters of the GSEs became more valuable than ever, but this ultimately made them dangerous. The events that caused this change were the Asian financial crisis, the long-term capital management crisis, and the Russian financial crisis—events that contributed to an atmosphere of panic that substantially reduced the liquidity of capital markets. Spreads for all types of debt instruments widened. The commercial real estate

---

4. Source: Statistical Abstract of the United States, 1982–1983, Table 1345.

market was especially hard hit; spreads not only widened, but in some instances, lending disappeared altogether. (See Maris and Segal 2002, Exhibit 1).

The one exception to the liquidity problem was the residential mortgage market. This market was cooking along while panics infected other markets. Presumably one of the reasons for this is that national markets presumed that Fannie Mae and Freddie Mac had the implicit backing of the US government behind them. There are a number of reasons why markets made this assumption despite the fact that in their prospectuses Fannie Mae and Freddie Mac insisted that they had no such backing.

To understand why investors assumed (correctly, as it turned out) that the government would bail out those with positions in mortgage-backed securities issued by Fannie Mae and Freddie Mac, we need to return to 1968 when Fannie Mae was privatized. One of Lyndon Johnson's motives for privatizing Fannie Mae was to remove its debt from the federal government's balance sheet.

While technically this happened, markets couldn't imagine that debt that had been issued with the backing of the US government would not ultimately continue to have the backing of the government. Perhaps investors should have assumed instead that once these debts had been run, they would be subject to the discipline of the market.

We have lots of evidence, however, that investors made no such assumption. For starters, rating agencies gave Fannie Mae and Freddie Mac the highest possible ratings. If one looks at Moody's and Standard & Poor's[5] judgments of the companies, however, the high ratings assigned to them reflected the rating agencies' assumption that the federal government would indeed backstop the obligations of the government-sponsored enterprises.

Because Fannie Mae and Freddie Mac received AAA ratings, they were deemed acceptable investments by foreign central banks, and hence got woven into foreign policy issues as well as financial markets.

Because of the implicit government backing, Fannie Mae and Freddie Mac were able to stay in the mortgage market while other lenders were leaving their respective markets. But while spreads on Fannie Mae and Freddie Mac securities did not widen as much as in other types of bond instruments, they did widen. Both GSEs aggressively purchased mortgages at these fairly wide spreads; in other words, they bought low. One of the reasons they were able to be aggressive was that the market perceived government backing.

When markets returned to normal around 1999, spreads narrowed and Fannie Mae and Freddie Mac mortgage-backed securities issued in 1998 became more valuable. Consequently the GSEs were able to profit from the crisis of 1997 and 1998. While a general rule of finance should be that extraordinary profits are a reflection of good fortune, in most cases the managers who earn

---

5. See, for example, www.moodys.com/research/MOODYS-AFFIRMS-DEBT-AND-PREFERRED-STOCK-RATINGS-OF-FREDDIE-MAC-PR_69297

those extraordinary profits believe they are the result of their brilliant invest-ment strategy. As such, profitability, whether it is the product of luck or invest-ment strategy, can lead to arrogance.

In the cases of Fannie Mae and Freddie Mac, this arrogance was reflected in their managements' views that the GSEs could ignore the usual rules of accounting. In the case of Freddie Mac, the senior management did not believe that generally accepted accounting principles produced accurate depictions of the company's well-being. Rather than explain their view in a management dis-cussion, an analysis, or an MDA statement, the senior management at Freddie Mac decided to ignore accounting rules and issue earnings statements based on their view of the economics of the company.

Ironically, the auditor of Freddie Mac was Arthur Anderson, which also audited Enron. The collapse of Enron brought about the collapse of Arthur Anderson, and so Freddie Mac needed to find a new auditor. The auditor selected, Price Waterhouse Coopers, in 2003 found irregularities in the com-pany's previous years' accounting practices. These irregularities forced the company to restate its earnings, and led to an internal investigation of the com-pany, which in turn led to the relief of the chairman, the president, and the chief financial officer of the company. In the wake of these revelations, the Office of Federal Housing Enterprise Oversight (OFHEO), which was the regulator of government-sponsored enterprises, placed sanctions on Freddie Mac. Among the most important of these was a requirement that Freddie Mac increase the amount of capital that it had behind the mortgages that it owned and/or guar-anteed. As Freddie Mac stood at this time in the wake of the scandal, it was not in the best position to raise capital by issuing new stock. Therefore it needed to scale back on its participation in the mortgage market. This would leave an opening for the private-label market to increase its market share. We will talk at greater length about the private-label market later.

In 2004, Fannie Mae had an accounting scandal of its own. In contrast to Freddie Mac, which actually understated its earnings in order to smooth them, Fannie Mae overstated its earnings. This was particularly problematic, because the overstated earnings produced large bonuses for Fannie Mae's senior man-agement. As with Freddie Mac, the entire senior management team of Fannie Mae was let go in the wake of its own accounting scandal. OFHEO would hand down similar sanctions to Fannie Mae as it had to Freddie Mac.

Figure 1.2 shows Fannie Mae and Freddie Mac market shares of mortgage loans outstanding from their beginning to the present. It is striking how much the market share of the two companies fell in the wake of their respective disgraces. And yet, the mortgage market hardly missed a beat as Fannie and Freddie slowly withdrew from it.

The reason for this was the rise of the private-label market. Private-label mortgage-backed securities are mortgage-backed securities that contain "non-conforming" mortgages. Nonconforming loans tend to fall into two categories: they are either loans that do not meet the underwriting requirements of Fannie

Mae and Freddie Mac, or they are loans whose balances are too large to be eligible for purchase by Fannie Mae and Freddie Mac. The loans that failed to meet the credit quality required by Fannie and Freddie are generally referred to as subprime mortgages.

One of the reasons for the success of the private-label market is that mortgages were deemed to be very low risk investments. There was some foundation for this view. Between 1997 and 2003, the incidence of default on mortgages was low. The cost of default to Fannie and Freddie over this period of time was less than one basis point, or 1/100 of 1 percent, per year. Ironically, some of those who would later criticize the GSEs for being too reckless criticized Fannie and Freddie for charging too much for their loan guarantee and for not doing enough to serve low-income borrowers.

But there was a specific reason why loans were so low over that time: house prices rose sharply and rose everywhere. Nearly all homeowners had substantial equity in their homes and therefore had no incentive to default. The breadth of strong housing performance throughout the United States was a phenomenon that had not been seen since the 1960s. This may well have lulled lenders and investors into complacency.

While we will cover the mortgage chain in greater depth in another chapter of this book, it is worth briefly describing here. Between 2002 and 2007, most loans were originated through the so-called retail channel. Brokers would accept applications from borrowers and shop them around to lenders. They would be compensated based on production—in other words, brokers would only get paid upon the successful completion of the loan origination. Their compensation was not tied in any way to loan performance.

Lenders, who had money available to fund mortgages, would compete for loan applicants. Between 2002 and 2007, the lending business was highly competitive, meaning that economic profits were driven to zero. This meant an environment where some lenders would inexorably lose money. The best-known lenders at this time included Countrywide, Washington Mutual, and Indy Mac, none of which are with us today.

Lenders sought to get the mortgages that they purchased off their balance sheets as quickly as possible. They would sell their loans into private-label mortgage-backed securities that were underwritten by investment banks. They would however retain the servicing rights on the loans that they funded. So long as the loans caused no trouble these servicing rights would be quite valuable. Servicing usually is simply the process of collecting principal and interest payments on current loans. When mortgages perform well, the cost of servicing remains low, and servicers can earn easy cash flow. Hence lenders have strong incentives to fund as many mortgages as possible. Figure 1.4 demonstrates the enormous run up in mortgage debt outstanding in the United States between 1997 and 2008.

At the same time, investment banks were eager to purchase loans from lenders, package them into securities, and sell them to investors. Investment banks,

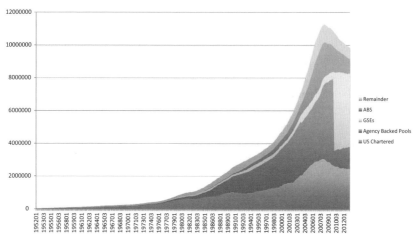

FIGURE 1.4   Holders of mortgage debt outstanding 1952–2012. *Source: Federal Reserve Flow of Funds Table L.218.*

like lenders, collected fees on consummated transactions. These institutions assured investors that mortgage-backed securities were safe using three mechanisms: First, they pointed out that default costs had been low for some time. Second, they chopped mortgage-backed securities into tranches, which we will discuss in greater depth in a later chapter. They were unlikely to face losses from their investments. Finally, investment banks would pay rating agencies a fee to rate mortgage-backed securities. Rating agencies often rated mortgage-backed securities AAA even with limited subordination.

The reassurances worked, as investor demand for mortgage-backed securities—particularly AAA-rated securities—was so large that the market needed to create synthetic securities in order to satiate demand. Synthetic securities are those that do not actually have underlying real assets, but rather perform based on the characteristics of a so-called reference set of assets.

But while there was hunger for AAA-rated securities, there was also hunger for less highly rated securities. We know this because nonconforming mortgages could not have been originated in the absence of demand for both senior and junior tranches. In fact, while many analysts (including, sadly, the author of this book) claimed that one of the problems that created the financial crisis was a lack of skin in the game on the part of many market participants, many investment banks did in fact have skin in the game. In particular, Lehman Brothers and Bear Stearns, as well as Merrill Lynch, owned the less highly rated securities. The reason for this is that the yields on the securities were handsome, and as we have already said, the costs appeared to be very low. Hence these highly leveraged institutions were able to earn very high returns on equity by investing in junior tranches of mortgage-backed securities.

Of course the underlying assumption for mortgage performance was that house prices would continue to rise. As long as house prices kept rising, borrowers would not have an incentive to default, so brokers would continue to do their business, lenders would continue to collect large servicing fees, and investment bankers would continue to collect fees and earn higher yields on junior tranche securities. The problem was that house prices merely had to stop rising for this all to fall apart. House prices on average are flat, and some borrowers see their house prices fall. In 2004, 2005, and 2006, mortgage underwriting essentially ceased to exist. Put all that together and a small pain from a flat housing market would lead to the beginning of the collapse in the mortgage market.

Ironically, the beginning of the end came with markets where prices declined not because a bubble was pricked, but rather because economies imploded. Those economies once again were in the upper Midwest. The first cities to see house prices fall, according to the Federal Housing Finance Agency, the successor agency of the Office of Federal Housing Enterprise Oversight, were Detroit and Cleveland—cities that suffered large losses in manufacturing employment.

Once house prices began falling in the cities, default rates started rising rapidly, as borrowers had negative equity and no income with which to repay their mortgages. Detroit made for a particularly spectacular case, as the median house price in that city fell to $7100 in 2009.[6] So mortgages backed by property in these cities began to default. The lower tranches of mortgage-backed securities were particularly hard hit, and this blow started the collapse of highly leveraged investment banks that owned junior tranches of mortgage-backed securities.

Other investment banks, such as Goldman Sachs, recognized the potential calamity arising from the mortgage meltdown. They responded by buying credit default swaps. These were essentially insurance policies against falling house prices. In the event that mortgage default rates rose, credit default swaps would pay those that owned them. Among the most famous investors in credit default swaps were Michael Berry, who was featured in Michael Lewis's book, *The Big Short*, and John Paulson, who was featured in Gregory Zuckerman's book, *The Greatest Trade Ever*.

But while Goldman Sachs was wise to hedge against mortgage risk by purchasing credit assault default swaps, it made the mistake of purchasing the swaps from a company, AIG, that did not have adequate capital to meet its contract obligations in the event that mortgage markets took a serious tumble. The collapse of the mortgage market thus emphasized the importance of two types of risk: credit risk and counterparty risk. The first of these is well understood, but the second is not, and continues to be a sticking point as we think about how to reform our financial system.

---

6. Michael M. Phillips, "In One Home, a Mighty City's Rise and Fall," *Wall Street Journal*, September 26, 2009. Accessed at http://online.wsj.com/article/SB125390841258341665.html

With private investors exiting the market mortgages, lenders such as Countrywide, Washington Mutual, and Indy Mac were no longer able to get loans off of their balance sheets. At the same time, these institutions did have loans on their balance sheets, but they tended to be second mortgages: piggyback seconds, which allowed borrowers to buy houses with little or no money down, and home equity lines of credit, which allowed borrowers to tap equity from their houses. Just as junior tranche mortgage-backed securities became vulnerable when house prices fell, so too did second mortgages. Lenders thus found themselves with mortgages that performed poorly and with mortgages they couldn't sell. The combination led to rapid insolvency.

And so it was that the mortgage crisis, which led to a deep economic crisis, developed. Between 2000 and 2005, Fannie Mae and Freddie Mac lost substantial market share to the purely private market. At the same time, both firms had new senior management. This management had limited experience in the mortgage market. In the face of losing market share, both Fannie and Freddie became much more aggressive. In particular they began to purchase large amounts of AAA-rated subprime mortgage-backed security tranches. Underwriting on subprime mortgages was poor: very often these mortgages lacked proper documentation, had very low down payments, were financed speculative purchases of houses, or were heady combinations of all three of these and other risk characteristics. Consequently, junior tranches sometimes became worthless and senior tranches began realizing losses. Because Fannie Mae and Freddie Mac were required to have small amounts of capital (even after sanctions were imposed by the OFHEO, the two firms needed to hold only 3% capital against their assets), small losses were catastrophic for the companies. In 2008 the Treasury Department placed both companies into conservatorship. Essentially, the treasury wiped out common shareholder valuation and took preferred shares in the companies. The companies owed the treasury dividend payments of 10 percent. In exchange, the treasury lent the companies money as needed and wound up paying out about $181 billion. In 2012, Fannie Mae and Freddie Mac became profitable again, and began repaying the Treasury Department. Surprisingly, the GSEs may wind up fully repaying all that they borrowed.

Fannie Mae and Freddie Mac, or at least their management, behaved badly. Note, however, that the GSEs followed the private market down the path of poor underwriting. Ultimately, the GSEs could not have bought AAA rated securities backed by subprime mortgages had there not been an appetite for lower rated securities. The market share of the GSEs dropped dramatically in the first few years that the subprime market began to wrap up.

In the aftermath of the crisis, mortgage lending had almost entirely fallen into the hands of Fannie Mae, Freddie Mac, and FHA. Between 2008 and 2012, the private sector showed little if any appetite for mortgage lending. At the same time, mortgage underwriting standards became stricter than they have been at any time since the 1990s, and in some ways they have become even more strict.

In particular, while people who draw regular salaries and receive W-2 forms from the Internal Revenue Service at the end of each year have fairly ready access to mortgage credit, self-employed people find it very difficult to obtain a mortgage. This is even true for people who can document a long history of self-employment income.

What are the lessons we can take away from the crisis? That will be the focus of Chapter 9.

REFERENCES

Brian, Maris A., Segal, William, 2002. Analysis of yield spreads on commercial mortgage-backed securities. Journal of Real Estate Research 23.3, 235–252.

Courtemanche, Charles, Snowden, Kenneth, 2011. Repairing a mortgage crisis: HOLC lending and its impact on local housing markets. The Journal of Economic History 71.02, 307–337.

Crossney, Kristen B., Bartelt, David W., 2005. The legacy of the home owners' loan corporation. Housing Policy Debate 16.3 (4), 547–574.

Peek, Joe, 1990. A call to ARMs: Adjustable rate mortgages in the 1980s. New England Economic Review Mar, 47–61.

"Resource Center: Daily Treasury Yield Curve Rates." U.S. Department of the Treasury, n.d. Web. 17 Apr. 2013.

Rose, Jonathan D., 2011. The incredible HOLC? Mortgage relief during the Great Depression. Journal of Money, Credit and Banking 43.6, 1073–1107.

Rose, Jonathan, Snowden, Kenneth, 2013. The New Deal and the Origins of the Modern American Real Estate Loan Contract. Explorations in Economic History.

Snowden, Kenneth A., 1987. Mortgage rates and American capital market development in the late nineteenth century. Journal of Economic History 47.3, 671–691.

United States, 5 July 2013. Senate Banking Committee. Testimony of Susan E. Woodward, Senate Banking Committee, October 20, 2010. By Susan Woodward N.p., n.d. Web.

Walter, John, 2006. The 3-6-3 Rule: An Urban Myth? FRB Richmond Economic Quarterly Winter 92.1, 51–78 Print.

Mortgage Originations and the Mortgage Chain

Many borrowers think their mortgage lender is a bank or other depository, such as a Savings and Loan (S&L) or a Credit Union. But it is a rare event for a borrower to go to an institution, apply for a loan at that institution, get approved for a loan by that institution, get funded for a loan by that institution, and then have that institution hold the loan and collect its payments until it is paid off.

We may divide the loan process and its institutions into five parts: origination, funding, securitizing, investment, and servicing. We shall discuss each in turn.

LOAN ORIGINATION

There are four channels through which loans originate: the brokerage channel, the mortgage banking channel, the correspondent channel, and the direct depository channel. Many, if not most borrowers assume they are getting their loan through the last channel ("Bank of America is my Lender"), but direct depository is in fact the least commonly used. With that in mind, let's describe each channel.

Brokers

Mortgage brokers, who may be found online through sites such as Lendingtree, are not lenders—they do not have money to fund loans. They are, in fact,

Introduction to Mortgages & Mortgage Backed Securities.
http://dx.doi.org/10.1016/B978-0-12-401743-6.00002-0

brokers—institutions whose purpose is supposed to be to consummate trans-actions that are mutually satisfactory to buyers (in this case, borrowers) and sellers (in this case, lenders).

A broker takes a loan application and then shops it around to lenders. In prin-ciple, this means that brokers should be able to take advantage of a competitive market and find a lowest cost option for borrowers. In particular, brokers can examine the wholesale rates offered by lenders, which come in the form of rate sheets, and then advise their clients, the potential borrowers, about the best deal. For a nice explanation of how to read a rate sheet, watch www.youtube.com/watch?v=fFZWehE763w. An example of a rate sheet is at www.pbmwholesale.com/rates/CA-Whlsle-Conv99(2).pdf.

The rate sheet does underscore a conflict of interest between brokers and borrowers: the Yield Spread Premium, or YSP. As the interest rate paid to the borrower rises, the YSP to the lender gets larger. Now the lender can pass the YSP to the borrower (this is how discount points lower the interest rate), but the lender can also keep the YSP for itself.

One of the good aspects of Dodd-Frank is that brokers are now required to disclose their YSP to borrowers. But there is a bit of a conundrum here. On the one hand, borrowers can shop across brokers to try to get the best deal possible. On the other hand, the purpose of brokers is alleged to be that they can get borrowers the best deal possible.

The thing that can be really bedeviling to consumers is that it is very difficult for them to know what costs actually are (and hence, it is diffi-cult for them to know how much the broker is getting in compensation). In particular, as we will discuss in Chapter 3, the cost of a mortgage is actu-ally dependent on two things that don't show up in the APR: the length of time the borrower had a mortgage before repaying it, and fees that are not included in an APR.

Mortgage Bankers

Mortgage bankers are different from brokers in that they actually have money with which to fund loans. They are different from regular banks in that they do not take deposits, but raise funds through capital markets.

Mortgage bankers are like warehouses that rely on rapid throughput—they originate and fund loans under the assumption that they will be able to resell them quickly, either to a longer-term portfolio lender or on the secondary mar-ket (more about this later).

Income comes through three sources for mortgage bankers: origination fees (in this they are similar to brokers), spreads (the difference between how much they pay for their debt and how much they sell their loans for), and servicing rights (also a subject for later in the chapter).

Unlike brokers, mortgage bankers actually underwrite loans, and make the decision as to whether to approve a loan for a borrower or not.

Correspondent Lenders

A correspondent lender is something of a hybrid between a mortgage broker and a mortgage banker. A correspondent, like a broker, does not fund loans with its own money. A correspondent, like a mortgage banker, underwrites loans and makes approval decisions.

Although correspondent lenders do not have their own money, they have direct access to someone else's money—this is what allows them to decide which loans to approve and which loans not to approve.

Direct Lenders

Finally, there are direct lenders (depositories)—institutions that use short-term money (i.e., deposits) to fund mortgages. But total deposits in the United States totaled about $1.06 trillion at the end of 2012,[1] while residential mortgage debt outstanding was $9.92 trillion. Needless to say, depositories could not fund mortgages using deposits alone, nor would they want to do so.

As a consequence, while depositories originate, underwrite, and fund mortgages, they too look to sell them as rapidly as possible.

Countrywide's Many Businesses

Countrywide was a lending brand—a brand that became notorious for being the source of many loans that went into default. But there were in fact many Countrywides; there was a Countrywide Mortgage Bank and a Countrywide Bank, which began as a nationally chartered bank but then became an S&L. Among the most important differences between a chartered bank and an S&L is that a chartered bank was regulated by the Federal Reserve and the Office of the Comptroller of the Currency, whereas an S&L was regulated by the Office of Thrift Supervision. (The OTS no longer exists.) Many argue that Countrywide, along with Washington Mutual and Indy Mac, wanted to have S&L charters because such institutions were not subject to the same rigorous regulation as banks.

The multiple channels for mortgage lending lead to multiple questions. The first question is which channel is best for consumers; Do they get the best pricing from brokers, mortgage banks, correspondent lenders, or depository-based direct lenders? As explained in the discussion of mortgage types in Chapter 4, it is difficult to answer this question, because the cost of a mortgage to a consumer is not a straightforward calculation, even when we are dealing with the most vanilla of mortgage products: the self-amortizing fixed-rate mortgage.

---

1. See Federal Reserve Statistical Release H.6. Money Stock Measures: http://www.federalreserve.gov/releases/h6/current/

The second question involves the incentives of originators, and whether those who have to "eat what they cook" have better outcomes than those who just originate to distribute. But again, the meaning of "originate to distribute" is not clear.

FUNDING

Mortgage funding can come from three sources: deposits, short-term capital markets, and long-term capital markets.

Deposit-based funding was the primary source of mortgage lending from the end of World War II through the later 1970s. S&Ls typically funded more than half of mortgage debt over that period, and banks funded another 10 to 15 percent (Green and Wachter, 2007).

This system worked well as long as two things were in place: a stable, upward-sloping yield curve, and an absence of runs by depositors. The yield curve was indeed stable and upward sloping for many years, leading to the joke that mortgage lending by depositories was the 3–6–3 business: an S&L executive would borrow at 3 percent, lend at 6 percent, and be on the golf course by 3 in the afternoon.[2] At the same time, deposit insurance gave adequate insurance to depositors to prevent bank runs.

But the beginning of the 1980s brought about the end of deposits as the principal source of mortgage funds. Two things happened to the yield curve. First, thanks to high rates of inflation in the 1970s, interest rates across the yield curve rose. This put depositories in an untenable position, because the interest rates they had to pay to keep depositors were above the interest rates they were receiving on mortgages originated 5, 10, and 15 years earlier. This upward shift in the yield curve created losses.

Over the course of the 1980s, deposits became a less important source of mortgage funding, and capital markets became more important. Ginnie Mae, Fannie Mae, and Freddie Mac were responsible for more and more mortgage funding, and for a long period, depositories liked it. The reason is that by expanding sources of funds to the mortgage market, the government-sponsored enterprises (GSEs) allowed lenders to develop more business and thus generate more in fees for origination and servicing, about which we will say more later.

Quite often, depositories would fund mortgages for short periods, and then sell them into mortgage-backed securities (MBS). The MBS were underwritten by investment banks, who would earn fees for setting up trusts within which to hold mortgages. A specific type of trust was the Real Estate Mortgage Investment Conduit, or REMIC.

The REMIC structure was a creature of Congress that allowed MBS to be pure pass-through (and thereby passive) entities; the pass-through nature of the entity allowed investors to avoid double taxes. If REMICs were set up like

---

2. Walter (2006) wrote a paper showing that while the 3–6–3 stereotype was not strictly true, it was not entirely false, either. See http://papers.ssrn.com/sol3/papers.cfm?abstract_id=2186150

corporations, their income would be taxed before it was distributed to holders, and then taxed again when the holders reported their incomes. The REMIC structure was put in place in 1987.[3]

THE SECURITIZATION PROCESS

When Fannie Mae and Freddie Mac issue securities, they most often issue them in a "to-be-announced," or TBA, market. That is, they sell new securities to investors before the investors know exactly what will be inside of them. As Vickery and Wright (2010) explain, investors in TBA MBS know only six things about the security they are investing into in advance: coupon, issuer, price, par amount, settlement date, and maturity.

For the TBA setup to work, investors in the securities must be confident about a number of things: that the credit guarantee behind the loans within the security is reliable, and that the loans share at least a broad set of features in common.

The second of these requirements brought about standardization for Fannie and Freddie loan underwriting. Everyone who applies for a loan and who is eligible for Fannie Mae or Freddie Mac Funding fills out the same loan application form: the Fannie Mae 1003 form. The form is attached at the end of this chapter.

Note the use of the word uniform in the Fannie Mae 1003 form. The fact that all borrowers fill out the same form means that investors in the TBA securities know that all loans contain basic information about property location, borrower income, borrower employment, and borrower assets and liabilities. Investors also know that, in general, the borrower information has been processed through an underwriting model (Desktop underwriter for Fannie and Loan Prospector for Freddie) that returns a score summarizing the safety of the loan, and only loans that meet certain safety standards are funded. It is worth noting that the home loans underwritten by Fannie and Freddie models generally performed better than other loans through the recent financial crisis—the GSEs got themselves into trouble largely because of investments in subprime loans and poorly documented loans—loans they made outside their core business.

Beyond the standard loan application, loans underwritten by Fannie and Freddie were appraised based on certain procedures that were largely codified by a form. All appraisals use three approaches (market comparable, income, and cost) to value, and require documentation about the house appraised, its condition, and the appropriateness of comparable sales.

The combination of uniformity and quality control gave (and once again gives) investors in MBS the confidence to invest in MBS whose loans have yet to be delivered. Because the market largely operates as a TBA market, borrowers are able to receive locks on their interest rates when they apply for their loan, because an investor has made a commitment to buy a security at some point in the future at some specified rate.

---

3. See Schwarcz, S.L. 2004, Securitization, Structured Finance and Capital Markets.

Susan Woodward and Robert Hall argue that the absence of information received by investors in the TBA market actually makes MBS more valuable:[4]

a…feature of Fannie and Freddie's MBSs is that they efficiently suppress information about the location of mortgages in individual MBS pools. Even with the guarantee against default, investors face another risk that varies slightly (much less than default risk) from one region to another: different speeds of loan prepayment. Some areas have higher turnover, and loans prepay when people move, and partly because from the point of view of an investor in an MBS with a default guarantee, a default looks like a prepayment: the investor gets her money back when the loan either prepays or defaults (with a guarantee.) So how do the GSEs keep the MBS market liquid despite some geographical differences in prepayment speeds? By not revealing the geography of loans in any given MBS. Wait! What about market transparency?

More transparency is not always better. This can be seen in another institution in the municipal bond market. A structure used for promoting liquidity in the municipal bond market is a random call feature used for bonds that fund small but long-lived projects. Take a dam, for example. Bondholders are repaid from citizens' water bills. Such bonds are often structured in sets that repay at different times, for example, 10 years, 11 years, and so on up to 40 years. For little projects, each slice may be too small to find a liquid market. Instead, the entire issue is given the same maturity, but a specified fraction of it is called at random for repayment each year. The investors buy many such issues, and thus have a good idea of when they will be repaid, easily tolerate the uncertainty, and value the greater liquidity.

Not all loans are sold into a TBA market—some loans are sold into "specified pools," where investors choose the loans that go into an MBS when it is originated.

Finally, we should note that Fannie Mae and Freddie Mac buy only conventional conforming mortgages. Conventional means a mortgage that is not backed by the US government via FHA or VA (such loans go into Ginnie Mae pools). Conforming means loans that comply with the conforming loan limit. Conforming loan limits are tied to the house price of a county. As of 2013, all places in the United States have a conforming loan limit of at least $417,000; limits are higher in high-cost areas such as California, Colorado, Connecticut, the District of Columbia, Florida, Georgia, Hawaii, Idaho, Massachusetts, Maryland, North Carolina, New Hampshire, New Jersey, New York, Pennsylvania, Rhode Island, Utah, Virginia, Washington, West Virginia, and Wyoming. For a list, see www.fhfa.gov/webfiles/24675/High_Cost_Area_Loan_Limits_CY2013_HERA.pdf.

Loans that are not conforming (known as Jumbo loans), have been funded largely by deposits since the financial crisis, as the appetite for private-label MBS (i.e., MBS that are not backed by Ginnie, Fannie, or Freddie) has shrunk dramatically (Figure 2.1). From the peak of the Private Label market in the second quarter of 2007, the Private Label market has shrunk by more than $1.4 trillion, or 62 percent.

---

4. See http://woodwardhall.wordpress.com/2009/01/28/what-to-do-about-fannie-mae-and-freddie-mac/

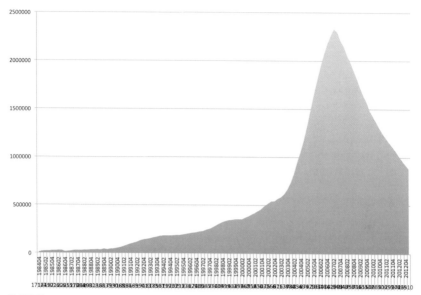

FIGURE 2.1   Private label holdings of mortgages. *Source: Federal Reserve Flow of Funds Data, Table L218.*

This also explains why the Jumbo market was, in general, moribund between 2008 and 2012, and why the Jumbo market was principally an Adjustable Rate market.

INVESTORS

Because GSE MBS are liquid and generally carry higher yields than treasury securities, they have some appeal to investors. Investors also relied on the implied guarantee of the US government when buying GSE MBS. This is why pension funds and foreign governments were large investors.

Figure 2.2 shows that in 2012, the largest holders of Freddie Mac MBS were commercial banks, the New York Fed (because of the Fed's program to buy MBS in order to stimulate the housing market), mutual funds, a catch-all category, and foreign investors. The GSEs themselves own a substantial amount of MBS, which are backed by debt; much of that debt is owned by foreign central banks.

Between 2002 and 2008, the investor market showed an appetite for Private Label Securities, which owned loans in one of two broad categories—those that the GSEs would not purchase, and those that GSEs could not purchase. Those in the first category were loans that failed to pass the underwriting standards embedded in Fannie Mae's Desktop Underwriting Model and/or Freddie Mac's Loan Prospector Model. Those in the second category were loans whose balances were above the conforming loan limit.

In Chapter 1 we discussed what made these securities appealing—at least for a while.

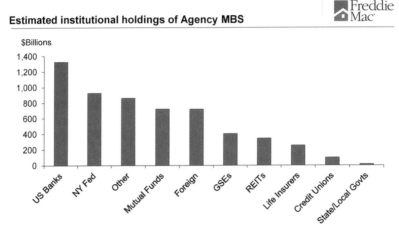

FIGURE 2.2 Estimated institutional holdings of agency MBS. Note: Other investors include hedge funds, structured investment vehicles, pension funds, saving institutions, nonprofits and individuals. *Source: Freddie Mac, Fannie Mae, Federal Reserve, Inside MBS & ABS, National Credit Union Administration, and the U.S. Treasury Department. Data as of December 31, 2012.*

SERVICING

Finally, there is a role for an entity that actually collects money from borrowers—the servicer. Servicers fall into one of two categories: master servicers and special servicers.

Master servicers collect principal and interest payments and pass them on to securities (trusts); in exchange for this, they receive a fee that is tied to the mortgage balance.

A special servicer takes over from the servicer when loans are delinquent. Because special servicing is deemed a more difficult thing to do, the fees for special servicing are higher.

The financial crisis put special servicers in a difficult position—sometimes, different investors within a troubled private label trust would have different views about how troubled loans should be disposed with. In Chapter 6, we will discuss how different investors in a trust receive different priorities for getting paid. An investor who gets paid first might want to foreclose as quickly as possible, because under such circumstances, it might recover its entire initial investment. An investor with a lower priority, however, might want to modify the loans in the trust in the hope that it will get most, if not all, of its principal back.

A SUMMARY: THE MORTGAGE CHAIN

For GSE loans, the mortgage chain is usually quite simple, and can be summarized by the diagram in Figure 2.3, which comes from a prospectus for Freddie Mac Securities.

Mortgage Securitizations

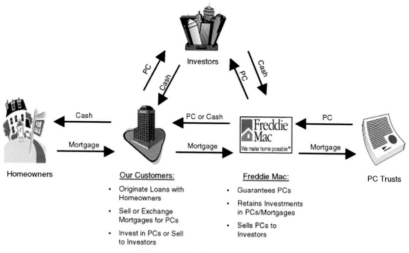

FIGURE 2.3   A mortgage chain.

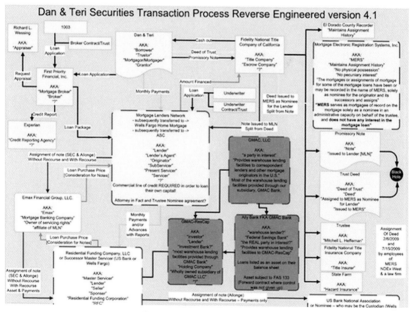

FIGURE 2.4   The mortgage chain.

Alas, as the private label market developed, so too did the complexity of the mortgage chain, as shown in the rather notorious diagram[5] in Figure 2.4.

---

5. Accessed at http://media.tumblr.com/tumblr_lc9nj9m3CQ1qdpyu8.jpg on July 22, 2013.

We will discuss how this came to happen in Chapter 9, "The Recent Financial Crisis."

REFERENCES

Green, Richard K., Wachter, Susan M., 2007. The Housing Finance Revolution. The Blackwell companion to the economics of housing: The housing wealth of nations, 414–445.

Schwarcz, Steven L., Markell, Bruce A., Broome, Lissa Lamkin, 2004. Securitization, Structured Finance, and Capital Markets. Lexis Nexis Matthew Bender.

Vickery, James, Wright, Joshua, 2010. TBA trading and liquidity in the agency MBS market. FRB of New York Staff Report 468.

Walter, John, 2006. The 3-6-3 rule: an urban myth? FRB Richmond Economic Quarterly 92.1, 51–78.

Uniform Residential Loan Application

This application is designed to be completed by the applicant(s) with the Lender's assistance. Applicants should complete this form as "Borrower" or "Co-Borrower," as applicable. Co-Borrower information must also be provided (and the appropriate box checked) when □ the income or assets of a person other than the Borrower (including the Borrower's spouse) will be used as a basis for loan qualification or □ the income or assets of the Borrower's spouse or other person who has community property or similar rights pursuant to applicable state law will not be used as a basis for loan qualification, but his or her liabilities must be considered because the spouse or other person who has community property or similar rights and the Borrower resides in a community property state, the security property is located in a community property state, or the Borrower is relying on other property located in a community property state as a basis for repayment of the loan.

If this is an application for joint credit, Borrower and Co-Borrower each agree that we intend to apply for joint credit (sign below):

_____   _____
Borrower   Co-Borrower

I. TYPE OF MORTGAGE AND TERMS OF LOAN			
Mortgage Applied for: □ VA □ USDA/Rural Housing Service □ FHA □ Conventional □ Other (explain):		Agency Case Number	Lender Case Number
Amount $	Interest Rate %	No. of Months	**Amortization Type:** □ Fixed Rate □ Other (explain): □ GPM □ ARM (type):

II. PROPERTY INFORMATION AND PURPOSE OF LOAN	
Subject Property Address (street, city, state & ZIP)	No. of Units
Legal Description of Subject Property (attach description if necessary)	Year Built

Purpose of Loan	□ Purchase □ Refinance □ Construction □ Construction-Permanent □ Other (explain):	Property will be: □ Primary Residence □ Secondary Residence □ Investment

Complete this line if construction or construction-permanent loan.

Year Lot Acquired	Original Cost	Amount Existing Liens	(a) Present Value of Lot	(b) Cost of Improvements	Total (a + b)
	$	$	$	$	$

Complete this line if this is a refinance loan.

Year Acquired	Original Cost	Amount Existing Liens	Purpose of Refinance	Describe Improvements	□ made □ to be made
	$	$			

Title will be held in what Name(s)	Manner in which Title will be held	Estate will be held in: □ Fee Simple □ Leasehold (show expiration date)

Source of Down Payment, Settlement Charges, and/or Subordinate Financing (explain)

Borrower				III. BORROWER INFORMATION	Co-Borrower			
Borrower's Name (include Jr. or Sr. if applicable)					Co-Borrower's Name (include Jr. or Sr. if applicable)			
Social Security Number	Home Phone (incl. Area code)	DOB (mm/dd/yyyy)	Yrs. School		Social Security Number	Home Phone (incl. Area code)	DOB (mm/dd/yyyy)	Yrs. School
☐ Married ☐ Separated		Dependents (not listed by Co-Borrower)			☐ Married ☐ Separated		Dependents (not listed by Borrower)	
☐ Unmarried (include single, divorced, widowed)		no.	ages		☐ Unmarried (include single, divorced, widowed)		no.	ages
Present Address (street, city, state, ZIP)	☐ Own ☐ Rent __No. Yrs.				Present Address (street, city, state, ZIP)	☐ Own ☐ Rent __No. Yrs.		
Mailing Address, if different from Present Address					Mailing Address, if different from Present Address			

If residing at present address for less than two years, complete the following:

Former Address (street, city, state, ZIP)	☐ Own ☐ Rent __No. Yrs.	Former Address (street, city, state, ZIP)	☐ Own ☐ Rent __No. Yrs.

Borrower		IV. EMPLOYMENT INFORMATION	Co-Borrower	
Name & Address of Employer	☐ Self Employed	Yrs. on this job	Name & Address of Employer ☐ Self Employed	Yrs. on this job
		Yrs. employed in this line of work/profession		Yrs. employed in this line of work/profession
Position/Title/Type of Business		Business Phone (incl. area code)	Position/Title/Type of Business	Business Phone (incl. area code)

If employed in current position for less than two years or if currently employed in more than one position, complete the following:

Name & Address of Employer ☐ Self Employed	Dates (from - to)	Name & Address of Employer ☐ Self Employed	Dates (from - to)
	Monthly Income $		Monthly Income $
Position/Title/Type of Business	Business Phone (incl. area code)	Position/Title/Type of Business	Business Phone (incl. area code)
Name & Address of Employer ☐ Self Employed	Dates (from - to)	Name & Address of Employer ☐ Self Employed	Dates (from - to)
	Monthly Income $		Monthly Income $
Position/Title/Type of Business	Business Phone (incl. area code)	Position/Title/Type of Business	Business Phone (incl. area code)

V. MONTHLY INCOME AND COMBINED HOUSING EXPENSE INFORMATION						
Gross Monthly Income	Borrower	Co-Borrower	Total	Combined Monthly Housing Expense	Present	Proposed
Base Empl. Income*	$	$	$	Rent	$	
Overtime				First Mortgage (P&I)		$
Bonuses				Other Financing (P&I)		
Commissions				Hazard Insurance		
Dividends/ Interest				Real Estate Taxes		
Net Rental Income				Mortgage Insurance		
Other (before completing, see the notice in "describe other income," below)				Homeowner Assn. Dues		
				Other:		
Total	$	$	$	Total	$	$

    *   Self Employed Borrower(s) may be required to provide additional documentation such as tax returns and financial statements.

      Describe Other Income

           Notice: Alimony, child support, or separate maintenance income need not be revealed if the Borrower (B) or Co-Borrower (C) does not choose to have it considered for repaying this loan.

B/C		Monthly Amount
		$

VI. ASSETS AND LIABILITIES

This Statement and any applicable supporting schedules may be completed jointly by both married and unmarried Co-Borrowers if their assets and liabilities are sufficiently joined so that the Statement can be meaningfully and fairly presented on a combined basis; otherwise, separate Statements and Schedules are required. If the Co-Borrower section was completed about a non-applicant spouse or other person, this Statement and supporting schedules must be completed about that spouse or other person also.

Completed   ☐
Jointly   ☐
Not
Jointly

ASSETS Description	Cash or Market Value	Liabilities and Pledged Assets. List the creditor's name, address, and account number for all outstanding debts, including automobile loans, revolving charge accounts, real estate loans, alimony, child support, stock pledges, etc. Use continuation sheet, if necessary. Indicate by (*) those liabilities, which will be satisfied upon sale of real estate owned or upon refinancing of the subject property.		
Cash deposit toward purchase held by:	$	LIABILITIES	Monthly Payment & Months Left to Pay	Unpaid Balance
List checking and savings accounts below		Name and address of Company	$ Payment/Months	$
Name and address of Bank, S&L, or Credit Union				
		Acct. no.		
Acct. no.	$	Name and address of Company	$ Payment/Months	$

VI. ASSETS AND LIABILITIES (cont'd)				
Name and address of Bank, S&L, or Credit Union		Acct. no.		
Acct. no.	$	Name and address of Company	$ Payment/Months	$
Name and address of Bank, S&L, or Credit Union				
		Acct. no.		
Acct. no.	$	Name and address of Company	$ Payment/Months	$
Name and address of Bank, S&L, or Credit Union				
		Acct. no.		
Acct. no.	$	Name and address of Company	$ Payment/Months	$
Stocks & Bonds (Company name/number & description)	$			
		Acct. no.		
Life insurance net cash value	$	Name and address of Company	$ Payment/Months	$
Face amount: $				
Subtotal Liquid Assets	$	Acct. no.		
Real estate owned (enter market value from schedule of real estate owned)	$	Alimony/Child Support/Separate Maintenance Payments Owned to:	$	$
Vested interest in retirement fund	$			
Net worth of business(es) owned (attach financial statement)	$	Job-Related Expense (child care, union dues, etc.)	$	
Automobiles owned (make and year)	$			
Other Assets (itemize)	$			
		Total Monthly Payments	$	
Total Assets a.	$	Net Worth (a minus b) $	Total Liabilities b.	$

Schedule of Real Estate Owned (If additional properties are owned, use continuation sheet.)

Property Address (enter S if sold, PS if pending sale or R if rental being held for income)	Type of Property	Present Market Value	Amount of Mortgages & Liens	Gross Rental Income	Mortgage Payments	Insurance, Maintenance, Taxes & Misc.	Net Rental Income
		$	$	$	$	$	$
	Totals	$	$	$	$	$	$

List any additional names under which credit has previously been received and indicate appropriate creditor name(s) and account number(s):

Alternate Name	Creditor Name	Account Number

VII. DETAILS OF TRANSACTION		VIII. DECLARATIONS				
a. Purchase price	$	If you answer "Yes" to any questions a through i, please use continuation sheet for explanation.	Borrower		Co-Borrower	
b. Alterations, improvements, repairs			Yes	No	Yes	No
c. Land (if acquired separately)		a. Are there any outstanding judgments against you?	☐	☐	☐	☐
d. Refinance (incl. debts to be paid off)		b. Have you been declared bankrupt within the past 7 years?	☐	☐	☐	☐
e. Estimated prepaid items		c. Have you had property foreclosed upon or given title or deed in lieu thereof in the last 7 years?	☐	☐	☐	☐
f. Estimated closing costs		d. Are you a party to a lawsuit?	☐	☐	☐	☐
g. PMI, MIP, Funding Fee		e. Have you directly or indirectly been obligated on any loan of which resulted in foreclosure, transfer of title in lieu of foreclosure, or judgment?	☐	☐	☐	☐
		(This would include such loans as home mortgage loans, SBA loans, home improvement loans, educational loans, manufactured (mobile) home loans, any mortgage, financial obligation, bond, or loan guarantee. If "Yes," provide details, including date, name, and address of Lender, FHA or VA case number, if any, and reasons for the action.)				
h. Discount (if Borrower will pay)		f. Are you presently delinquent or in default on any Federal debt or any other loan, mortgage, financial obligation, bond, or loan guarantee?	☐	☐	☐	☐
		If "Yes," give details as described in the preceding question.				
i. Total costs (add items a through h)		g. Are you obligated to pay alimony, child support, or separate maintenance?	☐	☐	☐	☐
j. Subordinate financing		h. Is any part of the down payment borrowed?	☐	☐	☐	☐
k. Borrower's closing costs paid by Seller		i. Are you a co-maker or endorser on a note?	☐	☐	☐	☐
l. Other Credits (explain)		j. Are you a U.S. citizen?	☐	☐	☐	☐
		k. Are you a permanent resident alien?	☐	☐	☐	☐
m. Loan amount (exclude PMI, MIP, Funding Fee financed)		l. Do you intend to occupy the property as your primary residence? If "Yes," complete question m below.	☐	☐	☐	☐
n. PMI, MIP, Funding Fee financed		m. Have you had an ownership interest in a property in the last three years?	☐	☐	☐	☐
o. Loan amount (add m & n)		(1) What type of property did you own–principal residence (PR), second home (SH), or investment property (IP)?	—	—	—	—
p. Cash from/to Borrower (subtract j, k, l & o from i)		(2) How did you hold title to the home– by yourself (S), jointly with your spouse or jointly with another person (O)?	—	—	—	—

ACKNOWLEDGMENT AND AGREEMENT

Each of the undersigned specifically represents to Lender and to Lender's actual or potential agents, brokers, processors, attorneys, insurers, servicers, successors and assigns and agrees and acknowledges that: (1) the information provided in this application is true and correct as of the date set forth opposite my signature and that any intentional or negligent misrepresentation of this information contained in this application may result in civil liability, including monetary damages, to any person who may suffer any loss due to reliance upon any misrepresentation that I have made on this application, and/or in criminal penalties including, but not limited to, fine or imprisonment or both under the provisions of Title 18, United States Code, Sec. 1001, et seq.; (2) the loan requested pursuant to this application (the "Loan") will be secured by a mortgage or deed of trust on the property described in this application; (3) the property will not be used for any illegal or prohibited purpose or use; (4) all statements made in this application are made for the purpose of obtaining a residential mortgage loan; (5) the property will be occupied as indicated in this application; (6) the Lender, its servicers, successors or assigns may retain the original and/or an electronic record of this application, whether or not the Loan is approved; (7) the Lender and its agents, brokers, insurers, servicers, successors, and assigns may continuously rely on the information contained in the application, and I am obligated to amend and/or supplement the information provided in this application if any of the material facts that I have represented should change prior to closing of the Loan; (8) in the event that my payments on the Loan become delinquent, the Lender, its servicers, successors or assigns may, in addition to any other rights and remedies that it may have relating to such delinquency, report my name and account information to one or more consumer reporting agencies; (9) ownership of the Loan and/or administration of the Loan account may be transferred with such notice as may be required by law; (10) neither Lender nor its agents, brokers, insurers, servicers, successors or assigns has made any representation or warranty, express or implied, to me regarding the property or the condition or value of the property; and (11) my transmission of this application as an "electronic record" containing my "electronic signature," as those terms are defined in applicable federal and/or state laws (excluding audio and video recordings), or my facsimile transmission of this application containing a facsimile of my signature, shall be as effective, enforceable and valid as if a paper version of this application were delivered containing my original written signature.

Acknowledgement. Each of the undersigned hereby acknowledges that any owner of the Loan, its servicers, successors and assigns, may verify or reverify any information contained in this application or obtain any information or data relating to the Loan, for any legitimate business purpose through any source, including a source named in this application or a consumer reporting agency.

Borrower's Signature	Date	Co-Borrower's Signature	Date
X		X	

X. INFORMATION FOR GOVERNMENT MONITORING PURPOSES

The following information is requested by the Federal Government for certain types of loans related to a dwelling in order to monitor the lender's compliance with equal credit opportunity, fair housing and home mortgage disclosure laws. You are not required to furnish this information, but are encouraged to do so. The law provides that a lender may not discriminate either on the basis of this information, or on whether you choose to furnish it. If you furnish the information, please provide both ethnicity and race. For race, you may check more than one designation. If you do not furnish ethnicity, race, or sex, under Federal regulations, this lender is required to note the information on the basis of visual observation and surname if you have made this application in person. If you do not wish to furnish the information, please check the box below. (Lender must review the above material to assure that the disclosures satisfy all requirements to which the lender is subject under applicable state law for the particular type of loan applied for.)

BORROWER	CO-BORROWER
☐ I do not wish to furnish this information	☐ I do not wish to furnish this information
Ethnicity: ☐ Hispanic or Latino ☐ Not Hispanic or Latino	Ethnicity: ☐ Hispanic or Latino ☐ Not Hispanic or Latino
Race: ☐ American Indian or Alaska Native ☐ Asian ☐ Black or African American ☐ Native Hawaiian or Other Pacific Islander ☐ White	Race: ☐ American Indian or Alaska Native ☐ Asian ☐ Black or African American ☐ Native Hawaiian or Other Pacific Islander ☐ White
Sex: ☐ Female ☐ Male	Sex: ☐ Female ☐ Male

1   To be Completed by Loan Originator

This information was provided:
☐ In a face-to-face interview
☐ In a telephone interview
☐ By the applicant and submitted by fax or mail
☐ By the applicant and submitted via e-mail or the Internet

Loan Originator's Signature		Date
Loan Originator's Name (print or type)	Loan Originator Identifier	Loan Originator's Phone Number (including area code)
Loan Origination Company's Name	Loan Origination Company Identifier	Loan Origination Company's Address

CONTINUATION SHEET/RESIDENTIAL LOAN APPLICATION

Use this continuation sheet if you need more space to complete the Residential Loan Application. Mark **B** for Borrower or **C** for Co-Borrower.	Borrower:	Agency Case Number:
	Co-Borrower:	Lender Case Number:

I/We fully understand that it is a Federal crime punishable by fine or imprisonment, or both, to knowingly make any false statements concerning any of the above facts as applicable under the provisions of Title 18, United States Code, Section 1001, et seq.

Borrower's Signature	Date	Co-Borrower's Signature	Date
X		X	

Uniform Residential Appraisal Report
File #

The purpose of this summary appraisal report is to provide the lender/client with an accurate, and adequately supported, opinion of the market value of the subject property.

S U B J E C T			
Property Address	City	State	Zip Code
Borrower	Owner of Public Record	County	
Legal Description			
Assessor's Parcel #	Tax Year	R.E. Taxes $	
Neighborhood Name	Map Reference	Census Tract	
Occupant ☐ Owner ☐ Tenant ☐ Vacant	Special Assessments $	☐ PUD HOA $	☐ per year ☐ per month
Property Rights Appraised ☐ Fee Simple ☐ Leasehold ☐ Other (describe)			
Assignment Type ☐ Purchase Transaction ☐ Refinance Transaction ☐ Other (describe)			
Lender/Client	Address		
Is the subject property currently offered for sale or has it been offered for sale in the twelve months prior to the effective date of this appraisal? ☐ Yes ☐ No			
Report data source(s) used, offering price(s), and date(s).			

CONTRACT

I ☐ did ☐ did not analyze the contract for sale for the subject purchase transaction. Explain the results of the analysis of the contract for sale or why the analysis was not performed.

Contract Price $ Date of Contract   Is the property seller the owner of public record? ☐Yes ☐No Data Source(s)

Is there any financial assistance (loan charges, sale concessions, gift or downpayment assistance, etc.) to be paid by any party on behalf of the borrower? ☐ Yes ☐ No
If Yes, report the total dollar amount and describe the items to be paid.

NEIGHBORHOOD

Note: Race and the racial composition of the neighborhood are not appraisal factors.

Neighborhood Characteristics			One-Unit Housing Trends			One-Unit Housing		Present Land Use %	
Location ☐ Urban ☐ Suburban ☐ Rural			Property Values ☐ Increasing ☐ Stable ☐ Declining			PRICE	AGE	One-Unit	%
Built-Up ☐ Over 75% ☐ 25–75% ☐ Under 25%			Demand/Supply ☐ Shortage ☐ In Balance ☐ Over Supply			$ (000)	(yrs)	2-4 Unit	%
Growth ☐ Rapid ☐ Stable ☐ Slow			Marketing Time ☐ Under 3 mths ☐ 3–6 mths ☐ Over 6 mths			Low		Multi-Family	%
Neighborhood Boundaries						High		Commercial	%
						Pred.		Other	%

Neighborhood Description

Market Conditions (including support for the above conclusions)

SITE

Dimensions	Area	Shape	View
Specific Zoning Classification	Zoning Description		

Zoning Compliance ☐ Legal ☐ Legal Nonconforming (Grandfathered Use) ☐ No Zoning ☐ Illegal (describe)

Is the highest and best use of the subject property as improved (or as proposed per plans and specifications) the present use? ☐ Yes ☐ No If No, describe

Utilities	Public	Other (describe)		Public	Other (describe)	Off-site Improvements—Type	Public	Private
Electricity	☐	☐	Water	☐	☐	Street	☐	☐
Gas	☐	☐	Sanitary Sewer	☐	☐	Alley	☐	☐

FEMA Special Flood Hazard Area ☐ Yes ☐ No FEMA Flood Zone   FEMA Map #   FEMA Map Date

Are the utilities and off-site improvements typical for the market area? ☐ Yes ☐ No If No, describe

Are there any adverse site conditions or external factors (easements, encroachments, environmental conditions, land uses, etc.)? ☐ Yes ☐ No If Yes, describe

IMPROVEMENTS

General Description		Foundation		Exterior Description	materials/condition	Interior	materials/condition
Units ☐ One ☐ One with Accessory Unit		☐ Concrete Slab ☐ Crawl Space		Foundation Walls		Floors	
# of Stories		☐ Full Basement ☐ Partial Basement		Exterior Walls		Walls	
Type ☐ Det. ☐ Att. ☐ S-Det./End Unit		Basement Area sq. ft.		Roof Surface		Trim/Finish	
☐ Existing ☐ Proposed ☐ Under Const.		Basement Finish %		Gutters & Downspouts		Bath Floor	
Design (Style)		☐ Outside Entry/Exit ☐ Sump Pump		Window Type		Bath Wainscot	
Year Built		Evidence of ☐ Infestation		Storm Sash/Insulated		Car Storage ☐ None	
Effective Age (Yrs)		☐ Dampness ☐ Settlement		Screens		☐ Driveway # of Cars	
Attic ☐ None		Heating ☐ FWA ☐ HWBB ☐ Radiant		Amenities ☐ Woodstove(s) #		Driveway Surface	
☐ Drop Stair ☐ Stairs		☐ Other Fuel		☐ Fireplace(s) # ☐ Fence		☐ Garage # of Cars	
☐ Floor ☐ Scuttle		Cooling ☐ Central Air Conditioning		☐ Patio/Deck ☐ Porch		☐ Carport # of Cars	
☐ Finished ☐ Heated		☐ Individual ☐ Other		☐ Pool ☐ Other (describe)		☐ Att. ☐ Det. ☐ Built-in	

Appliances ☐Refrigerator ☐Range/Oven ☐Dishwasher ☐Disposal ☐Microwave ☐Washer/Dryer ☐Other (describe)

Finished area **above** grade contains: Rooms   Bedrooms   Bath(s)   Square Feet of Gross Living Area Above Grade

Additional features (special energy efficient items, etc.)

Describe the condition of the property (including needed repairs, deterioration, renovations, remodeling, etc.).

Are there any physical deficiencies or adverse conditions that affect the livability, soundness, or structural integrity of the property? ☐ Yes ☐ No If Yes, describe

Does the property generally conform to the neighborhood (functional utility, style, condition, use, construction, etc.)? ☐ Yes ☐ No If No, describe

Uniform Residential Appraisal Report

File #

There are	comparable properties currently offered for sale in the subject neighborhood ranging in price from $		to $	
There are	comparable sales in the subject neighborhood within the past twelve months ranging in sale price from $		to $	

FEATURE	SUBJECT	COMPARABLE SALE # 1		COMPARABLE SALE # 2		COMPARABLE SALE # 3	
Address							
Proximity to Subject							
Sale Price	$		$		$		$
Sale Price/Gross Liv. Area	$ sq. ft.	$ sq. ft.		$ sq. ft.		$ sq. ft.	
Data Source(s)							
Verification Source(s)							
VALUE ADJUSTMENTS	DESCRIPTION	DESCRIPTION	+(-) $ Adjustment	DESCRIPTION	+(-) $ Adjustment	DESCRIPTION	+(-) $ Adjustment
Sale or Financing Concessions							
Date of Sale/Time							
Location							
Leasehold/Fee Simple							
Site							
View							
Design (Style)							
Quality of Construction							
Actual Age							
Condition							
Above Grade	Total Bdrms. Baths	Total Bdrms. Baths		Total Bdrms. Baths		Total Bdrms. Baths	
Room Count							
Gross Living Area	sq. ft.	sq. ft.		sq. ft.		sq. ft.	
Basement & Finished Rooms Below Grade							
Functional Utility							
Heating/Cooling							
Energy Efficient Items							
Garage/Carport							
Porch/Patio/Deck							
Net Adjustment (Total)		☐ + ☐ -	$	☐ + ☐ -	$	☐ + ☐ -	$
Adjusted Sale Price of Comparables		Net Adj. % Gross Adj. %	$	Net Adj. % Gross Adj. %	$	Net Adj. % Gross Adj. %	$

I ☐ did ☐ did not research the sale or transfer history of the subject property and comparable sales. If not, explain

My research ☐ did ☐ did not reveal any prior sales or transfers of the subject property for the three years prior to the effective date of this appraisal.

Data source(s)

My research ☐ did ☐ did not reveal any prior sales or transfers of the comparable sales for the year prior to the date of sale of the comparable sale.

Data source(s)

Report the results of the research and analysis of the prior sale or transfer history of the subject property and comparable sales (report additional prior sales on page 3).

ITEM	SUBJECT	COMPARABLE SALE # 1	COMPARABLE SALE # 2	COMPARABLE SALE # 3
Date of Prior Sale/Transfer				
Price of Prior Sale/Transfer				
Data Source(s)				
Effective Date of Data Source(s)				

Analysis of prior sale or transfer history of the subject property and comparable sales

Summary of Sales Comparison Approach

Indicated Value by Sales Comparison Approach $

Indicated Value by: Sales Comparison Approach $ Cost Approach (if developed) $ Income Approach (if developed) $

This appraisal is made ☐ "as is", ☐ subject to completion per plans and specifications on the basis of a hypothetical condition that the improvements have been completed, ☐ subject to the following repairs or alterations on the basis of a hypothetical condition that the repairs or alterations have been completed, or ☐ subject to the following required inspection based on the extraordinary assumption that the condition or deficiency does not require alteration or repair:

Based on a complete visual inspection of the interior and exterior areas of the subject property, defined scope of work, statement of assumptions and limiting conditions, and appraiser's certification, my (our) opinion of the market value, as defined, of the real property that is the subject of this report is
$, as of   , which is the date of inspection and the effective date of this appraisal.

Uniform Residential Appraisal Report

File #

ADDITIONAL COMMENTS

COST APPROACH TO VALUE (not required by Fannie Mae)

Provide adequate information for the lender/client to replicate the below cost figures and calculations.

Support for the opinion of site value (summary of comparable land sales or other methods for estimating site value)

COST APPROACH

ESTIMATED ☐ REPRODUCTION OR ☐ REPLACEMENT COST NEW

Source of cost data

Quality rating from cost service   Effective date of cost data

Comments on Cost Approach (gross living area calculations, depreciation, etc.)

OPINION OF SITE VALUE .... = $

Dwelling	Sq. Ft. @ $	.... =$
	Sq. Ft. @ $	.... =$
Garage/Carport	Sq. Ft. @ $	.... =$
Total Estimate of Cost-New		.... = $
Less	Physical	Functional	External
Depreciation			=$( )
Depreciated Cost of Improvements..........................		=$
"As-is" Value of Site Improvements........................		=$

Estimated Remaining Economic Life (HUD and VA only)   Years   Indicated Value By Cost Approach .... =$

INCOME APPROACH TO VALUE (not required by Fannie Mae)

INCOME

Estimated Monthly Market Rent $ X Gross Rent Multiplier   = $ Indicated Value by Income Approach

Summary of Income Approach (including support for market rent and GRM)

PROJECT INFORMATION FOR PUDs (if applicable)

PUD INFORMATION

Is the developer/builder in control of the Homeowners' Association (HOA)? ☐ Yes ☐ No   Unit type(s) ☐ Detached ☐ Attached

Provide the following information for PUDs ONLY if the developer/builder is in control of the HOA and the subject property is an attached dwelling unit.

Legal name of project

Total number of phases   Total number of units   Total number of units sold

Total number of units rented   Total number of units for sale   Data source(s)

Was the project created by the conversion of an existing building(s) into a PUD? ☐ Yes ☐ No   If Yes, date of conversion

Does the project contain any multi-dwelling units? ☐ Yes ☐ No   Data source(s)

Are the units, common elements, and recreation facilities complete? ☐ Yes ☐ No   If No, describe the status of completion.

Are the common elements leased to or by the Homeowners' Association? ☐ Yes ☐ No   If Yes, describe the rental terms and options.

Describe common elements and recreational facilities

Uniform Residential Appraisal Report

File #

This report form is designed to report an appraisal of a one-unit property or a one-unit property with an accessory unit; including a unit in a planned unit development (PUD). This report form is not designed to report an appraisal of a manufactured home or a unit in a condominium or cooperative project.

This appraisal report is subject to the following scope of work, intended use, intended user, definition of market value, statement of assumptions and limiting conditions, and certifications. Modifications, additions, or deletions to the intended use, intended user, definition of market value, or assumptions and limiting conditions are not permitted. The appraiser may expand the scope of work to include any additional research or analysis necessary based on the complexity of this appraisal assignment. Modifications or deletions to the certifications are also not permitted. However, additional certifications that do not constitute material alterations to this appraisal report, such as those required by law or those related to the appraiser's continuing education or membership in an appraisal organization, are permitted.

SCOPE OF WORK: The scope of work for this appraisal is defined by the complexity of this appraisal assignment and the reporting requirements of this appraisal report form, including the following definition of market value, statement of assumptions and limiting conditions, and certifications. The appraiser must, at a minimum: (1) perform a complete visual inspection of the interior and exterior areas of the subject property, (2) inspect the neighborhood, (3) inspect each of the comparable sales from at least the street, (4) research, verify, and analyze data from reliable public and/or private sources, and (5) report his or her analysis, opinions, and conclusions in this appraisal report.

INTENDED USE: The intended use of this appraisal report is for the lender/client to evaluate the property that is the subject of this appraisal for a mortgage finance transaction.

INTENDED USER: The intended user of this appraisal report is the lender/client.

DEFINITION OF MARKET VALUE: The most probable price which a property should bring in a competitive and open market under all conditions requisite to a fair sale, the buyer and seller, each acting prudently, knowledgeably and assuming the price is not affected by undue stimulus. Implicit in this definition is the consummation of a sale as of a specified date and the passing of title from seller to buyer under conditions whereby: (1) buyer and seller are typically motivated; (2) both parties are well informed or well advised, and each acting in what he or she considers his or her own best interest; (3) a reasonable time is allowed for exposure in the open market; (4) payment is made in terms of cash in U. S. dollars or in terms of financial arrangements comparable thereto; and (5) the price represents the normal consideration for the property sold unaffected by special or creative financing or sales concessions* granted by anyone associated with the sale.

*Adjustments to the comparables must be made for special or creative financing or sales concessions. No adjustments are necessary for those costs which are normally paid by sellers as a result of tradition or law in a market area; these costs are readily identifiable since the seller pays these costs in virtually all sales transactions. Special or creative financing adjustments can be made to the comparable property by comparisons to financing terms offered by a third party institutional lender that is not already involved in the property or transaction. Any adjustment should not be calculated on a mechanical dollar for dollar cost of the financing or concession but the dollar amount of any adjustment should approximate the market's reaction to the financing or concessions based on the appraiser's judgment.

STATEMENT OF ASSUMPTIONS AND LIMITING CONDITIONS: The appraiser's certification in this report is subject to the following assumptions and limiting conditions:

1. The appraiser will not be responsible for matters of a legal nature that affect either the property being appraised or the title to it, except for information that he or she became aware of during the research involved in performing this appraisal. The appraiser assumes that the title is good and marketable and will not render any opinions about the title.

2. The appraiser has provided a sketch in this appraisal report to show the approximate dimensions of the improvements. The sketch is included only to assist the reader in visualizing the property and understanding the appraiser's determination of its size.

3. The appraiser has examined the available flood maps that are provided by the Federal Emergency Management Agency (or other data sources) and has noted in this appraisal report whether any portion of the subject site is located in an identified Special Flood Hazard Area. Because the appraiser is not a surveyor, he or she makes no guarantees, express or implied, regarding this determination.

4. The appraiser will not give testimony or appear in court because he or she made an appraisal of the property in question, unless specific arrangements to do so have been made beforehand, or as otherwise required by law.

5. The appraiser has noted in this appraisal report any adverse conditions (such as needed repairs, deterioration, the presence of hazardous wastes, toxic substances, etc.) observed during the inspection of the subject property or that he or she became aware of during the research involved in performing this appraisal. Unless otherwise stated in this appraisal report, the appraiser has no knowledge of any hidden or unapparent physical deficiencies or adverse conditions of the property (such as, but not limited to, needed repairs, deterioration, the presence of hazardous wastes, toxic substances, adverse environmental conditions, etc.) that would make the property less valuable, and has assumed that there are no such conditions and makes no guarantees or warranties, express or implied. The appraiser will not be responsible for any such conditions that do exist or for any engineering or testing that might be required to discover whether such conditions exist. Because the appraiser is not an expert in the field of environmental hazards, this appraisal report must not be considered as an environmental assessment of the property.

6. The appraiser has based his or her appraisal report and valuation conclusion for an appraisal that is subject to satisfactory completion, repairs, or alterations on the assumption that the completion, repairs, or alterations of the subject property will be performed in a professional manner.

Uniform Residential Appraisal Report

File #

APPRAISER'S CERTIFICATION: The Appraiser certifies and agrees that:

1. I have, at a minimum, developed and reported this appraisal in accordance with the scope of work requirements stated in this appraisal report.

2. I performed a complete visual inspection of the interior and exterior areas of the subject property. I reported the condition of the improvements in factual, specific terms. I identified and reported the physical deficiencies that could affect the livability, soundness, or structural integrity of the property.

3. I performed this appraisal in accordance with the requirements of the Uniform Standards of Professional Appraisal Practice that were adopted and promulgated by the Appraisal Standards Board of The Appraisal Foundation and that were in place at the time this appraisal report was prepared.

4. I developed my opinion of the market value of the real property that is the subject of this report based on the sales comparison approach to value. I have adequate comparable market data to develop a reliable sales comparison approach for this appraisal assignment. I further certify that I considered the cost and income approaches to value but did not develop them, unless otherwise indicated in this report.

5. I researched, verified, analyzed, and reported on any current agreement for sale for the subject property, any offering for sale of the subject property in the twelve months prior to the effective date of this appraisal, and the prior sales of the subject property for a minimum of three years prior to the effective date of this appraisal, unless otherwise indicated in this report.

6. I researched, verified, analyzed, and reported on the prior sales of the comparable sales for a minimum of one year prior to the date of sale of the comparable sale, unless otherwise indicated in this report.

7. I selected and used comparable sales that are locationally, physically, and functionally the most similar to the subject property.

8. I have not used comparable sales that were the result of combining a land sale with the contract purchase price of a home that has been built or will be built on the land.

9. I have reported adjustments to the comparable sales that reflect the market's reaction to the differences between the subject property and the comparable sales.

10. I verified, from a disinterested source, all information in this report that was provided by parties who have a financial interest in the sale or financing of the subject property.

11. I have knowledge and experience in appraising this type of property in this market area.

12. I am aware of, and have access to, the necessary and appropriate public and private data sources, such as multiple listing services, tax assessment records, public land records and other such data sources for the area in which the property is located.

13. I obtained the information, estimates, and opinions furnished by other parties and expressed in this appraisal report from reliable sources that I believe to be true and correct.

14. I have taken into consideration the factors that have an impact on value with respect to the subject neighborhood, subject property, and the proximity of the subject property to adverse influences in the development of my opinion of market value. I have noted in this appraisal report any adverse conditions (such as, but not limited to, needed repairs, deterioration, the presence of hazardous wastes, toxic substances, adverse environmental conditions, etc.) observed during the inspection of the subject property or that I became aware of during the research involved in performing this appraisal. I have considered these adverse conditions in my analysis of the property value, and have reported on the effect of the conditions on the value and marketability of the subject property.

15. I have not knowingly withheld any significant information from this appraisal report and, to the best of my knowledge, all statements and information in this appraisal report are true and correct.

16. I stated in this appraisal report my own personal, unbiased, and professional analysis, opinions, and conclusions, which are subject only to the assumptions and limiting conditions in this appraisal report.

17. I have no present or prospective interest in the property that is the subject of this report, and I have no present or prospective personal interest or bias with respect to the participants in the transaction. I did not base, either partially or completely, my analysis and/or opinion of market value in this appraisal report on the race, color, religion, sex, age, marital status, handicap, familial status, or national origin of either the prospective owners or occupants of the subject property or of the present owners or occupants of the properties in the vicinity of the subject property or on any other basis prohibited by law.

18. My employment and/or compensation for performing this appraisal or any future or anticipated appraisals was not conditioned on any agreement or understanding, written or otherwise, that I would report (or present analysis supporting) a predetermined specific value, a predetermined minimum value, a range or direction in value, a value that favors the cause of any party, or the attainment of a specific result or occurrence of a specific subsequent event (such as approval of a pending mortgage loan application).

19. I personally prepared all conclusions and opinions about the real estate that were set forth in this appraisal report. If I relied on significant real property appraisal assistance from any individual or individuals in the performance of this appraisal or the preparation of this appraisal report, I have named such individual(s) and disclosed the specific tasks performed in this appraisal report. I certify that any individual so named is qualified to perform the tasks. I have not authorized anyone to make a change to any item in this appraisal report; therefore, any change made to this appraisal is unauthorized and I will take no responsibility for it.

20. I identified the lender/client in this appraisal report who is the individual, organization, or agent for the organization that ordered and will receive this appraisal report.

Uniform Residential Appraisal Report   File

21. The lender/client may disclose or distribute this appraisal report to: the borrower; another lender at the request of the borrower; the mortgagee or its successors and assigns; mortgage insurers; government sponsored enterprises; other secondary market participants; data collection or reporting services; professional appraisal organizations; any department, agency, or instrumentality of the United States; and any state, the District of Columbia, or other jurisdictions; without having to obtain the appraiser's or supervisory appraiser's (if applicable) consent. Such consent must be obtained before this appraisal report may be disclosed or distributed to any other party (including, but not limited to, the public through advertising, public relations, news, sales, or other media).

22. I am aware that any disclosure or distribution of this appraisal report by me or the lender/client may be subject to certain laws and regulations. Further, I am also subject to the provisions of the Uniform Standards of Professional Appraisal Practice that pertain to disclosure or distribution by me.

23. The borrower, another lender at the request of the borrower, the mortgagee or its successors and assigns, mortgage insurers, government sponsored enterprises, and other secondary market participants may rely on this appraisal report as part of any mortgage finance transaction that involves any one or more of these parties.

24. If this appraisal report was transmitted as an "electronic record" containing my "electronic signature," as those terms are defined in applicable federal and/or state laws (excluding audio and video recordings), or a facsimile transmission of this appraisal report containing a copy or representation of my signature, the appraisal report shall be as effective, enforceable and valid as if a paper version of this appraisal report were delivered containing my original hand written signature.

25. Any intentional or negligent misrepresentation(s) contained in this appraisal report may result in civil liability and/or criminal penalties including, but not limited to, fine or imprisonment or both under the provisions of Title 18, United States Code, Section 1001, et seq., or similar state laws.

SUPERVISORY APPRAISER'S CERTIFICATION: The Supervisory Appraiser certifies and agrees that:

1. I directly supervised the appraiser for this appraisal assignment, have read the appraisal report, and agree with the appraiser's analysis, opinions, statements, conclusions, and the appraiser's certification.

2. I accept full responsibility for the contents of this appraisal report including, but not limited to, the appraiser's analysis, opinions, statements, conclusions, and the appraiser's certification.

3. The appraiser identified in this appraisal report is either a sub-contractor or an employee of the supervisory appraiser (or the appraisal firm), is qualified to perform this appraisal, and is acceptable to perform this appraisal under the applicable state law.

4. This appraisal report complies with the Uniform Standards of Professional Appraisal Practice that were adopted and promulgated by the Appraisal Standards Board of The Appraisal Foundation and that were in place at the time this appraisal report was prepared.

5. If this appraisal report was transmitted as an "electronic record" containing my "electronic signature," as those terms are defined in applicable federal and/or state laws (excluding audio and video recordings), or a facsimile transmission of this appraisal report containing a copy or representation of my signature, the appraisal report shall be as effective, enforceable and valid as if a paper version of this appraisal report were delivered containing my original hand written signature.

APPRAISER

Signature_____
Name _____
Company Name _____
Company Address _____
_____
Telephone Number _____
Email Address _____
Date of Signature and Report _____
Effective Date of Appraisal _____
State Certification # _____
or State License # _____
or Other (describe) _____ State # _____
State _____
Expiration Date of Certification or License _____

ADDRESS OF PROPERTY APPRAISED

_____

APPRAISED VALUE OF SUBJECT PROPERTY $ _____
LENDER/CLIENT
Name _____
Company Name _____
Company Address _____
_____
Email Address _____

SUPERVISORY APPRAISER (ONLY IF REQUIRED)

Signature_____
Name _____
Company Name _____
Company Address _____
_____
Telephone Number _____
Email Address _____
Date of Signature _____
State Certification # _____
or State License # _____
State _____
Expiration Date of Certification or License _____

SUBJECT PROPERTY

☐ Did not inspect subject property
☐ Did inspect exterior of subject property from street
    Date of Inspection _____
☐ Did inspect interior and exterior of subject property
    Date of Inspection _____

COMPARABLE SALES

☐ Did not inspect exterior of comparable sales from street
☐ Did inspect exterior of comparable sales from street
    Date of Inspection _____

Chapter 3

The Work-Horse American Mortgage: The 30-Year Fixed-Rate Mortgage

The most common mortgage in the United States is the fixed-term, fixed-rate, prepayable mortgage. This mortgage is at once consumer friendly and expensive. Consumers bear no interest rate risk when they obtain this mortgage: if rates go up, they are protected, if rates go down, they can take advantage of the lower rate via refinancing.

Long-term fixed-rate mortgages have been around for 200 years, but they became the "default" mortgage for the United States in the aftermath of the Great Depression (a phenomenon we discuss in Chapter 1).

The mechanics of the 30-year mortgage are straightforward. A borrower obtains a mortgage of amount X, and makes payment based on a quoted interest rate and a term. The quoted interest rate on a mortgage does not exactly inform the borrower of the cost of credit, even for "no-cost origination" mortgages. Although the rate that is quoted is an annual rate, borrowers pay loans monthly, and interest to the lender compounds monthly. Hence, when a borrower is quoted an annual rate of r, he or she is actually paying a monthly rate of $r/12$. The effective annual yield for the mortgage is thus $(1 + r/12)^{12} - 1$, which is an amount that is slightly higher than r.

To understand how to calculate the payment on a fixed-rate, fixed-term payment, let us begin with the formula for the value of a perpetual annuity. If an annuity pays a constant cash flow (cf) each period at rate i of the principal, then the value (V) of the principal is just:

$$V = cf/i$$

If mortgages were infinitely lived, it would be easy to calculate the payment by rearranging (X):

$$cf = iV$$

As it happens, this is the payment formula for an interest-only mortgage, about which we will say more later.

The problem, of course, is that mortgages are not finitely lived. We thus must think about how we would value a finitely lived constant cash flow asset. The formula is:

$$V = cf/i - (cf/i)/(1+i)^\wedge T$$

or

$$V = cf\left(1/i - (1/i)/(1+i)^\wedge T\right)$$

where T is the number of periods over which the cash flow is paid. We can rearrange this and show that the payment is:

$$cf = Vi/\left(1/i - (1/i)/(1+i)^\wedge T\right)$$

Although memorizing formulas is not particularly useful, this action is important to understanding their derivation. Basically, if someone can remember the simple formula for a value of a perpetual annuity, and have a basic understanding of discounting, he or she can easily derive the formula for the annuity payment necessary to pay off a debt, given a rate and term.

Let us do a simple example. Suppose we want to find the payment for a $100,000 mortgage at an interest rate of 6 percent that has a term of 15 years. Now the monthly rate is 0.06/12, or 0.5 percent, and the mortgage amortizes over 180 months. The payment for this mortgage is:

$$cf = 100,0000/(1/0.005) - (1/0.005)/\left((1+0.005)^\wedge 180\right)$$

or $843.86.

Of course, we needn't do this manually (although it is good practice to do so!). We can use a calculator, and enter 100,000 for the PV, 0.005 for the rate, and 180 for the term (or N). We can also use a spreadsheet, such as Excel, and use the formula PMT(0.005,180,100,000). (See Spreadsheet 3.1.) The payment resulting from this formula is –843.86. Spreadsheets produce negative payments because payments are outflows—they are negatives to borrowers (conversely, the proceeds that they receive from the mortgage is an inflow). To generalize this process so that we can look at mortgages with annual or quarterly payments, see Box 3.1.

We now turn to a concept called Annual Percentage Rate, or APR. We can use a spreadsheet to find the monthly rate on this mortgage by using the function "rate." In particular, for the example we gave earlier, we can plug in: (180, –843.86, 100,000). We use a negative sign for the payment because it is a cash outflow. When we do this calculation, we get a rate of 0.005, or

> **BOX 3.1 Total Annual Payments with Different Numbers of Payments Per Year 15-year $100,000 Fixed Rate 6 Percent Mortgage**
>
> | One payment per year | ($10,296.28) |
> | --- | --- |
> | Four payments per year | ($10,157.37) |
> | Twelve payments per year | ($10,126.28) |

0.5 percent, which is as it should be, because that is the rate we paid in the first place.

But remember that this is a monthly rate. To find the annual yield produced by this rate, we must compound it by 12 periods. Hence the effective annual yield is $(1.005)\wedge 12 - 1$, or 6.17 percent. We can get the same outcome by using the EFFECT function in Excel, where we enter the nominal rate (0.06) and the number of payment periods with a year (12). In the event that the mortgage has no cost associated with its origination, this is also called the APR. So for a zero-cost mortgage, the relationship between that quoted mortgage rate (RATE) and the APR is:

$$APR = (1 + RATE/12)^{\wedge} 12 - 1$$

Mortgages rarely come with no cost, however. At minimum, borrowers must pay for an appraisal and title insurance. These costs mean that from the standpoint of a borrower, they receive less money than the stated mortgage balance. We will deal with these sorts of issues later.

In the meantime, however, let us consider mortgage origination fees and points. Suppose that to obtain a mortgage, we must pay an origination fee of 1 percent and a point (or another 1 percent). Let us stick with the mortgage we discussed earlier. The value begins with a balance of $100,000, has a quoted rate of 6 percent, and has a term of 180 periods. But if the borrower pays 2 percent of the loan up front in points and fees, she is effectively receiving only $98,000 to $100,000 for the mortgage, less $2,000 in points and fees. As a result of this, assuming the borrower fully amortizes the mortgage, the monthly cost of the mortgage to the borrower is:

$$Monthly\ cost = RATE\,(180,\ -843.86,\ 98,000)\ = 0.053\ percent$$

which is, of course, higher than 0.5 percent. The effective annual yield is now $(1 + 0.0053)\wedge 12 - 1$, or 6.5 percent annually. So the mortgage that is quoted at 6 percent costs *at least* 6.5 percent.

Now suppose the borrower pays off the mortgage early, either because she decides to refinance, or decides to move to another house, or just because she doesn't want to have any debt. She is borrowing money for a shorter period, and so she has less time to amortize her initial costs. This raises the effective periodic costs of the mortgage. Let's see by how much.

We can approach this from a number of perspectives. Let us assume our borrower repays her mortgage after five years, or 60 periods. This means that the mortgage at that time has 120 remaining periods of payments, so the value of the mortgage at that point is:

$$V = 843.86/0.005 - 843.86/0.005/(1.005)\hat{\ } 120$$

or, using an Excel function:

$$PV \ (0.005, \ 120, \ -843.86)$$

or, using another Excel function:

$$FV \ (0.005, \ 120, \ 843.86, \ 100{,}000)$$

The first function, the Present Value function, has a straightforward meaning. The Future Value function gives the future value of an investment given its original present value, and the payment that "chips away" at that present value. In all cases, this should produce a value of $76,009.10.

We can now calculate the true cost of the mortgage to this borrower. We need to solve for the rate that makes the following formula hold:

$$98{,}000 = \sum_{t=1}^{60} \frac{843.84}{1+r^t} + \frac{76{,}009.10}{1+r^{60}}$$

We can use the RATE formula to do this. If we calculate RATE(60,843.86, −90,000, 76, 009.10), we get 0.054 percent. If we take $(1.0054)\wedge 12 - 1$, we get 6.7 percent. So our mortgage that is quoted at 6 percent, and has an APR of 6.5 percent, has a true cost to the borrower of 6.7 percent!

But we are still not really finished. If the borrower needs to pay for an appraisal and title insurance, the effective cost of the mortgage is even higher. This needs to get built into the proceeds disbursed (the amount on the left-hand side of the previous equation). So, if the appraisal costs $500, the net to the borrower drops to $97,500. Now the true cost to the borrower increased to 6.6 percent (see Table 3.1).

The point is that the cost of a mortgage—even the most straightforward of mortgages—is not straightforward.

One more point. Suppose a borrower decides to pay off the mortgage before it fully amortizes. We will use five years as an example. We can use the RATE function in Excel again, but now we add the option of placing the mortgage balance in the future value slot, the fourth slot in the rate function. The balance after five years is $76,009.10, and so we enter that value (as a negative, because it is a payment). Now the effective rate, or cost, rises even further to 6.87 percent. With less time to amortize the up-front costs, the effective rate rises even more.

THE POPULARITY OF THE 30-YEAR FIXED-RATE MORTGAGE

Fixed-rate mortgages are, over the long-term, the most popular type of mortgage product in the United States. Fuster and Vickrey (2013) show that since 1996, FRM market share in the US has nearly always been above 50 percent, is usually above 70 percent, and is sometimes nearly 100 percent. Clearly, consumers like the certainty that the 30-year fixed-rate mortgage gives them about their payments, and are willing to spend the extra cost that comes with such mortgages. No less an eminence than Alan Greenspan thought that Americans spent too much on their mortgages:[1]

TABLE 3.1

Points and Fees as Share of Mortgage Balance (Fully Amortized)	Monthly Rate	True Cost of Mortgage (Fully Amortized)
0	0.50%	6.17%
0.01	0.51%	6.33%
0.015	0.52%	6.42%
0.02	0.53%	6.50%
0.025	0.53%	6.59%
0.03	0.54%	6.67%
0.035	0.55%	6.76%
0.04	0.55%	6.85%
0.045	0.56%	6.94%
0	0.50%	6.17%
0.01	0.52%	6.44%
0.015	0.53%	6.58%
0.02	0.54%	6.72%
0.025	0.55%	6.87%
0.03	0.57%	7.01%
0.035	0.58%	7.15%
0.04	0.59%	7.30%
0.045	0.60%	7.44%

1. See http://www.federalreserve.gov/boarddocs/speeches/2004/20040223/default.htm.

One way homeowners attempt to manage their payment risk is to use fixed-rate mortgages, which typically allow homeowners to prepay their debt when interest rates fall but do not involve an increase in payments when interest rates rise. Homeowners pay a lot of money for the right to refinance and for the insurance against increasing mortgage payments. Calculations by market analysts of the "option adjusted spread" on mortgages suggest that the cost of these benefits conferred by fixed-rate mortgages can range from 0.5 percent to 1.2 percent, raising homeowners' annual after-tax mortgage payments by several thousand dollars. Indeed, recent research within the Federal Reserve suggests that many homeowners might have saved tens of thousands of dollars had they held adjustable-rate mortgages rather than fixed-rate mortgages during the past decade, though this would not have been the case, of course, had interest rates trended sharply upward.

American homeowners clearly like the certainty of fixed mortgage payments. This preference is in striking contrast to the situation in some other countries, where adjustable-rate mortgages are far more common and where efforts to introduce American-type fixed-rate mortgages generally have not been successful. Fixed-rate mortgages seem unduly expensive to households in other countries. One possible reason is that these mortgages effectively charge homeowners high fees for protection against rising interest rates and for the right to refinance.

American consumers might benefit if lenders provided greater mortgage product alternatives to the traditional fixed-rate mortgage. To the degree that households are driven by fears of payment shocks but are willing to manage their own interest rate risks, the traditional fixed-rate mortgage may be an expensive method of financing a home.

At the time this book is being written, the interest rate on a typical five-year adjustable rate mortgage is 2.9 percent, and on a 30-year fixed-rate mortgage it is 4.2 percent. So while the five-year mortgage's rate can rise, in the short run, consumers are paying 130 basis points in order to get the benefits of locking in a rate. (See, for example, www.zillow.com/mortgage-rates/#sortBy=lenderFees.)

Consumers pay for something else as well—the embedded call option in a mortgage. Americans can, under almost all circumstances, repay their mortgage at any time they like, at very little cost. This is like a call option (the right to buy an asset at a particular price, which is known as the strike price; in the case of a mortgage, the strike price is the mortgage balance outstanding).

Americans take the ability to repay their mortgage at any time for granted, and yet it is a feature that is not ubiquitous around the world. Mortgages in Canada and Germany carry prepayment penalties—in fact, some German mortgages forbid prepayments altogether.

Mortgages with prepayment penalties often contain yield maintenance clauses, which work in the following way. Suppose a borrower has a $100,000 mortgage with an 8 percent rate of interest and mortgage rates fall to 5 percent, so the borrower wishes to refinance. Suppose the mortgage also has 10 years remaining on its life. Now finally suppose 10-year Treasury rates are 3 percent. Under a yield maintenance arrangement, if the borrower prepays, he owes the lender the difference between the mortgage rate (8 percent) and the Treasury rate (3 percent) multiplied by the mortgage balance multiplied by the remaining number of years, or (0.08 − 0.05) * 100,000 * 10, or $30,000. Prepayment will obviously not be an appealing option under these circumstances.

So even though the absence of prepayment penalties (or a free call option) makes a mortgage consumer friendly, such an absence comes with a cost— the spread between mortgage rates and Treasury rates in the United States is higher than in other countries, because investors in US mortgages need to earn a spread to compensate for the risk that they acquire when they invest in fixed-rate mortgages. We will discuss the computation of that spread from the investor's perspective in Chapter 11.

REFERENCE

Fuster, Andreas, James Vickery, 2013. Securitization and the fixed-rate mortgage. FRB of New York Staff Report 594.

Other Types of Mortgages

In Chapter 3, we discussed the workhorse American mortgage—the 30-year fixed-rate mortgage. Since the financial crisis of 2008, this has been the preponderant mortgage in the United States, with a market share in excess of 80 percent.[1]

But even before the potential crisis, other types of mortgages, while not preponderant, were popular. The most important of these has been the one-year adjustable-rate mortgage (ARM).

We should clarify that when we say one year, we are not referring to the term of the mortgage, but rather to the maturity of the security to which its rate is tied. Typically, the one-year ARM is tied either to the one-year Constant Maturity Treasury Rate (CMT), or the one-year London Interbank Offered Rate (LIBOR).

The mechanics of the one-year ARM are quite straightforward. Typically, the lender will set an initial rate for the mortgage, and then specify how the mortgage adjusts each year that the mortgage ages. For example, a mortgage might begin with a 3 percent annual rate on January 20, 2013. Then on January 20, 2014, the rate will reset to the one-year CMT as measured by the Treasury Department on that day, plus 275 basis points. This is the most straightforward type of ARM.

Sometimes the one-year ARM will have other features such as annual caps and floors, and lifetime caps and floors. For example, the mortgage contract may specify that rates may neither increase nor decrease by more than 2 percent per year and that they may neither increase nor decrease by more than 6 percent

---

1. See Fuster and Vickery (2013), p. 45.

Introduction to Mortgages & Mortgage Backed Securities.
http://dx.doi.org/10.1016/B978-0-12-401743-6.00004-4

over the lifetime of the loan. Currently, because initial rates are so low, the lifetime floor might be specified as something like 1.5 percent.

Because the rate on ARMs resets, so too does the payment necessary to amortize the mortgage at any particular point in time. Let's give an example:

Suppose an ARM starts out with a 3.5 percent interest rate. Let us also assume that it is a $100,000 mortgage and that it amortized over 30 years with monthly payments. The initial payment on that mortgage will be $449.04 (use a spreadsheet to check this out yourself).

Now let's say that after one year it is time for the one-year ARM to reset, at the CMT plus 2.5 percent. As it happens today is June 25, 2013, and on this day the one-year CMT is 0.16 percent. Thus the new rate that will be applied to this mortgage is 2.66 percent.

After we have amortized this mortgage for one year at a 3.5 percent interest rate, it has a balance of $98,080.87. We now find that the payment amortizes $98,080.87 over 29 years, which is the remaining term of the mortgage. This yields a new payment of $404.68. Again, check this out for yourself.

Exercise

Assume a loan that is tied to one-year LIBOR begins with a mortgage rate of 6 percent and has a term of 15 years. The loan origination has a balance of $250,000. It is a fully amortizing loan. The margin on the loan (the difference between LIBOR and the rate the borrower pays) is 225 basis points. Let's say the loan is two years old and ready to adjust and that LIBOR is 3 percent. What is the payment that the borrower will make on this loan between months 25 and 36?

Analysts are sometimes puzzled about why borrowers do not take up one-year ARMs more often. That will be the subject of another chapter of this book. But, in general, the payments made on an ARM will be lower than those on a fixed-rate mortgage. Of course, one reason for this is that the borrower takes on more risk with an ARM than with a fixed-rate mortgage (although if it has caps on annual and lifetime rates, to some extent it provides the best of both the fixed-rate and adjustable-rate product). Another reason is that the prepayment option on an ARM is less valuable than it is on a fixed-rate mortgage, simply because when interest rates fall, the rates on ARMs also fall automatically.

In any event, the one-year ARM is a fine and sustainable mortgage product. In fact, it is the default product in many parts of the world including the United Kingdom and Singapore.

Similarly, for many people, the five-year ARM is an excellent product. This loan keeps its rate fixed for five years and then adjusts, again typically with changes in life or with a one-year constant maturity treasury security, every year thereafter. The initial rate on five-year ARMs is almost always lower than that on a 30-year fixed-rate mortgage. For those borrowers who do not plan on keeping a mortgage for more than five years, the five-year ARM is unambiguously a better product than the 30-year fixed-rate mortgage.

INTEREST-ONLY MORTGAGES

Interest-only (IO) mortgages are mortgages that require borrowers to make no interest payments for a specified period of time, and then begin amortizing at a later time. Let us return to our example of a $100,000 mortgage with a fixed rate of 6 percent. The monthly rate is 0.005, so it is simple to calculate the IO mortgage payment, which is $100,000 * 0.005 = $500.

This payment is considerably lower than the payment on the 15-year amortizing mortgage payment of $843.86. Real estate lenders and brokers have been known to sell these mortgages as "affordable" products, because the initial payments are considerably lower than those on the fixed-rate products.

But IO loans, in the end, do have to amortize. Let's say that in our example, the loan has IO payments for five years, but then the payments are reset to amortize the loan for the 15 years that follow (so that the loan is paid off in 20 years). The payment jumps from $500 per month to $843.86 per month, for an increase of 70 percent. Now let's think about the implications this has for affordability.

Suppose we call an "affordable" loan one in which the mortgage payments are not more than 30 percent of gross income (this leaves some income for property taxes and insurance). So, if a household has a monthly income of $1667, or an annual income of $20,000, a mortgage with a $500 monthly payment is just affordable.

But what happens in five years, particularly if the household's income hasn't changed? Instead of paying 30 percent of income on mortgage payments, the household will be spending a little more than half of its monthly income on payments.

Is such a situation likely? Perhaps not, but from 2006 to 2011, nominal income in the bottom two income quintiles remained flat (inflation-adjusted income fell). Perhaps this is a better way to look at it; For the mortgage to remain "affordable" for the household that acquired it at the margin of affordability, its income would have to rise 70 percent in five years. This scenario is, in fact, unlikely.

This does not mean that the IO loan is inherently a bad product; for certain types of households, it makes a lot of sense. Suppose a household has lots of equity, and its heads are looking to retire in 20 years. Affordability is not an issue. A sensible financial strategy would be refinancing into an IO mortgage, and to use the difference between an IO payment and an amortizing payment to invest in a stock index fund. This plan allows the household to become more diversified financially and invest in growth opportunities.

Households that can only barely afford a house, however, rarely have much equity in anything. For such households, the IO mortgage is a potentially explosive product. It should not be used to make housing "affordable."

PAY OPTION ARMS, PLAMS, AND OTHER NEGATIVE AMORTIZATION MORTGAGES

The inflationary period of the 1970s produced a dilemma for the mortgage market. High rates of inflation meant that nominal interest rates were also high (see Figure 4.1 for an illustration of the relationship between the Consumer Price Index (CPI) and 10-year Treasury rates).

High nominal rates and inflation produced the problem of "tilt." Suppose we think that inflation will rise by 10 percent per year for 10 years, and as a consequence of this, the rate on fixed-rate mortgages is 14 percent. Suppose a household has an income of $50,000, and wished to buy a house for $150,000 (a common heuristic is that you can afford a house that is three times your annual income). If the buyer has a 20 percent down payment, this means they will be making payments on a $120,000 mortgage. Assuming amortization of 30 years, this produces a payment of $1422 per month or $17,062 per year, or about 34 percent of income, which might be a stretch.

But if the household's income grows at just the rate of inflation for 10 years (that is, its inflation-adjusted income remains constant), its income will increase to about $130,000, at which point the payment on the mortgage is quite low relative to income. So in this scenario, real payments are "tilted" toward the beginning of the mortgage, hence making mortgages less affordable at origination.

In response to this, various nongovernment organizations, including the World Bank, introduced the PLAM (Price Level Adjustable Mortgage). PLAMs worked in the following way: Borrowers paid a real (i.e., inflation adjusted) rate of interest, and had their balance reset with inflation every year.

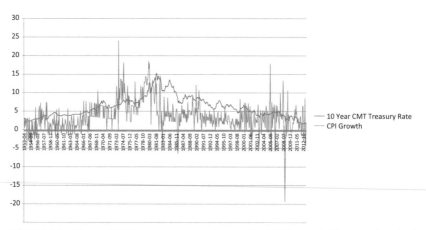

FIGURE 4.1 10-year CMT treasurey rate and annualized CPI growth. *Sources: Board of Governors of the Federal Reserve System and Bureau of Labor Statistics.*

Let us do this with the previous example. The rate of inflation is 10 percent, so the real interest rate is 4 percent. The borrower makes payments for the first year based on the 4 percent rate, or $572.90. This is 14 percent of income, so quite affordable. But after one year, the balance, which is $117,886.76 before the PLAM adjustment, is increased by the 10 percent inflation rate, to $129,654.73. The new payment, based on 4 percent interest and 29 remaining years, is $630.19, which, not coincidentally, is 10 percent higher than the previous payment.

If incomes and house prices move in lock-step with inflation, this all works well. An increase in income to $55,000 would mean that payment-to-income would remain at 14 percent, and an increase in the value of the house to $165,000 would mean that the loan-to-value (LTV) ratio would remain below 80 percent.

Problems arise, however, if incomes and/or house prices do not move with inflation. Indeed, even if incomes and prices move *on average* with inflation, individual incomes and house prices might not. The impact of those that don't keep up with inflation is asymmetric with respect to mortgage performance relative to those that do better. People whose houses go up in value more than inflation will only be slightly less likely to default, whereas those whose prices fall will be substantially more likely to default (income changes have the same effect).

EXOTIC MORTGAGES

Whereas one-year and five-year ARMs could be called consumer-friendly products, the exotic mortgages that largely made up the subprime mortgages responsible for the recent financial crisis almost certainly were not. We will discuss why they are not consumer friendly after we discuss the mechanics of these mortgages.

Three types of exotic mortgages predominated between 2002 and 2007, the height of the "subprime era": The interest-only mortgage, the two–28[2] ARM, and the pay option adjustable rate mortgage, or pay-option ARM.

A two–28 mortgage largely operated like any other ARM, with two exceptions. First, the initial rate on the mortgage was a teaser rate: a rate that was less than the sum of the underlying index rate (e.g., LIBOR or CMT) and the margin. Second, the margin would be very high. The idea was that the consumer would pay a low rate that would allow him or her to qualify for large mortgage origination, and make up for the low rate by paying a higher rate later in the life of the loan. The higher rate would be enforced via a third characteristic of these loans: a prepayment penalty.

How should we think about a prepayment penalty? Consider a loan that has a 30-year amortization period. Suppose in the first two years of its existence it

---

2. Also the three–27 ARM, which was the same as the two–27 except for the time of reset.

has an interest rate of 2 percent, but that if it is prepaid before five years the borrower owes a prepayment penalty of 10 percent.

Mechanics of this mortgage are the same as the previous mortgages we have discussed, with one exception. If the borrower pays off the loan before it is five years old, he or she will own the mortgage balance plus 10 percent. Therefore, what is the cost of this loan to the borrower in the event it pays off in two years? Our cash flows will include 24 months of mortgage payments plus the mortgage balance at the end of month 24 + 10 percent of the mortgage balance. The annual cost of this loan is 6.48 percent. (Use an example with a $100,000 loan to confirm this result. Make the assumption that this mortgage has no cost at origination.)

Paul Willen (2009) and others have shown that these types of mortgages did not explode because their payments got much higher. Instead, they defaulted before their payments would reset. The real problem was that the underwriting methods for these mortgages were not sustainable. Specifically, these mortgages allowed households to qualify for houses they could not afford in the long run. As it happened, the unaffordability of the mortgages became clear before they even reset.

An even more dangerous mortgage was the pay-option ARM. For this mortgage, borrowers have the option to pay less than the amount of interest due at any point in the life of the mortgage. Like the PLAM, these mortgages featured negative amortization; that is, the mortgage balance increased every period that the borrower did not pay the full interest accumulated.

This caused mortgages to be dangerous from two perspectives. First, these mortgages ensured that once house prices stopped rising, as they inevitably would, equity would deteriorate and in many cases turn negative. Second, these mortgages would have even bigger payment shocks than interest-only mortgages once amortization began. As it happened, the first effect was much more important than the second effect. Negative amortization mortgages such as pay option ARMs performed so badly that few actually reached the point where they would begin amortization. According to JP Morgan, as quoted in a Bloomberg Article by Gopal and Shenn (2011), the default rate of pay-option ARMs could approach 70 percent.

SECOND LIEN MORTGAGES

To this point we have confined ourselves to first lien mortgages. Until the financial crisis, second lien mortgages were quite common in the US market. As the name implies, these mortgages have lower priority for payment than first lien mortgages. For example, in the event that a borrower defaults, proceeds from the sale of the house acquired due to foreclosure are first distributed to first lien lenders. Second lien lenders are repaid only if first lien lenders get entirely repaid first.

Because of their lower priority for repayment, second lien loans carry higher interest rates than first lien loans. Two common types of second lien loans are piggyback loans and home equity lines of credit.

Piggyback loans are typically made when a borrower purchases a house. Such loans are constructed to allow borrowers to avoid paying private mortgage insurance. Under Fannie Mae and Freddie Mac rules, borrowers must pay mortgage insurance in the event that their loan-to-value ratio at the time of origination is greater than 80 percent. However, this 80 percent rule applies only to loans purchased by Fannie Mae or Freddie Mac.

In order to help borrowers avoid mortgage insurance, which can be quite expensive, lenders sometimes offered borrowers a second loan equal to 10 percent of the purchase price of the house. Then, Fannie Mae or Freddie Mac would purchase the first loan, which would have an 80 percent loan-to-value ratio, while the lender originating the first lien loan would keep the 10 percent second mortgage in portfolio. This mortgage would typically carry an interest rate that was considerably higher than the rate on the first mortgage and also have a short amortization period.

The 90–10–10 loan has been around for many years but was usually reserved for banks' most credit-worthy customers. Between 2002 and 2006, some lenders saw second liens as an opportunity to earn high yields. Examples of such lenders include Countrywide and Washington Mutual. Not coincidentally, these lenders are now out of business.

The 90–10–10 loan can be a good product for both lenders and borrowers when it is used judiciously. However, when it is used in the absence of strong underwriting, it becomes very vulnerable, even to small negative changes in the housing market. In the recent financial crisis, the Case-Shiller Index fell by more than 30 percent nationally from its peak in 2006. This means that nearly every second lien piggyback mortgage that originated in 2006 was vulnerable. Indeed, in states such as Florida, Arizona, and Nevada, as well as the Inland Empire of California, many piggyback loans had no equity at all to back them up as house prices fell enough for first lien mortgages to be in a negative equity position.

The second common type of second lien mortgage is a home equity line of credit (HELOC). Again, the mortgage is self-descriptive. The mortgage allows homeowners to borrow against their home equity and then to repay the loan when they wish, or at some specified point in the life of the mortgage. With a home equity line of credit, borrowers are required to make full payment of interest every month.

In a recent paper, Nakajima and Telyukova (2011) showed that home equity lines of credit or HELOCs have been a crucial tool, helping those who were house-rich, cash-poor, and elderly to remain in their houses while paying for needed medical care. Like many of the other products discussed here, the HELOC is an excellent product when properly underwritten.

REFERENCES

Fuster, Andreas, Vickery, James, 2013. Securitization and the fixed-rate mortgage. FRB of New York Staff Report 594.

Gopal, Prashant, Shem, Jody. Option ARM Time Bomb Blows Early. Easing Damage to U.S. Housing, Bloomberg February 15, 2011. Accessed at. http://www.bloomberg.com/news/2011-02-15/option-arm-time-bomb-blows-early-limiting-damage-to-u-s-housing-market.html.

Nakajima, Makoto, Telyukova, Irina A., 2011. Home equity in retirement. Age 65.75 85.

Willen, Paul S., 2009. Testimony before The U.S. Senate Committee on Banking, Housing, & Urban Affairs Hearing on "Preserving Homeownership: Progress Needed to Prevent Foreclosures." (July 16).

Underwriting Mortgages and Mortgage Default

INTRODUCTION

Investors in mortgages, whether they are banks or securities holders, seek to hold mortgages that have an optimal expected default rate. As we shall discuss in another part of this book, the optimal expected default rate is *not* zero. A zero default rate means that lenders are passing on good business opportunities, because there will always be profitable pools of borrowers that include a few that for a variety of reasons will not perform (even Harvard has a few students who flunk out).

The key to obtaining an optimal expected default rate is good underwriting. We can think of mortgages as being a lot like insurance: lenders charge a premium (the spread between their cost of funds and the cost of a loan to the borrower) whose price is based on perceived risk. The perception of risk is based on underwriting.

In the case of mortgages, underwriting is based on a number of criteria, six of which are especially important: income, down payment, credit history, documentation, assets beyond down payment, and residency status. We will discuss each of these in turn, as well as some of the other, less important criteria. We will then discuss how these can be used in a statistical model of default to determine expected probability of default, and the impact of those probabilities on expected mortgage losses.

Introduction to Mortgages & Mortgage Backed Securities.
http://dx.doi.org/10.1016/B978-0-12-401743-6.00005-6

UNDERWRITING CRITERIA

Income

Documentation

We might expect that household income would be an especially important deter-minant of mortgage performance. After all, it just makes sense that borrow-ers who spend a smaller part of their income on their mortgage would be less stressed in the face of adverse life-events, and would therefore be more likely to continue to pay their mortgage under most circumstances.

Before characterizing the relationship between income and mortgage perfor-mance, we should discuss the mundane issue of documenting income. For many borrowers, particularly those who have been employed with the same employer for two years or more, income documentation is straightforward. Lenders ask for payroll stubs from the borrower's employer, typically for the most recent two months; IRS W-2 forms from the borrower's employer, typically for the most recent two to three years; and IRS 1040 forms, again, usually from the pre-vious two years. Lenders like W-2 income, and will usually take it at face value.

In the aftermath of the crash, however, lenders view income that arises from activities other than salaried employment more skeptically. This is an issue for two groups in particular: the newly employed, and the self-employed.

Consider a recent college graduate with a job that pays $44,000 per year.[1] As we shall see, in a market where mortgage interest rates are less than 5 percent, this graduate should be able to swing a $125,000 mortgage without difficulty. The graduate may also be able to demonstrate that this income is steady because of a signed contract, and, perhaps, a few months of payroll stubs. But in the aftermath of 2008, lenders are hesitant about borrowers without a track record of earning sufficient income steadily—the evidence of such a track record is the W-2 statement. The absence of two years of sufficient reported income for mort-gage payments is leading newly hired people to leave the conventional market (see definition in Chapter 13) for the FHA market—a market where mortgages are more expensive for borrowers.

It is even more problematic now for potential borrowers who are self-employed to obtain a mortgage. The self-employed include many physicians, dentists, attor-neys—people who have reliable income. But the very nature of self-employment is that income is volatile, in part because business waxes and wanes, and in part because self-employed people will choose to work more in some years and less in others. Self-employed people document their income using the IRS 1099-MISC form, and although such a form provides reliable evidence of income, the income reported tends to vary from year to year. Lenders are thus not entirely sure how to underwrite self-employment income.

---

1. See www.forbes.com/sites/susanadams/2013/01/11/starting-salaries-jump-3-4-for-new-grads/ Adams 2013.

It is perhaps ironic that many loan officers are themselves self-employed people. Mortgage brokers are rarely employees compensated through a salary, but rather independent contractors who work on commission. Needless to say, there were large swings in income for loan officers over the period from 2002 to 2012, as loan origination volumes changed dramatically over this period, reaching a peak of $2.9 trillion in 2005 and a trough of 1.5 trillion in 2008.[2]

For a long period of time, one of the purposes of low documentation loans, or Alt-A loans, was to provide a mechanism by which self-employed people could obtain mortgages. Before the go-go years of 2002 to 2006, however, these loans would have compensating factors, such as high down-payments, to offset the uncertainty arising from hard-to-document steady income.

Ratios

Until roughly the late 1990s, mortgages were underwritten using the 28/36 ratio test: borrowers were expected to pay no more than 28 percent of their gross income for the carrying cost of a house (mortgage payments, property taxes and casualty insurance, or PITI) and no more than 36 percent of their gross income on the carrying cost of the house plus other long-term debt, such as student loans, car loans, and minimum credit card payments. While the expectations of lenders have obviously changed, it is worth doing an example using this standard to understand how we might determine the maximum acceptable mortgage given a certain income.

Let's take a family with an income of $75,000 per year. Let's also assume that they live in a market where property taxes are equal to 1.5 percent of a property's value, and where casualty insurance costs 0.1 percent of the value of the house. The family plans to make a 20 percent down payment, and has a car loan with payments of $400 per month.

The general formula for the carrying cost of a house for a borrower is:

$$CC = V*LTV*DSC + V*\tau_p + V*INS \qquad (5.1)$$

where

CC = carrying cost
V = House Value
LTV = Loan-to-value
DSC = Debt Service Constant
τ_p = Property Tax Rate
INS = Insurance Rate

Suppose the family can obtain a 6 percent, self-amortizing, 30-year fixed-rate mortgage. The Debt Service Constant for this loan is:

$$pmt(0.06/12, 360, 1) *12 = 0.07915$$

---

2. See www.census.gov/compendia/statab/2012/tables/12s1194.pdf

The carrying cost of the house for this family thus will be:

$$(0.8 \, (0.07915) + 0.015 + 0.001) * V = 0.07356 * V$$

We are now close to determining the size of the loan the family can afford using the 28/36 standard. But first, we must ask whether or not mortgage debt is more than 8 percent of gross income. We assume the family has car payments of $400 per month, so their nonmortgage debt obligations as a share of income are:

$$\$4800/\$75,000 = 0.064$$

Because this is less than 8 percent, we can use the 28 percent standard to determine the price of the house the family can afford and the loan amount it can obtain. So now we have that a family can afford a house where the carrying cost is equal to 28 percent of its $75,000 income. Thus we have:

$$0.28 * 75,000 = 0.07356 * V$$

Solving for V, we get a house value of $285,493. The mortgage the family will need is 0.8 * $285,493, or $228,395. Note that this mortgage is roughly three times the family's income. Therefore, in a 6 percent interest rate market, using old-fashioned underwriting standards, we find that a family can comfortably afford a mortgage that is three times larger than its annual income.

Exercise

Suppose this household has student and automobile debt payments of $800 per month. How large a mortgage can the household now afford?

Loan-to-Value Ratio

Documentation

When a lender is evaluating a borrower with respect to loan-to-value ratio, or LTV, two elements come into play: the source of a borrower's down payment, and the value of the property.

When borrowers put money down on a house, lenders want to be sure that the money actually belongs to the borrower—that is, that the borrower hasn't borrowed money in order to produce a down payment. Suppose, for example, that a borrower used a credit card to borrow 20 percent to put down on a house. The borrower under such circumstances has done nothing to demonstrate financial capacity, which is one of the characteristics of a borrower that a lender is interested in. And though it is true that a mortgage obtained with a borrowed down payment is secured by a property that is worth more than the mortgage, it is not clear that such a borrower will, in the presence of financial distress, choose to honor the mortgage.

Analysis

The most important criterion for determining the riskiness of a loan is loan-to-value ratio. The reason for this is straightforward. Suppose a borrower purchases a house with a 50 percent down payment. If that borrower faces financial troubles, she has a choice between selling a house that she might no longer be able to afford, or defaulting on her loan and allowing it to go into foreclosure. So long as she has equity in the house, she will not default; in other words, house prices would have to fall by 50 percent for her to consider default.[3]

The relationship between down payment (or its inverse, LTV) and default propensity is nonlinear. Suppose house prices move as a Weiner Process:

$$dP = \mu + \sigma\sqrt{t} \tag{5.2}$$

Suppose we put $\mu = 0.03$ and $\sigma = 0.05$ To make things easy, let's also assume that we are looking at an interest-only (IO) mortgage.

Now consider the distribution of values of a house relative to a mortgage under LTVs at origination varying from 50 percent to 95 percent five years after the mortgage is originated. The standard deviation of house prices is $0.05\sqrt{5}$, or about 0.11. For the full distribution of house prices over the first 10 years of the mortgage, see Figure 5.1. Let's think about mortgages that originate with a 50 percent LTV. For house prices to have fallen 50 percent (to the point where equity gets wiped out) in 5 years means that house prices have to fall by almost 6 standard deviations relative to expected house prices. To see this, consider that:

$$E[P_5] = P_0 + 0.03 * 5$$

and

$$\sigma_5 = 0.05 * \sqrt{5}$$

Our expected house price to loan after 5 years is thus 1.15. The standard deviation of this is 0.11. The difference between 1.15 and 0.5 (the point at which the value of the loan is equal to the value of the house) is 0.65, which is slightly less than 6 standard deviations. The probability of observing such an outcome is very small.

We should note that there were markets where house prices did fall by 50 percent and more during the crisis, but we should also note that even in the presence of the crisis, there were not many such markets. Based on Federal

---

3. This is an approximation, because other things determine whether or not default is a net benefit. On the one hand, there are generally costs associated with selling a house, which means a borrower might find default beneficial even if they technically have some equity in their house. On the other hand, there are costs associated with default (about which we shall say more elsewhere), meaning a borrower might find default detrimental even if they have no equity in their house.

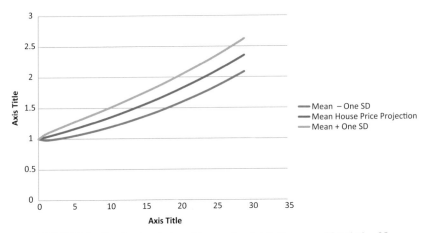

FIGURE 5.1   Simulated evolution of house price distribution mu = .03 and sd = .05.

Housing Finance agency data, the number of metropolitan areas where prices fell more than 50 percent was 21.

We can turn this data around to examine confidence intervals. If the parameters of the mode specified earlier are correct, in 5 years, we expect that house prices on average will be 15 percent higher, thus reducing the probability of default. On the other hand, we expect the standard deviation of prices to rise to about 11.2 percent. Essentially, the 95 percent confidence region for house prices will be $P_0 * 1.15 \pm 0.11 * 1.96$, or ± 0.22.

We have shown that a 50 percent LTV loan is quite safe, if not absolutely bullet proof. Now let's look at a loan that has an 80 percent LTV at origination. In 5 years, the expected house value to loan ratio is 1.15/0.8, so house prices would have to drop by 35 percent, or about 3 standard deviations, for house values to be even with the loan amount. Again, this is a low probability event that occurs about 0.14 percent of the time.

Now let's try 90 percent. Expected house value to loan value in 5 years now becomes 1.15/0.9, so prices would have to drop by 25 percent, or a little more than two standard deviations, for the loan value to equal the house price. We would expect to see this happen about 4 percent of the time.

Note how a large change in LTV—from 50 percent to 80 percent—produces a small change in the probability that a borrower goes underwater, while a smaller change in LTV—from 80 percent to 90 percent—produces a large change in the probability of whether a borrower goes underwater.

Exercise

Using the model of house prices assumed earlier, compute the probability that a loan with an LTV of 95 percent at origination goes under water.

It is thus fair to say that for low LTVs, LTV is not an important predictor of default; however for high LTVs—say those above 80 percent—measuring LTV correctly is crucial to loan performance.

The Appraisal

Appraisals are supposed to provide lenders with reassurance that the collateral being borrowed against is worth what the borrower claims. But appraisal methods and appraisal outcomes both encumber that reassurance.

Appraisers of owner-occupied houses typically fill in a standard form, called the Fannie Mae X form (see Figure 5.2). This form essentially walks appraisers through their job.

The form asks appraisers to provide value using three approaches: the market comparison approach, the cost approach, and the income approach. We will say more about each of these approaches later. The appraiser is supposed to reconcile disagreements among the three approaches, to the extent that the approaches do disagree when it comes to producing a house value. He usually does this by giving a weight to each approach, and then providing a weighted average that expresses his opinion of value.

In the market comparison approach, an appraiser looks for houses (usually at least three) that are comparable to the house being appraised. This is a strength of the market comparison approach, in that it allows an appraiser to use houses that might have individual features that are difficult to value as a foundation for valuing a house that has its own difficult-to-value features.

To give one example, we know that certain architects have built houses that are desirable in the marketplace, but perhaps not enough within one neighborhood to reveal an implicit value, or shadow price, using the sort of statistical analysis we will discuss later. But if a neighborhood has two such houses, and the two houses have sold within a reasonably short period of time before a lender is contemplating a loan on a house by the same architects, those two houses can be good comparables for the house looking to get a loan (also known as a subject property).

The problem, however, is that no two houses are exactly alike, and so appraisers need to make adjustments to value to reflect differences between the comparables and the subject property. If one of the comparables has less dwelling space than the subject property, for instance, the appraiser needs to take that into account, and adjust the value of the appraisal upward.

Very often, however, these types of adjustments seem rather *ad hoc*— appraisers rarely justify how they perform their adjustments. Appraisers might do such a justification in all manner of ways. For example, they could go to cost services, such as RS Means, to find the cost of adding a square foot to a house of a given quality or style. They could also recover adjustments from hedonic regression coefficients, something we will discuss later.

Another approach appraisers use to determine value is the cost approach, which simply totals the cost of producing all the components of a house, depreciates the cost based on age, and then produces a number.

There are two areas in which the cost approach becomes problematic: calculating depreciation, and figuring out the value of land.

Let's start with depreciation. We might think that the easiest way to tackle depreciation is to simply apply straight-line methods to individual components of a house. For example, if a typical composition shingle roof lasts for 15 years, and the roof is 10 years old, we could depreciate the cost of the roof by 2/3.

The problem is that there is no evidence that the market actually values depreciation in this way. Specifically, markets do discount items that need immediate repair (such as a 14-year-old roof), but do not seem to discount items that are just, shall we say, sort of old.

But more ambiguous than depreciation is the valuation of land. Work from Davis and Palumbo (2006) shows that while the value of structures remains more or less constant (on an inflation-adjusted basis) across time, the value of land swings dramatically.

There are two reasons for this. First, land is, by its very nature, inelastic. Although there are examples of places around the world where developable land supply changes through government control (South Korea and Hong Kong release land from government to private control over time), in general, land is in fixed supply. We could argue that certain types of land—for instance, land in successful Central Business Districts or beachfront properties—has little in the way of substitutes, and so is quite inelastically supplied.

When a good's supply is inelastic, changes in demand show up in prices rather than quantities. We can adjust the supply of structures (particularly in growth periods), but we cannot easily adjust the supply of land.

But land is also the aspect of real estate that is affected by speculative bubbles. Structure costs are grounded in commodities prices and labor costs: lumber costs what lumber costs, as does gypsum, as does an hour of a carpenter's labor. So when expectations get frothy, they show up in the value of land (see Chapter 9 for a more detailed description of modeling house price bubbles).

This poses a dilemma for appraisers. When it comes to valuing land, appraisers use the market comparison approach.

Estimating land value is especially difficult in built-up areas. The reason for this is that vacant land sales are hard to come by. Consider, for example, Midtown Manhattan. Vacant lots are rare, and sales of vacant property are even rarer. On the other hand, to acquire property, developers tear down improvements and build new structures. Under such circumstances, they are essentially buying vacant land. The value of such land as vacant is equal to the acquisition price of the property plus the cost involved in demolishing the existing building.

But the market comparison approach reflects what the market is willing to pay for land and this includes bubble markets. So even good appraisers confirm values based on the wisdom or lack thereof of markets. The experience of 2002 to 2008 tells us that markets are not always wise.

This presents problems for investors in mortgages. Even if an appraisal is well constructed, they provide no insight as to whether markets are near their tops (or at their bottoms), and loan-to-value ratios are always measured with some uncertainty.

Before providing broader evidence of the inefficacy of appraisal, let us briefly discuss the income approach to valuation of residential property. This approach is fraught with difficulties. First, we need to assume that an owner-occupied house is rented. To assign a rent to the house, appraisers need to find comparable houses for rent. There are some markets in the United States with active single-family rental markets (indeed, over one-quarter of renters in the United States live in single-family detached houses[4]), but more often than not, single-family neighborhoods principally contain owner-occupied housing.

Once a rent is assigned, it must be converted into a value using a capitalization rate. This once again involves finding comparables—and a sufficient number of them to give some confidence about the capitalization rate. We can understand why appraisers—and lenders—rarely take seriously the income approach to valuing single-family houses.

Yet there is a lot to be gained from using the income approach as a valuation method. When the value obtained via the market comparison approach varies substantially from the income approach, it may be showing that house prices are detached from fundamentals, and that there is thus a possibility of falling house prices. We don't need to believe the precise result arising from the income approach to still glean warnings from it.

In any event, we have good reason to believe that appraisers tend not to provide a truly independent measure of a house's value. The reason is simple: an appraiser's valuation of a house is usually bigger than a property buyer's valuation. This was true 20 years ago, when Lacour-Little and Green (1998) showed that appraisals in Boston matched or exceeded the price of a house paid by an owner 94 percent of the time. It is also true now: Pinto (2013) has shown similar numbers for today.

AUTOMATED VALUATION METHODS

Hedonic Regression

Appraisers, being human, will always feel pressure to provide appraisals that support the issuing of loans. The reasons for this can range from benign (they don't want to upset the ability of a nice young couple to buy their first house) to

---

4. See American Housing Survey (2009), Table 1.1.

malignant (they think they get more business by making sure loan originators get more business).

An alternative method of valuation that removes human emotions, whether empathy or greed, is the automated valuation model, or AVM. Such models generally come in one of two flavors.

The first type of model is a hedonic regression model. Hedonic regressions attempt to uncover the value of individual characteristics of houses by estimating regression coefficients. The models generally take the form:

$$Value = f(X, Z) + \varepsilon \qquad (5.3)$$

where X is house characteristics and Z is neighborhood characteristics.

Spreadsheet 5.1 contains a sample of housing sales data from a large US city in 2006. Included is information for each house about the sale price of the house, the dwelling area in square feet, the size of the lot on which the house sits, the number of bedrooms, the number of bathrooms, the month in which the house sold, the vintage of the house, and the school district in which the house sold.

We will now make some changes. First, we will change the continuous variable "month" into a set of categorical variables, or dummy variables, called M1, M2, and so on. These variables contain on-off switches reflecting the month in which the house was sold. For houses sold in January, M1 takes on a value of 1, otherwise 0; for those sold in February, M2 takes on a value of 1, otherwise 0, and so on. We do this to reflect that fact that house prices are seasonal—they tend to be higher in the summer (when the market is thicker) and lower in the winter.

We will make a second transformation of the data, by converting vintage to age. The data I am using are from 2006, so the age of a house is just 2006-vintage. This will allow me to interpret the meaning of my regression coefficients better; it will tell me how an increase in the age of the house contributes to value. I am also going to transform age into a set of categorical variables, because the relationship between the age of a house and its value, while more often than not negative, is not linear.

Suppose, for example, that houses built in the 1920s that still exist are particularly nice, because the bad houses from the 1920s have been demolished. This means that houses from the 1920s might be, on average, more valuable than those from the 1930s. If my model divides age into categories, such as age is between 0 and 1 (or new), between 2 and 5, and so on, I can see how the impact of vintage changes the value of a house.

I will also create categorical variables for whether a house has a fireplace, whether it has more than one fireplace, whether it is a townhouse, whether it is a condo, how well cared for it is, and whether it has been renovated. I will also create categorical variables for the zip code the house is in.

Let us start with a very simply regression model. We can estimate a regression taking data from Excel and exporting it into the program Stata (there are many programs that do regressions).

We begin by lining up our data such that sales price (our "y" variable, or dependent variable) is on the left-hand side and the other variables (the "x" or explanatory variables), are on the right-hand side. For the time being, we will leave out zip code. Note that we have labels for each of the variables—this is going to be helpful when we get our regression results.

Now click on the Stata icon, and you will get a menu. Go to the toolbar, click Statistics, then Regression, and then Linear Regression. Now go through the menus and select sales price as the dependent variable and the other characteristics as the independent variable.

Now you should be able to see regression results. Each coefficient is like a price—it reflects the marginal value of each characteristic on house prices. The coefficient on dwelling space is 85.40; this means that each square foot adds $85.40 to the value of the house. The coefficient on a new house is $75,000—this means a new house is worth on average $75,000 more than a 50- to 70-year-old house (the excluded age category). But note that a new house is worth less than houses in our oldest category! We can graph what this means about the impact of age on value—note that it rises for a little while, and then falls until the house is 70–100 years old, at which point it begins to rise again.

Before we start to discuss the problems with this approach to valuation, let's take a few minutes to determine how to use it to value a house. We can easily take the characteristics of the house we are attempting to value, and plug them into the model. Suppose we have a house with the following characteristics:

Dwelling Size:	2200 square feet
Age:	70 years
Lot Size:	0.13 Acres
Bedrooms:	4
Full Bathrooms:	2
Half Bathrooms:	1
Quality:	Renovated
Fireplaces:	1
Month sold:	August
Zip code:	12

We plug these numbers into our regression model, and we get a value of $473,386. Alternatively, we could have our computer scan the market for comparables, and find three that are "nearest neighbors" statistically, using methods proposed in Vandell (1993). We could then use the regression coefficients as adjustment factors.

Exercise

Given that we specify the impact of the age as a categorical variable, how can we use this information to develop adjustment factors?

Remember that there is something missing from this model—zip code. A long literature, beginning with Oates (1969), shows that school quality, or at least perception of school quality, has a very large influence on the value of a house. While zip codes are not school districts, some have better schools than others.

The impact of being in a desirable location—such as a good school district— on house prices is colloquially known as the "Disneyland Effect," because of a paper written by Oi (1971) on pricing at Disneyland. In Disneyland, people pay to get in, but not for individual rides. Similarly, people may pay substantial amounts to live in particular neighborhoods, because of schools or other ameni- ties associated with those neighborhoods.

Let us suppose (with some reason) that desirable neighborhoods tend to have older houses than other neighborhoods. What will happen if we perform regressions that take into account dwelling space without controlling for neigh- borhood? We will overstate the value of a vintage. This is why controls for loca- tion are quite important when using hedonic regression as the foundation for an automated valuation model.

Exercise

Perform another regression, only now do so creating categorical variables, or dummy variables, for school districts. What happens to the coefficient on dwelling size?

Getting individual coefficients right is important if we want to know the true value of the individual characteristics of a house. And this will be the case if we are going to use the coefficients as adjustment factors.

But the individual coefficients are not so important if all we care about is estimating the value of the house. If a relatively small number of coefficients fit the data well, they might be able to give us an automated estimate of value.

The most commonly used measure of goodness-of-fit is R^2. In our regres- sion example, we get an R^2 of 0.55. This means that 55 percent of the variation in sales prices can be explained by the variation in the explanatory variables.

But what does this mean? It actually doesn't mean as much as many people think, because it only gives the level of accuracy of the regression *assuming that we have true knowledge of regression coefficients*.[5] The problem is that we do not have such knowledge—we only have an estimate of the coefficients.

---

5. Goldberger (1991) has a superb explanation about why R^2 should not be taken as any kind of standard for how well a model predicts outcomes.

These estimates have standard errors that reduce our confidence in our ability to explain sales prices well. R^2 does not take these standard errors into account.

To determine how reliable a regression-based estimate of value is, we must find the standard error of the fitted value we get by using this model. This standard error is calculated using the following formula:

$$x\sigma_{se} = \sqrt{X \sum X' + \sigma_r^2}$$

(5.4)

where X is the vector of house characteristics, Σ is a variance covariance matrix of the regression coefficients, and σ_r^2 is the variance of the regression, which is the sum of squared error terms from the regression divided by its degrees of freedom, which is the number of observations on which the model is fitted less the number of regression coefficients. Formally,

$$x \cdot \sigma_r^2 = \frac{\sum_{i=1}^{N} e_i^2}{N - k}$$

(5.5)

where e_i is the error term, or residual, or unexplained part, from each observation in the regression; N is the number of observations; and k is the number of regression coefficients.

So let us take the example of the house we were valuing earlier. We can get most of the information we need from Statplus: it automatically gives us σ_r^2.

To calculate the variance covariance matrix, we need to know that the expression for a covariance matrix is:

$$\sum = \sigma_r^2 (X'X)^{-1}$$

where X is now a matrix of the explanatory variables. We can take care of this in Excel, using matrix functions. We begin by taking our matrix of explanatory variables, which we shall call X, and copying and pasting them using Transpose in Excel. That is, we select the explanatory variables, select Copy from the Edit menu, and then Paste while checking the box for Transpose. This transposed data is X'.

Now, go to another, clear place in the spreadsheet (or even better, another tab), and type =MMULT(Transposed X,X). You will get one number in one cell. Keep the cursor over that cell, and press Control-U; then press Command-Return. You will now get a matrix populated with numbers. Let's call this XPRIMEX.

Go to a space aligned below, and type MINVERSE(XPRIMEX). Once again press Control-U and then Command-Return. This will give you $(X'X)^{-1}$. We are nearly done now—we multiply all the elements in $(X'X)^{-1}$ by σ_r^2. We now have estimated Σ, which in turn allows us to estimate σ_{se}^2.

Now we can begin to see the problem. Our automated valuation of the house in our example is $508,694. But our 95 percent confidence interval is ± 1.96* σ_{se}^2. *In our context, the confidence interval is* $7391 to $1,009,996 Suppose we think we are underwriting a house with a loan-to-value ratio of 80 percent.

With the automated valuation system, we can be 95 percent sure that the true loan-to-value ratio is between about 40 percent and 5.7 million percent. This is not entirely helpful.

We can turn the model around and use it to ask whether the offer price a buyer makes on a house is within the confidence interval. If that is the case, it provides some evidence that the buyer is not overpaying for the house. Perhaps more important evidence is the size of the down payment itself. Let's say a buyer offers $250,000 for a house, and makes a $50,000 down payment. Given that according to the 2010 *Survey of Consumer Finances*, the median financial net worth of an American household was $77,300, this $50,000 is a powerful signal that the borrower believes the house is worth what she is paying for it. This fact does provide information about the value of the house that allows the lender to be more confident that the true LTV is equal to what the borrower posits it to be.

But this poses a dilemma about how to underwrite very low down payment loans—say FHA loans that require down payments of as little as 3 percent. We now have the duel problem that the regression has precision issues, and the buyer is not sending a strong signal about values. This is a reason low down payment loans are riskier than we can accurately measure.

Repeat-Sales Regression

An alternative regression method to hedonic regression is repeat-sales regression. This method was devised by Richard Muth (Muth 1963), and was popularized by Karl Case and Robert Shiller in the late 1980s Case and Shiller (1987). The repeat sales method has strengths and weaknesses relative to the hedonic method, but before discussing those, let's describe how repeat-sales regression works.

The first thing to note is that two of the most popular current measures of house prices are the Case-Shiller Index and the Federal Housing Finance Agency Index. Both indices start with a similar model specification, which is:

$$x\ln (price_t) - \ln (price_{t-1}) = \alpha + \sum_{t=1}^{T} \beta_t I(t)_t + \varepsilon \qquad (5.6)$$

where X_t takes on a value of 1 if a house is purchased at time t and a value of -1 if is it is sold at time t. The β_t coefficients can be interpreted as an index number for time t, relative to time zero, which is represented by α.

The virtue of repeat sales regression is that it allows us to take into account all the characteristics of a house—both observed and unobserved. Note, though, that this assumes the characteristics of the house remain unchanged between the time of one sale and the next. We will discuss some of the implications of this assumption when we discuss strengths and weaknesses.

In any event, while the application of repeat-sales may seem straightforward, it is not. Users of the procedure need to make a variety of decisions.

The first decision is whether to give each house the same weight in the regression, or to give each house a weight based on its value. From the standpoint of individual homebuyers (or underwriters of individual mortgages), equal-weight measure is the more appropriate; from the standpoint of investors in portfolios of mortgages, the value-weighted measure is more appropriate. The FHFA Index is an equal-weight index; the Case-Shiller Index is a value-weighted index.

The second decision deals with "unusual" sales, such as distressed sales—that is, sales arising from a foreclosure. Campbell et al. (2009) have found that distressed sales sell at a 28 percent discount to normal sales. Suppose you are appraising a house selling under normal circumstances, but are using an index that contains an unusual number of distressed sales. You will probably understate the value of the house (and the converse is true when valuing distressed sales, because ordinary sales are included in the data used in the regression underlying the index).

Third, we must take into account the fact that as the distance between a house's sales increases, the variation of the impact of maintenance on value also increases. Consider two owners who hold their houses for one year, and who bought houses that are in similar condition. One owner might take loving care of a house, and the other might ignore maintenance all together. When both owners go to sell, however, the houses will still be in fairly similar condition, because the consequences of low maintenance for one year are marginal.

But now let's say we have two owners who hold their houses for 15 years. The well-maintained house will still be in very good shape, but the poorly maintained one will not. This difference in quality is known in statistics jargon as unobserved heterogeneity. Case and Shiller's (1989) classic paper on repeat sales discusses techniques for dealing with unobserved heterogeneity, and readers who are interested in doing repeat sales analysis on their own are recommended to that reading.

Finally, we must make a decision about whether houses that sell more than once within a particular time period are representative of the overall housing stock. Heckman suggests that the answer to that question is no, but there is no particularly good method for correcting for the problem.[6] This may be a reason to use hedonic regression instead of repeat-sales regressions, because hedonics incorporate all houses that sell, not just those that sell more than once.

---

6. When a sample does not represent the underlying population being studied, we run into an issue known as "selection bias." Heckman (1979) developed a well-known technique for addressing this bias, but it is hard to implement in the context of repeat sales. The problem arises because addressing selection means having a convincing exclusion restriction, which means finding a variable that explains whether or not someone puts his house on the market without also explaining the value of the house. Whereas in principle, we could look at factors such as the demographic characteristics of home sellers, which explain a decision to sell but not the value of the house, in practice we can rarely access such personal information about homeowners.

Beyond all of this, repeat-sales methods make an important implicit assumption—that the relative price of individual housing characteristics remain constant over time. This is because the model underlying repeat-sales is:

$$\ln(price_t) - \ln(price_{t-1}) = X_t\beta_t - X_{t-1}\beta_{t-1} + I(t)\gamma_t - I(t-1)\gamma_{t-1}$$
$$+ \delta_t - \delta_{t-1} + \varepsilon_t - \varepsilon_{t-1} \tag{5.7}$$

where $I(t)$ is an indicator variable that takes a value of 1 at times 1, and 0 otherwise. The Xs and βs are presumed to remain constant, as are the unobservable characteristics δ and hence drop out, leaving us with Equation (5.7). But of course, the Xs change a little bit (or sometimes a lot) over time, and if we ran hedonic regressions each year, we would find that the βs change too.

But repeat-sales regressions are usually more precise than hedonic regressions, because they deal with unobserved characteristics. The point is that both techniques have limits, which is why they are not a magic bullet to the appraisal problem. AVMs do have the virtue, however, of being free of human bias, even if they are not free of statistical variety.

Cumulative Loan-to-Value Ratio

We have to this point discussed two issues that are key to determining home equity: the size of the borrower's down payment, and the true value of the house the borrower is purchasing.

But another issue bedevils lenders and investors trying to determine the safety of a loan—cumulative LTV, or CLTV.

For many years, when a lender offered a borrower a first lien loan, she often evaluated that loan as if the property secured no other debt. This is because the lender was in first position in the event that anything went wrong, so she had some confidence that the existence of second (or higher) liens was not so important: such liens would get wiped out before the first lien had to bear any cost.

As we discussed in Chapter 4 when listing types of mortgages, second lien mortgages usually come in one of two varieties: piggy-back loans (such as a 10 percent second lien for a 90-10-10 loan, which allows a borrower to put only 10 percent down and avoid mortgage insurance), and home equity lines of credit, or HELOCs, which allow households to extract equity from their houses. Of course because borrowers generally take out HELOCs after they have purchased their house, lenders making first lien loans often don't—in fact can't—know of their existence.

In any event, one of the surprises arising from the subprime crisis is that some borrowers continue paying their second liens after they cease to pay their first liens. Jagtiani and Lang (2010) write:

We … find that negative equity, proxied by LTV and/or CLTV exceeding 90 percent, has been the primary reason for homeowners to default on their mortgages overall. Negative equity is a necessary but not sufficient condition for strategic mortgage default. While some of these homeowners default on both first mortgages and second lien home equity lines, a large portion of the delinquent borrowers actually keep their second lien current. This behavior is generally more common with people who have HELOCs (rather than HELOANs) and is more common when there is a larger unused line of credit. These second liens that are current, but behind a seriously delinquent first mortgage, are subject to a high risk of default if the default on the first mortgage results in a foreclosure.

Perhaps because HELOCS are like revolving credit accounts, they are useful to borrowers looking to survive rough economic times.

The other issue is that first lien lenders have had a difficult time enforcing their priority over junior liens. If a first lien borrower is delinquent, but a second lien borrower is not, it is in the interest of the second lien lender to fight foreclosure. In the end, the first lien holder has priority, but it can be costly for a first lien holder to act, given that legal processes are usually expensive.

Credit History

After loan-to-value ratio (or perhaps more accurately, down-payment size), the most important predictor of default is credit history—whether, and for how long, a borrower has paid her bills. Although measures of credit history received considerable criticism, a Federal Reserve Board report to Congress on credit scores show that FICO does a reasonably good job of predicting whether and how well borrowers repay their debts.[7]

The most widely used credit score comes from Fair Isaac, and is known as the FICO (for Fair Isaac Company) score. FICO scores range from 300 to 850, and underwriters use the score to determine whether borrowers get credit, and if so, how much they pay for that credit. On March 20, 2013, FICO reported the following relationship between FICO score and interest rates available to borrowers for a $150,000, 30-year fixed rate mortgage:[8]

Your FICO® Score	Your Interest Rate	Your Monthly Payment
760–850	3.23%	$651
700–759	3.45%	$669
680–699	3.62%	$684
660–679	3.84%	$702
640–659	4.27%	$739
620–639	4.81%	$788

Borrowers with FICO scores below 620 are generally considered to be subprime borrowers. In 2013, such borrowers would find it difficult to obtain any mortgage financing.

---

7. http://www.federalreserve.gov/boarddocs/rptcongress/creditscore/creditscore.pdf, accessed on April 1, 2013.

8. http://www.myfico.com/FICOCreditScoreEstimator/AboutScores.aspx, accessed on March 20, 2013. The table varies daily.

FICO scores contain a number of ingredients, which can be largely gleaned from FICO's web site. They include:

1. The number of open credit cards the borrower has.
2. How long it has been since the borrower received her first loan.
3. How many loans or credit cards have been applied for recently.
4. How many loans or credit cards have been opened recently.
5. How many credit cards have a balance.
6. What the total balances are.
7. Whether any payments have been missed.
8. How many loans are past due.
9. What percent of your total credit card limits credit card balances represent.
10. Whether the borrower has had a severe adverse financial event, such as a bankruptcy.

So this gives us a pretty good idea about the ingredients in the FICO sauce, but how they mix together is proprietary.

FICO in the end develops three scores based on credit reporting from three agencies: Experien, Equifax, and Transunion.

FICO is helpful, as far as it goes. It has historically had some ability to predict default. But as Yuliya Demyanyk (2008) showed in a note for the Federal Reserve Bank of St. Louis, borrowers with high FICO scores who took out loans that had subprime characteristics (about which we will say more later) had high rates of serious delinquency (see Figure 5.2).

So while it is evident that borrowers with high FICO scores had lower serious delinquency rates than borrowers with lower scores, within the subprime market, their loans were still sufficiently troubled that they were not sustain-

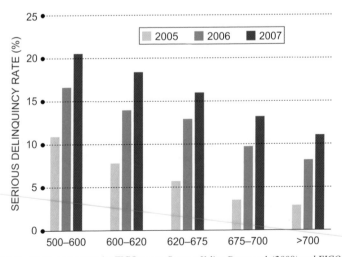

FIGURE 5.2 Delinquency rate by FICO score. *Source: Yuliya Demyanyk (2008) and FICO (2013).*

able as a product. Part of this may be that borrowers who had good measured credit characteristics, but who also sorted themselves into subprime product, had unmeasured credit characteristics that, if known, would predict a greater propensity to default.

Other Underwriting Standards

We have listed the most important underwriting standards: home equity, or loan-to-value ratio, documentation, debt-to-income ratio, and credit history. There are other underwriting standards as well.

1. **Use of the residence.** Loans backed by residences that are occupied by the owners are lower-risk loans than those backed by investment properties, because investment property owners are more likely to be speculators, and are also more likely to ruthlessly default.
2. **Job tenure.** Lenders deem those who have been in a particular job for more than two years to be lower risk borrowers.
3. **Reserves.** Lenders want borrowers to have in liquid accounts sufficient reserve to make payments for a number of periods, in the event that borrowers face economic dislocation, such as job loss and/or illness.

PUTTING IT TOGETHER

Perhaps the best way to demonstrate how underwriting works is to look at a sample underwriting matrix for Fannie Mae loans from 2012 (Figure 5.3).

Let's look at the requirements for a purchase-money loan for a single-family home with a LTV ratio of 90 percent. First, because the loan is greater than a 75 percent LTV loan, the borrower must have a credit score of at least 680, assuming that the borrower's debt-to-income ratio is less than 36 percent. If it is more than 36 percent, the FICO must be at least 700. The borrower's FICO can be a little lower if she has at least six months in reserves.

It is fair to ask where such a matrix might come from. A detailed answer involves knowledge of the estimation of hazard functions, which is beyond the scope of this book. Suffice it to say that modelers can estimate econometrically a function of the form:

$$\text{Prob (default)} = f(X) + e$$

where the X's are a series of variables that might influence default (and therefore the cost of default), such as LTV ratio, payment-to-income ratio, and FICO score.

Such models are the foundations of automated underwriting systems such as Freddie Mac's loan prospector, Fannie Mae's Desktop Underwriter, and the proprietary systems of private sector lenders. When we discuss the financial crisis, we will also discuss the strengths and limitations of these models.

ELIGIBILITY MATRIX

The Eligibility Matrix provides the comprehensive LTV, CLTV, and HCLTV ratio requirements for conventional first mortgages eligible for delivery to Fannie Mae. The Eligibility Matrix also includes credit score, minimum reserve requirements (in months), and maximum debt-to-income ratio requirements for manually underwritten loans. Other eligibility criteria that are not covered in the Eligibility Matrix may be applicable for mortgage loans to be eligible for delivery to Fannie Mae, e.g., allowable ARM plans. See the *Selling Guide* for details. Refer to the last two pages of this document for exceptions to the requirements shown in the matrices.

Acronyms and Abbreviations Used in this Document

ARM: Adjustable-rate mortgage, fully amortizing

DTI: Debt-to-income ratio

DU®:   Desktop Underwriter®

FRM: Fixed-rate mortgage, fully amortizing

LTV: Loan-to-value ratio

CLTV: Combined loan-to-value ratio

HCLTV: Home equity combined loan-to-value ratio

Credit Score/LTV: Representative credit score and highest of LTV, CLTV, and HCLTV ratios

Effective Dates:

DU loan casefiles – Loans underwritten with DU Version 9.1

Manually underwritten loans – Loans with application dates on or after January 10, 2014

September 24, 2013
1

FIGURE 5.3   Eligibility matrix for Fannie Mae loans.

REFERENCES

Adams, Susan, 2013. Starting Salaries Jump 3.4% For New Grads. Forbes. Forbes Magazine, 11 Jan. Web. 28 Mar. 2013.

Campbell, John Y., Giglio, Stefano, Pathak, Parag, 2009. Forced sales and house prices. National Bureau of Economic Research, No. w14866.

Case, Karl E., Shiller, Robert J., 1987. Prices of Single Family Homes Since 1970: New Indexes for Four Cities. New England Economic Review Sept.-Oct, 45–56. Web.

Davis, Morris A., Palumbo, Michael G., 2006. The Price of Residential Land in Large U.S. Cities. Washington, D.C.: Divisions of Research & Statistics and Monetary Affairs. Federal Reserve Board. Print.

Demyanyk, Yuliya, 2008. Did Credit Scores Predict the Subprime Crisis. Federal Reserve Bank of St. Louis, The Regional Economist Oct, 12–13. Web.

Eligibility Matrix. 2012. Fannie Mae, Web.

FICO Score Estimator. N.p., n.d. Web. 20 Mar. 2013.

Goldberger, Stanley, Arthur, 1991. A course in econometrics. Harvard, Cambridge, MA.

Green, Richard K., LaCour-Little, Michael, 1998. Are Minorities or Minority Neighborhoods More Likely to Get Low Appraisals? Journal of Real Estate Finance & Economics 16.3, 301–315. Print.

Heckman, James J., 1979. Sample Selection Bias as a Specification Error. Econometrica 47.1, 153–161. Print.

Isakson, Hans R., 1986. The Nearest Neighbors Appraisal Technique: An Alternative to the Adjustment Grid Methods. Real Estate Econ 14.2, 274–286. Print.

Jagtiani, Julapa, Lang, William W., 2010. Working Paper No. 11-3: Strategic Default on First and Second Lien Mortgages During the Financial Crisis. Philadelphia Fed. Federal Reserve Bank of Philadelphia 9 Dec. Web.

Muth, Richard, Bailey, Martin, Nourse, Hugh, 1963. A Regression Method for Real Estate Price Index Construction. Journal of the American Statistical Association 48, 933–943. Print.

Oates, Wallace E., 1969. The Effects of Property Taxes and Local Public Spending on Property Values: An Empirical Study of Tax Capitalization and the Tiebout Hypothesis. Journal of Political Economy 77.6, 957–971. Print.

Oi, Walter Y., 1971. A Disneyland dilemma: Two-part tariffs for a Mickey Mouse monopoly. The Quarterly Journal of Economics 85.1, 77–96.

Palumbo, Michael G., Davis, Morris A., 2008. The Price of Residential Land in Large U.S. Cities. Journal of Urban Economics 63.1, 352–384. Print.

Pinto, Edward J., 2013. Realty, Unreality: Are Low Appraisal Values a Problem in Housing? American Enterprise Institute. N.p., 11 Mar. Web. 28 Mar. 2013.

Mortgage-Backed Securities and Derivatives

The US mortgage, with its long-term fixed-rate and prepayment option, creates a dilemma for investors: term risk. Financial intermediaries funded with short-term money, such as banks and Savings and Loans (S&Ls), have problems with the fixed rate feature; those funded with long-term money, such as pension funds and insurance companies, have problems with the refinance feature. Until the recent financial crisis, in fact, investors in mortgages worried far more about market risk and prepayment risk than credit risk.

In an attempt to redress these issues, Salomon Brothers invented the Collateralize Mortgage Obligation, or CMO, in 1983. The idea of the CMO was to pool together mortgages and then split (tranche) them into pieces, such that the pieces are more attractive to different classes of investors than a whole loan would be. We have in a previous chapter discussed the benefits of pooling per se, so in this chapter we will focus on the perceived benefits of tranching. We will begin by focusing on interest rate and prepayment risk, and then move on to discuss credit risk.

TYPES OF TRANCHES

We will discuss five types of tranching: pro rata tranching, sequential tranching, strips, floaters, and planned amortization class tranching.

The definitions of each type of tranche are intuitive; with a pro rata tranching, each tranche pays principal on a pro rate basis to investors. With a

Introduction to Mortgages & Mortgage Backed Securities.
http://dx.doi.org/10.1016/B978-0-12-401743-6.00006-8

sequential tranche, mortgage pools are sliced into classes (for instance, A, B, and C), and each class's principal repaid in sequence. Sometimes, pools are split such that there is a Z-tranche, which mimics a zero-coupon bond. That is, the last tranche receives no cash flow—not even interest, until more senior tranches are paid off.

Strips are securities that split cash-flows from mortgage pools into their two fundamental components, with one class of investors receiving all principal payments, while another class of investors receives all interest payments.

Floaters arise from a tranching structure where cash flows from underlying long-term fixed-rate securities are broken up to mimic cash flows from shorter-term securities. Floaters generally move in step with London Interbank Offered Rate (LIBOR), while inverse floaters move in the opposite direction from LIBOR.

Finally, planned amortization class (PAC) securities are securities that guarantee the timing of cash flows to an investor, so long as prepayment speeds remain within a specific band.

To illustrate how each of these types of securities work, we hold constant the underlying pool of mortgages.

The Mortgage Pool

Our model pool will consist of 30 $100,000 mortgages. They have an initial coupon rate of 6 percent, and are self-amortizing, fixed-rate mortgages. The scheduled amortization is given in Spreadsheet 6.1, tab 1. Tab 2 presents amortization at a baseline PSA of 100. We also show amortization if interest rates fall after 1 year to 5 percent. We assume a PSA of 400. This is in Spreadsheet 6.1, tab 3. Finally, we show amortization if interest rates rise to 7 percent. This is accompanied by a PSA of 50. The cash flows under this scenario are in Spreadsheet 6.1, tab 4.

Just to review, both the duration and the weighted average life of the security change with prepayment behavior. Note that in the absence of any prepayment, the duration of the pool is 10.78 years and the weighted average life is 19.31 years. At baseline (100 percent) PSA, duration drops to 7.4 years and WAL to 11.35. At the fast PSA, duration drops to 3.92 years and the WAL to 4.76. At the slow PSA, duration rises to 8.75 years and WAL to 14.43 years.

We will put the pool into a Freddie Mac GOLD PC. This will allow us, for the time being, to not worry about credit risk.

Pro Rata Tranching

Pro rata tranching is straightforward, and is essentially the same thing as providing *pari passu* shares in a mortgage pool. Suppose there are 30 investors at 100,000 each. Each investor would receive 1/30 of all cash flows at the time they are paid. Interest rate and prepayment risks are the same for everyone.

Investors benefit from the diversification of having a piece of many different mortgages, but are taking equal risks.

Sequential Tranching

We now move on to sequential tranching. With a sequential tranche, cash flows are divided into sequences: the first tranche collects the first principal, the second collects principal only after the first tranche is retired, and so on. With a standard setup, all tranches receive interest until the underlying pool of mortgages is retired.

Let's start with a simple example. We can divide the cash flows from the pools into two tranches, which we shall call Tranche I and Tranche II. We will assign the first $1 million of principal to Tranche I, and the remaining $2 million to Tranche II. We will also assign a coupon rate of 4 percent to the first tranche (more on this later).

Tab 5 of Spreadsheet 6.1 presents that total principal and interest cash flows going to Tranche I and Tranche II, assuming a baseline case of interest rates remaining constant, and prepayment staying at the baseline of 100 percent.

Note that in the setup, Tranche I receives all the principal until it is paid off. Tranche II receives all principal that is not paid to Tranche I—in other words, zero—until Tranche I is fully repaid.

The initial interest payment to Tranche I is $1,000,000 * 0.04/12, or $3333.33. The interest not paid to Tranche I is paid to Tranche II. This goes on for 75 periods, at which point Tranche I is paid off and Tranche II receives all the cash flows.

What return, or implicit coupon, does Tranche II earn? To find this, we need to find the internal rate of return on the cash flows for Tranche II. The Tranche II cash flows are presented in column Q. Tranche II gets an IRR of 6.33 percent.

A couple of other things are worth noting. First, note that the duration and weighted average life on Tranche I are considerably smaller than on Tranche II. This is, of course, by design. By breaking up the mortgage pools into two tranches, the CMO allows investors mortgage instruments that to some degree mimic the yield curve.

Second, Tranche I is completely protected from a return perspective. Tranche II, on the other hand, faces some return risk. When prepayment slows, the Tranche receives more interest payments (a positive thing), but also receives principal later (a negative thing). As such, it looks a little like an interest-only (IO) strip security, about which we will say more later.

Exercises

1. You have been given spreadsheets for the scenario where mortgage rates stay constant and where mortgage rates fall. Please change the spreadsheet to reflect the scenario in which interest rates rise by 100 basis points after one year and in which PSA drops to 50 percent.

2. Find the Present Value of the two Tranches under all three scenarios.
3. Suppose I decided to break the underlying mortgage pool into three tranches with equal principal. The first tranche earns a return of 4 percent, and the second 5 percent. Compute the IRR on Tranche III under all three scenarios.

Z-Tranches

To this point, we have discussed sequential tranches, where one tranche receives all the principal before the second, but both tranches receive interest throughout their lives. With a Z-tranche structure, the final tranche in a sequence receives no cash flows at all until the others are retired. For investors who wish to time tax events, this structure can be appealing.

To see how this works, let us consider a simple two-tranche structure (tab 6). Tranche I receives all the cash flows until it is retired, and then the Z-tranche gets all the cash flows until the underlying mortgage pools are retired. Note that relative to the sequential tranche case, the duration shortens on the first tranche and lengthens on the second. Note also that the IRR on the second tranche drops a little bit. This is, of course, because the payments are delayed.

We might wonder why any investor would be interested in the Z-tranche, given that it is riskier than the second sequential tranche and earns a lower IRR. First, in structuring the deal, the underwriter of the MBS might assign a lower coupon to the first tranche, and as such, allow the Z-tranche to pick up more yield. But the Z-tranche structure also allows the investor to defer taxes—it is accumulating principal (essentially a capital gain) without paying taxes on that accumulation of wealth. When taxes are deferred, their effective rate is lowered. We will illustrate this in greater detail in a later chapter.

Exercise
Add a second tranche to the example discussed earlier. Specifically, create a structure with three $1 million tranches: two sequential tranches with coupon rates of 3.5 and 4.5 percent, followed by a Z-tranche. Compute the IRR on the Z-tranche.

Stripped Securities

Another method of creating derivatives out of mortgage pools is the stripped security. The construction of these securities is quite simple: one class of investor owns all the principal payments, and the other owns the interest payments.

Before getting into a specific example, let us work through the implication of such securities. For the time being, we worry only about interest rates and prepayment risk, and ignore default.

Investors in a principal-only (PO) strip know the sum total of the cash flows they receive—in the absence of default—is simply the original principal balance of the mortgage pool. So the only things that vary over the evolution of a PO strip are the timing of the cash flows and the rate at which they are discounted.

Consider what happens when interest rates rise. Prepayment slows, which means investors in the PO strip get their money back later, which reduces the value of the investment (money received later is not as valuable as money received sooner). At the same time, because interest rates have risen, the cash flows, when received, are more heavily discounted. The reverse is true when interest rates fall. Consequently, PO strips have very long duration.

Let us return to our example pool to see how this works. Let's take two cases: in one, interest rates rise to 7 percent and PSA drops to 50.5; in the other, interest rates fall to 5 percent and PSA rises to 400 (see tab 8). Under the 7 percent scenario, the value of the principal cash flows is $1,284,651. Now change the input values in tab 7 to a PSA of 400 percent and a discount rate of 5 percent: the value of the PO strip rises to $2,417,084, or an increase in value of 88 percent!

So let's calculate the implications of this. An instantaneous two percentage point drop in interest rates produces an 88 percent increase in value: the duration of this security is 88/2, or 44 years. This is almost five times as long as the duration of the underlying mortgage-backed security.

We might reasonably ask why such a security even exits. After all, it appears that it takes a security that already has a substantial amount of interest rate risk embedded into it—a mortgage-backed security—and makes it even riskier.

The answer is that PO strips can be good hedging instruments for institutions with negative duration. An example of such an institution is a life insurance company.

Life insurance companies can use actuarial studies to predict their payout requirements with a great deal of certainty. While no one knows for sure when an individual might die, it is possible to know with a great deal of certainty the share of people in an insurance pool that will die. Suppose a company has 10,000 50-year-olds in a pool, and the probability of any one 50-year-old dying in the next year is 0.001 percent. Then the insurance company can be sure with 95 percent confidence that $\pm 1.96 * \sqrt{(0.001 * 0.999/1000)}$ of their pool will die in the following year. The company can do similar calculations for any age group for any particular year.

While a life company can predict with confidence how much money it will owe in any particular year, it is much harder for it to predict how it will get to that point. Suppose it invests money today and expects to get an 8 percent return, and counts on that 8 percent to produce what is necessary to pay policy holders in 20 years. If it invests in short maturity assets at 8 percent, and then interest rates fall, it will find itself in trouble in 20 years when it needs to pay off its policy holders.

In financial terms, the way to think about this is that when interest rates fall, the present value of short-term assets stays about the same, while the present value of long-term liabilities increases. This creates a gap between funding and obligations. Life companies under such circumstances will need to raise premiums in order to fulfill their obligations.

But if a life company is not managed well financially, increases in premiums could lead to a loss of business, which could ultimately produce insolvency. This is the reverse side of the depository coin. For depositories with short liabilities and long assets, increases in interest rates can lead to insolvency; for insurance companies with short-term liabilities and long-term assets, *decreases* in interest rates can lead to insolvency.

Under such circumstances, derivatives with extremely long duration, such as PO strips, can be extremely useful as hedges. A life insurance company might

Orange County California

In the later 1980s, Robert Citron, the Treasurer of Orange County California, one of the most affluent counties in the United States, began investing county funds into mortgage-backed securities derivatives with long duration (including principal-only strips). Between 1985 and 1993, interest rates fell secularly (see Figure 6.1), because inflationary expectations dropped as the Federal Reserve, as led by Paul Volker and then Alan Greenspan, emphasized reducing inflation over stimulating employment.

As we have already discussed, in periods when interest rates are falling, fixed income securities with long duration will see strong capital gains. Because Orange County, via Robert Citron, invested in long duration securities in the later 1980s, the assets of Orange County increased in value, allowing for it to improve government services while not raising taxes.

While this strategy is very appealing when interest rates are falling, it is inevitably dangerous, because a small change in interest rates will lead to a large reduction in the value of government assets. But Citron (and to be fair, his advisors from investment banks such as Merrill Lynch) not only invested in long duration securities, he levered up using short-term debt to invest in such securities.

This placed Orange County at enormous risk, because, like a Savings and Loan, the present value of its liabilities was largely independent of interest rates, while the present value of its assets was highly sensitive to them. For Orange County, the chickens came home to roost in 1993: interest rates flattened in that year and then began rising. As a consequence, when Orange County needed to rollover its municipal debt, it could not post the necessary collateral: the value of its assets (which were sensitive to interest rates) was less than the value of the liabilities that came due. Consequently, in 1993, one of the richest counties in the United States became a deadbeat county, and declared bankruptcy.

Robert Citron and Orange County can teach us many lessons. First, extraordinary returns are more likely a function of good fortune than brilliance. Smart people will not let riches give way to hubris. Second, risky securities are, well, risky, and levering up to buy more of them just produces more risk. Third, while many derivatives are useful for hedging, they can prove very dangerous when used for speculation.

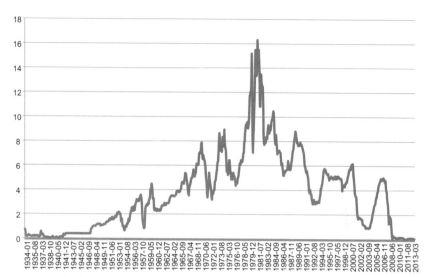

FIGURE 6.1   3-month treasury rates 1934–2013. *Source: Board of Governors of the Federal Reserve System.*

invest in PO strips in order to increase the duration of its book from negative toward zero.

At the same time, IO strips see countervailing influences affect their value when interest rates rise. On the one hand, slower prepayments mean that they collect more interest than otherwise. On the other hand, the higher discount rates make the value of those interest payments lower, offsetting the benefits of the greater number of interest payments. This tends to mean IO strips have short duration.

Consider the extreme case where interest rates drop precipitously and Public Securities Administration (PSA) rises dramatically. The value of the security drops to nearly zero, because interest payments drop to nearly zero. Thus dropping interest rates produce a reduction in security value, which is negative duration.

Let's turn again to tab 7. Under the 7 percent, 50 percent PSA scenario, the value of the IO strip is 1,470,300. Under the 5 percent, 400 percent PSA scenario, the value is $658,231. In this instance, the IO strip has very negative duration!

While the duration is still positive, it is considerably smaller, coming in at (2,066,243/1,775,309-1)/2, or 8 years.

Exercise

What happens to the duration of the two strips if PSA rises to 1000?

Adding Default

To this point, we have assumed that mortgages are guaranteed, and so the owners of derivatives backed by mortgages needn't worry about default.

But to understand the mortgage crisis, we need to understand the impact of default on holders of derivatives backed by private label securities. Because holders of junior tranches took first loss positions, their returns were far more vulnerable to default events than senior tranche holders. To see how that works, go to tab 8.

Our setup is the same as before, except we add two assumptions and two columns. First, we assume an annualized default rate of 1 percent. To convert an annual default rate into a monthly default rate, we use the same procedure we used to convert an annual prepayment rate into an annual default rate:

$$MONTHLY\ DEFAULT = \left(1 - \sqrt[12]{1 - ANNUAL\ DEFAULT}\right) \quad (6.1)$$

We then need to make an assumption about loss conditional on default. When a lender forecloses on a house, he is usually able to recover some part of the mortgage balance once the house is acquired and sold.

We now add two columns that reflect (1) how much the mortgage balance declines as a result of a default (column L) and (2) how much cash flow mortgage investors received as a result of default (column M), which is essentially a discounted prepayment. This allows us to compute a total principal payment, as well as an interest payment, for the pool, given a set of default assumptions.

As before, the first tranche collects all of its principal before the second tranche collects any. Under this scenario presented in tab 8, where the annual default rate is 1 percent and the loss conditional on default is 50 percent, the first tranche's cash flows are untouched by default. On the other hand, the second tranche loses both principal and interest, as it is in a first loss position. The loss of principal owed is straightforward, but because there is less principal generating interest, it loses interest as well. The return to the second tranche drops from 6.33 percent to 5.58 percent, which is a 12 percent reduction in its return. At a discount rate of 6.33 percent, the present value of the second tranche's cash flows drops from $2,000,000 to $1,917,838, for a reduction in value of 4.1 percent. While this may seem small, for highly leveraged financial institutions, such as Lehman Brothers in 2008, losses from large investments in second tranches such as the one modeled in tab 8 would be sufficient to wipe out all equity.

Moreover, an investment in the second tranche modeled earlier would be quite conservative in the context of the private label tranches that typified that time.

Exercise

Try modeling three sequential tranches using the default assumptions in tab 8. Now what is the loss in value arising from default compared with the no default case?

Inverse Floaters

Sometimes, investors will want to break up a fixed-rate mortgage into two floating rates: one that moves with a short-term rate, such as LIBOR, and another than moves in the opposite direction of that same short-term rate. The tranche that moves with a short rate is called a floater; the tranche that moves in the opposite direction is called an inverse floater.

Suppose we want to break the investment into two tranches, each with a 50 percent claim on the mortgage principal. The average return paid to each class must be the mortgage coupon. We might set up something that looks like this:

$$0.5 * [LIBOR + x] + 0.5 * [K - L * LIBOR] = Mortgage\ Coupon \quad (6.2)$$

Let us pick a margin of 0.05 for the floater, and a coefficient of 2 for the inverse floater. Then in our case, we must have

$$0.5 * [LIBOR + .005] + 0.5 * [K - 2 * LIBOR] = 0.06 \quad (6.3)$$

Solving for K, we see that we have

$$0.5K = 0.06 - 0.005 + 0.5\ LIBOR$$

or

$$K = 0.11 + 0.5\ LIBOR$$

Exercise

Once again do not worry about default. Assume that there are two *pari passu* tranches, where one is a floater and the other is an inverse floater. Each gets 50 percent of the mortgage pool. Assume the floater gets a margin of 50 basis points, and the coefficient for the inverse floater is 2. Model the cash flows of each tranche assuming LIBOR of 0.03. Do the same assuming LIBOR of 0.05.

1. What sort of investor do you think might be interested in a floater?
2. What sort of investor do you think might be interested in an inverse floater?

Planned Amortization Class Securities

Finally, mortgage pools can be divided into two types of securities known as planned amortization class securities and companion securities. The planned amortization class security, or PAC, is a mechanism under which investors can be assured the timing of both principal and interest payments, so long as PSA speeds remain within a specified range, known as the "collar." Companions receive all cash flows that do not flow to the PAC tranche from the underlying mortgage pool; companions thus carry large risk with respect to the timing of cash flows.

The design of the PAC is pretty straightforward. It starts with modeling two sets of cash flows based on a relative low PSA (the lower collar) and a relatively high PSA (the upper collar). The idea is that the PAC takes the minimum principal cash flows from the two schedules at any point in time. So long as actual PSA is in between the upper and lower collar, there will at all times be adequate principal payments to meet the obligations of the PAC.

To see this, go to the example in tab 10. In this example, the collars on the PAC are 100 and 275. Columns W and AH give the expected principal payments for the slow and fast prepayments, respectively. These principal payments are graphed in the upper chart on the left-hand side of tab 9.

Note that early on in the life of the PAC, the lower collar produces less principal than the upper collar. So long as the prepayment speed is at least 100, there will be at least enough cash flow to pay the PAC in a timely manner—if PSA is any higher, there will be more than enough. A crossing point happens in period 76, at which point the principal from the upper collar falls below that of the lower collar. But because the lower collar has paid so little early in its life, it will have plenty of cash flow to pay the PAC, which is now attached to the low cash flow upper collar.

On the other hand, the companion tranche will see its payment timing become quite volatile. Tabs 9 and 10 compare cash flows to the PAC and companion under PSA scenarios of 150 and 250. The cash flows to the PAC do not change—this is of course by design. The total principal to each tranche also remains the same. But at a PSA of 250, the companion gets lots of cash flow early on, and none toward the end of the mortgage pool, whereas with a PSA of 150, it gets a smoother set of cash flows over a longer period of time. Not surprisingly, investors in companions expect higher returns than investors in PACS.

Exercise

Based on our past discussion of sequential tranche securities, explain to yourself the meanings of columns AL, AM, AQ, and AR in tab 10.

Multifamily Mortgages

Multifamily mortgages have many parallels with single-family residential mortgages, but in one important way, they are different. Commercial mortgages tend to be bespoke products, tailored as the result of one-on-one negotiations, whereas residential mortgages tend to be standardized.

Moreover, unlike residential loans, commercial loans are generally not fully amortizing. A typical commercial loan will have a 30-year or longer amortization schedule, but will come due with a bullet payment after 5 to 10 years. This means that commercial mortgages must be refinanced on a fairly regular basis.

In the meantime, however, let us discuss the standard ingredients of a commercial mortgage: the underwriting setup that is fairly common to all commercial loans.

PROPERTY-BASED UNDERWRITING STANDARDS

Unlike residential loans, where underwriting the borrower is considered just as important (if not more so) than underwriting the property, with commercial loans, underwriting the property is considered more important than underwriting the borrower. This is because, among other things, properties are usually owned by a specific partnership that, upon dissolution, would have no assets, and because commercial loans generally are without recourse.

Property-based underwriting generally involves a series of ratios: the loan-to-value (LTV) ratio, the debt-cover ratio (DCR), the break-even ratio, and (most recently) the debt-yield ratio (DYR). We will discuss each in turn.

Introduction to Mortgages & Mortgage Backed Securities.
http://dx.doi.org/10.1016/B978-0-12-401743-6.00007-X

Loan-to-Value Ratio

Commercial loans are generally written to conform to maximum loan-to-value ratios. These ratios vary with property types: apartments can usually get loans with higher LTVs than office buildings, shopping centers, and industrial buildings, which in turn can get higher LTVs than hotels. The reason for this is straightforward—apartments usually produce steadier incomes over time than other property types, whereas hotels, with their one-day leases, produce the least steady income.

The question, then, is how to measure LTV. When lenders are behaving prudently (something they seem to do about half the time), the value part of the LTV ratio is taken to be the lowest of three numbers: the amount of money a purchaser of a property is willing to spend, the appraised value based on a static appraisal, and the appraised value based on a discounted cash flow analysis.

Let's take a simple example. Consider the following pro forma for an office building in Spreadsheet 7.1. We will assume an entry cap rate of 8 percent and an exit cap of 9 percent. With the entry rate of 8 percent, we use the simple income capitalization method to get a value. The method is just:

$$Value = \frac{NOI_1}{0.08}$$

or

$$77,109,375 = \frac{6,168,750}{0.08}$$

The problem with this method in this context is that it doesn't take into account the fact that the owner of the property will take on large capital expenses to lease the property at the time of acquisition, and five years after. It also doesn't take into account the fact that expenses for office buildings generally grow more rapidly than rents. These assumptions are built into the discounted cash flow analysis. When we discount cash flows at 8 percent, we get a value of $51,677,518.23. Note that we assume we sell the building in year 10 based on projected year 11 income and a 9 percent cap rate.

Clearly, in this instance, we use the Discounted Cash Flow (DCF) method for underwriting value. This will not always be the case, however, as there are trade-offs between direct capitalization and DCF. One advantage of the DCF method should already be clear—it explicitly takes into account capital expenses and vacancy rates—it also allows us to model expense growth, although that can also be taken into account in the income capitalization method. Higher expense growth simply means that we expect future income to grow less rapidly, which means that the cap rate should be higher.

But direct capitalization has one profound advantage over DCF. We usually have a pretty good idea of what a building's income will be in the following year, so long as there are leases in place. The further we go into the future, the less we know about modeling rents, vacancy conditions, expenses, capital markets, and so on. The numbers we must place in pro forma beyond a year or two are generally pretty tenuous.

In any event, with this example, we can see that the highest valuation for underwriting should be that produced by the DCF method, which is $51,677,518. If an LTV ratio maximum for office buildings is 0.7, the largest loan available for this building is $36,174,263 under the LTV test.

Debt-Cover Ratio

Another test is the DCR debt, which simply asks how much free cash flow there is after debt service payments are made. Think of this as an analogue to the PITI to Income ratio tests used for residential lending. Again, the formula for DCR is pretty simple:

$$DCR = \frac{NOI}{DS}$$

where again NOI is net operating income and DS is debt service.

Let's assume in our example that we get a 70 percent LTV loan (or $36,174,263) at a 5 percent interest rate and that it amortizes over 30 years. Our payment will be $2,330,295, and so our debt cover ratio will be $6,168,750/$2,330,295, or 2.65. DCRs are rarely above 1.5, and usually range between 1.25 and 1.35, so this mortgage easily clears the DCR requirement. In an era of low interest rates and LTVs, the DCR will rarely be binding.

Debt-Yield Ratio

In the aftermath of the financial crisis, debt-yield has become an increasingly popular underwriting criterion. Again, the calculation is elementary:

$$DYR = \frac{NOI}{Loan\ Amount}$$

In our case, the DYR is $6,168,750/$36,174,263, or 0.17. Typical debt yield requirements are 10 percent. The idea is two-fold: first, in the event the borrower defaults, the lender knows more or less what its yield on equity will be. Second, because commercial loans generally have balloon payments, lenders want to make sure they can be refinanced when they are due. By insisting on a large DYR, lenders can assure themselves that when a refinance date arrives, a property will have sufficient cash flows to pay for the subsequent loan, even if interest rates rise.

The break-even ratio is simply the occupancy rate at which a property breaks even. A simplified version of it is

(Debt Service + Operating Expenses)/Gross Potential Income.

This is the share of Gross Potential Income (that is, the revenue expected from a fully leased building) that would go toward expenses, and therefore, is the occupancy rate required for a building to break even.

In our example, operating expenses are $(5,250,000.00)$, debt service is, $(2,330,295.17)$, and gross potential income is $13,125,000.00$, so the break-even ratio is $(5.25+2.33)/13.13$, or .58. Lenders generally want a break-even ratio of less than 80 percent, meaning that a property could be 20 percent vacant and still service its debt.

UNDERWRITING THE BORROWER

Geltner et al. (2010) note that regarding income property, evaluation of the borrower is extremely important. In particular, lenders want to avoid borrowers that bleed properties or those that might use Chapter 11 to reduce their loan obligations.

Because apartment loans are generally nonrecourse loans, borrowers facing any financial difficulties have a strong incentive to walk away from their worst performing apartment assets. Sometimes, to avoid this problem, lenders will insist on cross-collateralization, where more than one property serves as collateral for a loan.

COMMERCIAL LOAN COVENANTS

Another difference between single-family and multifamily mortgages is that multifamily mortgages contain covenants that are put in place to assure that underwriting ratios remain in place over the life of the loan. Suppose, for example, that an apartment owner acquires a $100 million property with a $70 million, interest-only loan. Market conditions change, and an appraisal estimates that the value of the property drops to $90 million. The loan has a covenant that requires that the contemporaneous LTV ratio never exceeds 70 percent. The borrower may be required to make a payment of $7 million in order to reduce the loan balance to $63 million, so that the LTV returns to 70 percent.

Similarly, if loans at any point during the life of the loan fail to meet DCR or DYR standards, the borrower may need to pay down the loan. Interestingly, the requirement to repay part of the loan in the event of changing market conditions may come into conflict with another typical loan term—a lock-out clause or prepayment penalty clause with respect to prepayment.

Lock-Out Clauses and Prepayment Penalties

In the United States (unlike the rest of the world) prepayment penalties for single-family residential mortgages are rare. But for multifamily mortgages, they are common. The idea is simple—by making it difficult for borrowers to prepay their loans, lenders can be sure of their loan yield over a period of years (5- and 10-year terms are most typical). For institutions with long-term liabilities, such as life insurance companies and pension funds, this feature makes loans appealing. It also means the multifamily borrowers pay lower interest rates than they would in the presence of the ability to prepay.

A lockout clause does exactly what it says—it forbids borrowers from repaying any part of their loan early. An exception will be carved out in the event that the borrower needs to prepay in order to meet covenants.

Prepayment penalties generally have a yield maintenance feature, where the prepayment penalty is generally:

$$Penalty = Loan\ Balance * \left(r_{loan} - r_{treasury}\right) * \tau$$

where r_{loan} is the interest rate on the mortgage, $r_{treasury}$ is a short-term Treasury rate (or LIBOR), and τ is the remaining term on the loan at the time of prepayment.

Under these circumstances, should borrowers ever prepay? Let's do an example. Suppose a borrower has a loan with a 6 percent interest rate, with two years left on the loan. It finds itself in a market where loans with five-year terms carry 3 percent mortgage rates; the one-year Treasury rate is 1 percent. In order to "buy" the 3 percent rate, the borrower needs to pay a penalty equal to 10 percent of the loan balance. So the borrower gets a 6 percent benefit in exchange for a 10 percent cost. It doesn't seem to make any sense.

If borrowers could know with certainty that interest rates won't rise, then they should never bear the prepayment penalty. But of course, they cannot know this—they might find themselves confronted with higher interest rates if they wait until their loan comes due to refinance.

A clue about whether to bear the cost of refinancing exists in the yield curve. Because multifamily mortgages typically have terms of five years, we can use the yield curve to infer the two-year forward five-year Treasury rate. Let's do this by looking at the yield curve on maturities of up to seven years on August 19, 2013:

1 Mo	3 Mo	6 Mo	1 Yr	2 Yr	3 Yr	5 Yr	7 Yr
0.03	0.06	0.08	0.13	0.36	0.76	1.63	2.29

We can use the seven-year and two-year spot rates to calculate the two-year forward five-year rate. Remembering that Treasury securities make payments every six months, we can calculate:

$$r_{2,7} = \left(\sqrt[5]{\frac{1.01145^{14}}{1.0018^{4}}} - 1 \right) * 2 = 0.00307$$

So the yield curve is telling us that markets expect five-year rates to rise by 78 basis points between now and two years from now. This means that, assuming spreads remain constant, by locking in today at a new rate, the borrower can expect undiscounted savings of a total of 234 basis points in years 3 to 5 of the refinanced loans. But the net cost of the refinance for the first two years of the new loan would be 400 basis points. Under these circumstances, it makes sense to pay off the original loan.

Exercise

Keeping everything else the same, at what seven-year rate does refinancing the loan early begin to look attractive?

Borrowers may sometimes "detach" their properties from a loan through a process known as defeasance. Defeasance means that borrowers exchange the collateral they post from their property into government securities. The securities must produce enough cash flow to make the regular payments and fully pay the principal at the time the loan comes due.

Exercise

Why would a borrower prefer defeasance to prepayment?

SOURCES OF MULTIFAMILY FINANCE

For small properties (those with 1–4 units), investors in residential properties can obtain single-family loans from Fannie Mae and Freddie Mac. These loans have similar down payment requirements, and amortize fully over long terms. About 55 percent of the rental market in the United States is contained within these small properties (see Figure 7.1).

Traditionally, loans for larger multifamily housing came from banks and insurance companies. Figure 7.2 uses the Federal Reserve Flow of Funds Accounts to show the market shares of multifamily loans outstanding, by source of funds. Note that at the beginning of this history, nearly 70 percent of multifamily loans came from these sources. Government Sponsored Enterprise (GSE) direct lending, and GSE mortgage pools didn't exist until the late 1960s, and only became a large part of the market around 2000; but since the financial crisis, their market share has grown to nearly 40 percent. Indeed, between 2008 and 2012, when multifamily lending actually shrank, the GSEs kept the market from shrinking further (see Figure 7.3).

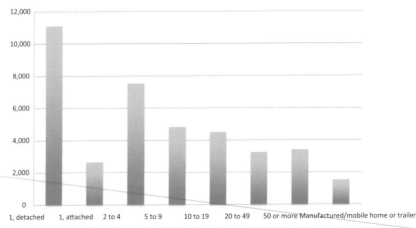

FIGURE 7.1 Number of rental units by size and type of building. *Source: American Housing Survey.*

The source of lending that grew dramatically from 1990 until 2008 was the private Commercial Mortgage-Backed Security (CMBS) market. The size of this market peaked in the third quarter of 2007; as capital markets started to retreat in general, so too did the CMBS market, which essentially shut down from 2008 to 2010 (see Figure 7.4). Default rates on CMBS soared to 20 percent, not so much because properties couldn't produce sufficient cash flow to meet debt service obligations, but because many loans went into technical default, as covenants were violated or properties backing loans that came due could not be refinanced.

The year 2013 has produced some recovery in CMBS issuance, but even still, total issuance is unlikely to surpass 50 percent of the 2007 peak.

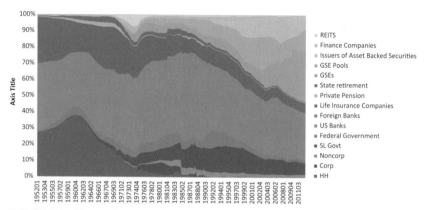

FIGURE 7.2 Shares of sources of multifamily mortgage debt outstanding. *Source: Federal Reserve Flow of Funds Table L219.*

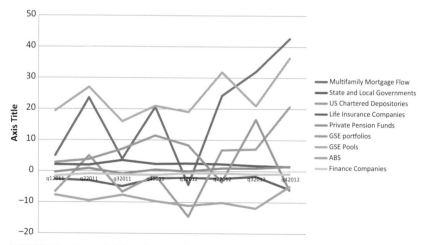

FIGURE 7.3 Net capital flows into multifamily housing. *Source: Federal Reserve Flow of Funds Table F.219.*

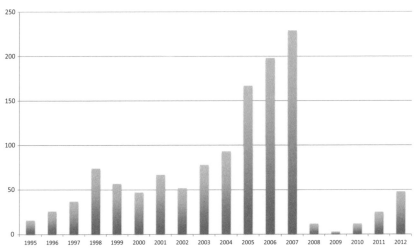

FIGURE 7.4   CMBS issuance in $billions. *Source: Commercial Mortgage Alert.*

Nevertheless, it is worth describing how CMBS markets work, and how their structures look relative to Residential Mortgage-Backed Security (RMBS) markets.

The two major categories of CMBS are large-loan and conduit. Large-loan CMBS securitize loans on one property, whereas conduits securitize loans on many properties. The advantage of the large-loan CMBS is the relative absence of complexity; the disadvantage is the lack of diversification. To some extent, large apartment buildings are diversified because they have many tenants, and thus many leases, although because all tenants are subject to a common economic shock, there are correlations across the performance of various leases.

CMBSs often are broken up into a Collateralize Mortgage Obligation (CMO) structure, but the structures are typically pretty simple: the security will be divided into an A piece and a B piece, where the A piece is senior to the B piece. The mechanism for distributing cash flows between the A piece and B piece is the same as the mechanism discussed for two tranche residential CMOs in Chapter 6.

THE 5–50 PROBLEM

Lenders are not enthusiastic about lending for small apartment developments, which are generally defined as those with five to 50 units.[1] Schneider and Follain (1998) wrote:

Originators indicated a fairly large demand for small project loan products. Banks, mortgage companies, thrifts, and other lending institutions are currently meeting some of the demand for financing small projects. Yet national lenders, especially Fannie Mae and Freddie Mac, are still reluctant to become active in financing smaller projects because they believe they could be unprofitable. Lenders agreed that the

---

1. See Segal (2002).

high administrative costs and low fees generated from this market compared with those received from larger loans discourage typical commission-based originators. These lenders favored loans to larger multifamily projects, where each transaction produced higher fees. Institutions significantly involved in making small loans typically have a small, specialized staff dedicated to that effort; those employees are paid a salary rather than on a commission basis. Some lenders forecasted, however, that the conventional market's interest in making smaller loans could increase if spreads on larger transactions continue to tighten (that is, the difference between the comparable U.S. Department of the Treasury rate and mortgage interest rates).

Since Schneider and Follain wrote this, the government has developed programs through the GSEs to make mortgage capital available to the smaller apartments. From an affordable housing perspective, small buildings are important, because they are often the only type of multifamily properties that are economically feasible in small to medium cities.

SECTION 42 LOW INCOME HOUSING TAX CREDIT PROGRAM

By far, the largest affordable housing production program currently in the United States is the Section 42 Low Income Housing Tax Credit Program (LIHTC). Typically, at least one-quarter of multifamily properties built in the United States are LIHTC developments. LIHTC deals are generally complicated, but to give you a sense of how they work, we present an outline and a simple example here.

Developers apply to a state housing finance agency for a LIHTC allocation. The federal government allocates each state $2.20 per capita of tax credits,[2] and states use various criteria for determining how the credits are allocated to developers. In one sense, the rules are straightforward: a developer can receive up to 9 percent of the hard costs of building a complex per year for 10 years in the form of tax credits. Tax credits are dollar for dollar reductions in tax liabilities, and are therefore as good as cash for entities that have federal tax liabilities.

In exchange for getting the tax credits, developers must agree to charge rents of no more than 30 percent of 60 percent of their area median income (AMI), where AMI is defined by HUD.[3] At a minimum, rents are limited for 15 years; typically, as part of the credit allocation process, states require longer periods (sometimes as long as 30 years) where rents are limited.

The restrictions on rent make LIHTC deals unattractive to typical private sector lenders, so LIHTC deals usually involve government financing along with the tax credits. Sometimes, these loans require very small DCRs, because lenders assume that the tax credits give developers adequate incentive to keep current.

---

2. See www.treasurer.ca.gov/ctcac/program.pdf
3. AMIs for 2013 may be found at http://www.huduser.org/portal/datasets/il/il13/index_mfi.html.

Spreadsheet 7.2 lays out an example of a LIHTC deal. The assumptions are listed on the left-hand side of the spreadsheet. The pro forma itself is arranged vertically instead of horizontally so it is easier to visualize the parts.

We begin by determining the loan amount. Rents are based on an area median income of $50,000 per year, and so are 60 percent of 30 percent of that amount, or $9,000 per year per unit or $750 per month. The 120 units thus generate $1,080,000 per year. After expenses, the developer nets $756,000 in income. The state housing finance agencies offer a mortgage with a DCR of 1, so the loan available to the developer is PV(9%/12,360,$756000/12) = $7,829,758.

Note that the before-tax cash flows in the first year on this deal are zero—all net income goes toward a loan payment. But the owner of the property will have a negative tax liability because (1) it gets a deduction for depreciation[4] and (2) because of the credit. Note that the owner needs to earn passive taxable income from some other investment in order to be allowed to use the money the IRS owes as the result of the negative tax liability. If a nonprofit develops a LIHTC project, it will sell its credits to a for-profit entity that it can then use to reduce taxes.

In this example, we assume that the property depreciates fully after 30 years, and that the value of land grows by the rate of rent growth. This allows us to determine the value we receive at reversion.

Now let's look at some features of the deal. At time of acquisition, the property has a present value of $4,494,574. Yet the developer/owner put only $1,170,242 into the deal. Thus the deal has an NPV of $4,494,574-$1,170,242, or $3,324,332. The present value of the credits is $3,893,101; so the vast majority of the subsidy is going to the property owner, rather than the tenants. Many, but not all states are seeking to prevent this large arbitrage opportunity by having developers bid for the tax credits, rather than just receive them via an allocation.

The second thing to note is that the benefits of the deal are highly front-loaded. Owners do need to keep their projects affordable for at least five years after they receive their last credit, or else they can be subject to a recapture provision whereby they pay some or all of the credits back. But after 15 years, the incentives to default rise, although through 2006, the default rates for LIHTC properties were low (Novogradic 2011).[5]

MODELING THE COST OF DEFAULT FOR A MULTIFAMILY PROPERTY

Because commercial lenders generally do not receive loan guarantees, they need to determine how much to charge for potential future default, particularly in light of the fact that commercial loans are generally non-recourse loans.

---

4. The US federal tax code assigns a 27.5 year life to apartments, and allows owners to expense depreciation to improvements on a straight line basis.
5. See http://www.novoco.com/products/special_reports/Novogradac_HAG_study_2011.pdf

We turn to Spreadsheet 7.3, which presents a simple model of default on a five-year mortgage. We lay out a binomial value tree for the value of apartments, and, in this example, assume that apartment values can rise by 10 percent in a year or fall by 25 percent in a year (while this assumption may seem far-fetched, we do actually see very large swings in property value for income properties from one year to the next).

We assume also that up years are three times more common than down years, so that the probability of a particular year being an up year is 75 percent, while the probability of a down year is 25 percent. We use this information to create a price tree and a probability tree. The price tree appears starting in cell E10 and continues to the right (to make things simple, we assume the borrower buys the apartment for $1); the probability tree appears starting in cell E24. The price tree gives a set of potential price nodes across time for five years; the probability tree gives the probability of reaching any one of those price nodes.

Along with price nodes, we have starting in cell E38 equity nodes, which are just the value of the property less the mortgage balance at each period. The amortization schedule is contained in cells L4 to R8. Note that we have cells with negative values; if borrowers are ruthless, and there is no cost of default, we would default at these nodes. These are identified beginning in cell E51 as points at which the default option is "in the money."

But here is where things become a little less obvious. Suppose an investor owns an underwater building, but thinks the value of that building might rise again. Ideally, from his perspective, he would give the building back to the lender, buy it at its current low value, and then get the benefit of future price increases. But lenders underwrite to prevent this sort of behavior—the mortgage lending game is a repeated game. Lenders will forgive commercial borrowers who default, but they will not forgive borrowers who take brazen advantage.[6]

This implies that having a default option in the money is not sufficient reason for a borrower to default. This means that to model default behavior, we need to start in the last period of the loan and look backward. For the time being, we will assume cash flows are trivially small, and have little to do with the default decision.[7]

Let us look at where we are at the end of period 5. There are three nodes where the borrowers' equity is negative. It is here that the borrower surely defaults—he can't get a new loan (because he has no equity) and it is cheaper to give away the building than to repay the mortgage principal. The incentives in the final period of the loan are quite unambiguous.

---

6. This statement is based on conversations I have had with large apartment lenders.
7. Liu, Jabbour, and Green (2007) find that equity is a far more important determinant of default than cash-flow, so this assumption is innocuous.

Let us step back one year earlier. At equity node I38, there are two paths: up, in which case the borrower will have 5.2 cents of equity, or down, at which point the borrower defaults, which is equivalent to having zero equity. The weighted average of a positive number and zero is positive, which means the expected payoff of not defaulting is greater than the payoff of defaulting (which would be zero in period 4). The borrower does not default.

What about cell I40? In this cell both the up and down paths lead to negative equity, and so a default will take place here. Using this reasoning, we can populate a tree that gives the nodes at which default does, indeed, take place.

So now we are close to being able to calculate something a lender cares about when making a decision about how much to charge borrowers for the potential cost of default: the probability of default. This might seem obvious— we just take the probabilities from the nodes in the probability tree that correspond to the nodes in the default tree where default takes place. But this is not correct.

Consider the bottom-most node on the tree. While there is an incentive to default there, we will never reach that point, because a default has taken place on the path to reaching that node. Once a borrower defaults in a period before the final period, they are done, and the probability of a default occurring in the final period goes to zero.

Taking this into account, there are only three places on this particular default tree where we would actually observe default. This produces the result that we have a 1.6 percent probability of default in period 3, a 3.5 percent probability in period 4 and a 5.3 percent probability in period 5.

Exercise

Use the formulas in the spreadsheet cells to convince yourself that these probabilities are correct.

From these probabilities, we can get expected losses in each of these periods. We use the formula

$$E\left[Loss\right] = pr\left(default\right) * loan\ balance * loss\ conditional\ on\ default$$

The loan balance comes from the amortization schedule, and the loss conditional on default is assumed to be 35 percent. We now have expected losses in each period.

We are nearly done. We take the present value of the losses at the mortgage rate to get total losses. We find that the losses on a 0.75 loan are 0.0281. In order to convert this into a rate, we want to amortize this amount over the five years and gross it up so it is an annuity loss per $1 of loan amount. This is done in cell E92. We find that we need to add 89 basis points to our loan in order to compensate for expected losses or, to use another term, mitigate yield degradation. (Note: This technique may also be used as part of a g-fee calculation for mortgage insurers.)

REFERENCES

Geltner, David M., Miller, N.G., Clayton, J., Eichholtz, P., Calhoun, J.W., Shaut, D., Design, C.M., 2010. Commercial real estate analysis and investments. West Group, Egan, Minnesota.

Liu, Yi-kang, Jabbour, George M., Green, Richard K., 2007. The performance of option-based default risk models on commercial mortgages: An empirical investigation. The Journal of Fixed Income 17.2, 63–76.

Schneider, Drew, Follain, James, 1998. A New Initiative in the Federal Housing Administration's Office of Multifamily Housing Programs: An Assessment of Small Projects Processing. Cityscape, 43–58.

Segal, William, 2002. Segmentation in the multifamily mortgage market: Evidence from the residential finance survey. Journal of Housing Research 13.2, 175–198.

International Comparisons of Mortgages

The US mortgage market is highly unusual. First, it is overwhelmingly a fixed-rate, free prepayment market. Second, it is a market that relies on an unusual type of security for mortgage finance: the mortgage-backed security (MBS). Other countries do rely on capital markets as sources of mortgage finance, but they usually use bonds, covered and otherwise, to do so.

In this chapter, we shall examine differences in mortgage markets in four dimensions: mortgage type, source of mortgage finance, size of mortgage market, and "consumer friendliness" and mortgage performance. The discussion will draw on work Green and Wachter (2007), Duebel (2005), Jaffe (2011) and especially Michael Lea (2010), who wrote the most comprehensive description of mortgage markets around the world.

TAX TREATMENT OF MORTGAGES

Before we discuss mortgages per se, it is important to note that different countries have different tax treatment for mortgages: in some countries, mortgage interest is tax deductible, while in others, it is not; in others still, it is partially deductible. This will have an incentive on borrower behavior—borrowers in

Introduction to Mortgages & Mortgage Backed Securities.
http://dx.doi.org/10.1016/B978-0-12-401743-6.00008-1

countries where interest is not tax deductible have more incentive to pay off their loans quickly. In particular, because return on equity for owner-occupied housing (net imputed rent) is not taxed, households in countries without a mortgage interest deduction are going to want to prepay their loans quickly, so as to move from nonpreferred debt to preferred equity.

Mortgage Type

Mortgages have a number of dimensions: size of down payment, term, amortization, recourse, ability to prepay, and variability of interest rate. To set the context, we begin by describing the US mortgage briefly.

In the United States, borrowers may obtain mortgages with as little as 3 percent down. These are FHA mortgages. However, FHA mortgages do not provide borrowers with the best possible terms. For borrowers to get the best possible terms, they generally need a minimum down payment of 20 percent. Borrowers in the United States may also get mortgages with fixed rates for terms as long as 30 years (or sometimes, although unusually, 40 years).

American mortgages usually have a self-amortizing feature as well. Loans in the United States are often nonrecourse loans, which is to say that if the mortgage borrower turns their house over to the lender, their debt is discharged. This is true in 11 of the 50 states and the District of Columbia (Ghent and Kudlyak 2011). In the remaining states, mortgages come with recourse, but the recourse is rarely enforced. As we shall see, this stands in contrast to many other countries around the world. Finally, while prepayment penalties are permissible in the United States, they are rarely observed. We will discuss prepayment penalties further when we review the mortgage features found in other countries.

Mortgage interest in the United States is tax deductible so long as a mortgage balance is less than $1 million. Mortgage interest is deductible for both first and second homes.

Canada

Let us begin our international comparison with America's neighbor to the north, Canada. Canada does have an entity that is similar to FHA, the Canadian Housing Finance Corporation. As is the case in the United States, borrowers in Canada may make loans with small down payments, but only if they pay for mortgage insurance. Canadian borrowers may choose between obtaining insurance from the Canadian Housing Finance Corporation or from private mortgage insurance companies. Discussions with Canadian banking officials reveal that banks often choose the insurer for the borrower.

The fact that Canadians may borrow with little money down is where similarities between mortgages in Canada and mortgages in the United States end. Canadian mortgages generally have short terms and are not self-amortizing. For example, a Canadian can get a loan with a 30-year amortization schedule that comes due after five years at which point it owes a balloon payment to the bank. Notice that I use the word bank, because most Canadian mortgages are funded by banks.

Canadian mortgages are also recourse loans. This means that if the borrower defaults and the value of the house that the borrower deeds to the bank is worth less than the amount due to the bank (an amount that includes accrued interest and the costs of recovering the house), the lender may attempt to recover the difference from the borrower. A common method for doing so would be the garnishment of wages. Another method would be the seizing of other borrower assets.

At the same time, Canadian mortgages generally come with prepayment penalties or lockout clauses. Suppose a borrower has a mortgage but carries a 6 percent interest rate and that market rates fall to 4 percent. This means that if the borrower repays the mortgage before it is due, the borrower will owe the bank mortgage balance multiplied by 2 percent (which is the difference between the coupon rate on the loan and the market rate available to the lender) multiplied by the remaining life of the loan in years. This assures the lender that it will get the return that was specified at the time the loan was originated. As such, the Canadian system reduces interest rate risk for lenders while preventing borrowers from benefiting from reductions in interest rates. There is one exception—borrowers may accelerate the payoff of 20 percent of the loan balance each year without penalty.

So the Canadian mortgage is on its face far less consumer friendly than the American mortgage. Canadian borrowers get one advantage over their American counterparts; because Canadian borrowers have less valuable options in their mortgages (that is, the option to freely default and the option to prepay) they usually pay lower rates of interest for a given maturity than their American counterparts.

We now move to Europe and head broadly from west to east.

United Kingdom

The United Kingdom did have low down-payment loans—loans with loan-to-value (LTV) ratios in excess of 95 percent made up more than 10 percent of the market for first-time homebuyers through 2007. Since the financial crisis, however, such mortgages have largely ceased to exist.[1]

The United Kingdom is a variable rate market, where lenders can decide to reset rates nearly as they please—as such, the process for setting interest rates for mortgages in the United Kingdom is similar to the process for setting interest rates for credit cards in the United States. This variable rate reflects the fact that money for mortgage finance in the United Kingdom overwhelmingly comes from banks, something we shall discuss further later in this chapter.

---

1. See http://www.fsa.gov.uk/static/pubs/cp/cp11_31.pdf, p 57

David Miles (2004) has argued that the United Kingdom's reliance on variable rate mortgages has contributed to volatility in that country's housing markets. But when the United Kingdom has experimented with making more fixed rate mortgages available, consumers have not been interested, perhaps because they are more costly (see Miles 2004). A majority of mortgages amortize (typically over 30 years) in the United Kingdom, but interest-only (IO) mortgages make up more than 40 percent of the mortgages outstanding in that country. The FSA (2011)[2] has expressed concern that large numbers of Britons are using IO loans because they are "affordable," but have no capital repayment strategy in place.

As is the case in Canada, loans in the United Kingdom come with recourse. As we shall see, the United States is highly unusual in that it has jurisdictions with nonrecourse loans.

Even though mortgages in the United Kingdom have variable rates, and therefore relieve lenders from interest rate risk, they also have prepayment penalties. Lea (2010) notes that borrowers who have loans with initial discounts or fixed rates will pay a penalty of 2 to 5 percent of the loan balance if they repay early.

Spain

Before the financial crisis, borrowers could obtain loans with very small down payments, but now financial regulation discourages lenders from offering LTVs in excess of 80 percent. Specifically, banks must set almost three times as much capital for mortgages with LTVs above 80 percent than with those below 80 percent (Financial Stability Board 2011).

Like the United Kingdom, Spain relies principally on variable rate mortgages. Unlike the United Kingdom, rates are linked to an underlying index, such as LIBOR. Spaniards can pay off 10 percent of their loans without penalty each year; if they pay off more they incur a 0.5 percent of loan balance penalty (Lea 2010). While Spain has recourse, during the crisis, lenders sometimes chose to repossess houses without further penalizing borrowers in order to get the costs of bad loans behind them as swiftly as possible (Wall Street Journal 2013). Loan terms in Spain are generally 20 years, but can be longer.[3]

France

The typical mortgage in France requires a 20 percent down payment. At least one lender, however, will offer French citizens 20-year loans with 110 percent LTV financing![4]

---

2. See http://www.fsa.gov.uk/static/pubs/cp/cp11_31.pdf p 123
3. The determination of a 20-year length comes from the author's search of Spanish bank web sites in 2013.
4. http://www.frenchmortgagedirect.com/mortgageguide.php

France is the only country other than the United States in Lea's (2010) review where a majority of borrowers finance their houses with fixed rate mortgages. The typical amortization period is 20 years, although terms range between 5 and 25 years. IO loans are uncommon in France; loans have recourse, and typically have small prepayment penalties. Mortgage interest is not tax deductible in France and indeed has been deemed unconstitutional there.[5]

Germany

Germany has a low homeownership rate by world standards, standing at 43 percent, yet its mortgage market is fairly large. A reason that Germany has such a low homeownership rate may be that tenant protections are very strong there, meaning that renters have many of the benefits of home-owning (i.e., security of tenure and hedges against rising rents). Germany is also noteworthy as a country where house prices have been more or less stagnant for some time.

Germany is a medium-term to long-term fixed-rate market, and typically has yield maintenance prepayment penalties—those penalties expire after 10 years, do not apply to variable rate mortgages, and do not apply when households decide to move. Duebel (2005) describes the structure:

In the indemnity model practiced in Germany the lender may compensate his reinvestment loss when investing the prepaid sums through a yield maintenance prepayment indemnity. However, a reinvestment gain that may arise when interest rates have risen, does not have to be disbursed to the consumer, with the result that prepayments in those phases, for instance because of a move, are associated with a financial disadvantage ("lock-in")

Like every other country in Europe, German loans come with recourse. Mortgage interest is not tax-deductible in Germany. German mortgages typically require large down payments; according to the European Central Bank, the typical German mortgage has an LTV of 70 percent at origination, whereas in the remainder of Europe higher LTVs are typical.

Denmark

Denmark's mortgages are most similar to those in the United States: they have longer terms than those in most other countries (although as short-term interest rates have fallen, variable rate mortgages have become more popular) and are generally prepayable, although the prepayment method is different from that in the United States.

Danish borrowers may purchase their mortgage back from the lender at any time at the market price. This means borrowers (or issuers) can prepay at the

---

5. See http://taxfoundation.org/blog/frances-highest-court-strikes-down-mortgage-interest-deduction

market's perception of the present value of the remaining cash flows. Because the ability to prepay shortens the duration of the Danish mortgage, the impact of a decrease in interest rates is smaller than it would be for a noncallable bond. On the other hand, because borrowers do not get to automatically repay at par (as Americans generally do), the call option is less valuable to a Danish borrower than it is to an American borrower.

Denmark has some tax deductibility for mortgages, but it is limited; mortgages are recourse loans.

The Netherlands

The Netherland has the largest mortgage market (relative to GDP) in the world. This is because (1) The Netherlands now has the loosest down-payment requirements of any developed country and (2) mortgage interest in The Netherlands is fully deductible. Borrowers in The Netherlands can receive loans without making a down payment, so long as the lender is convinced that in the event the house securing the loan is foreclosed upon, its value will be sufficiently high to repay the mortgage. Loans in The Netherlands come with recourse. Most loans in The Netherlands are medium-term fixed rate loans (Lea 2010), but long-term fixed rate mortgages are available. As in Canada, borrowers in The Netherlands can make partial prepayments on their loans, but there is a yield maintenance clause for prepayments beyond a specified limit.

Italy

The Italian mortgage market is relatively small—in fact, the mortgage debt outstanding to GDP ratio in Italy is the smallest in Western Europe (ECB 2009). Biasin and Smith (2010) lay out some of the characteristics of Italian mortgages.

The maximum LTV in Italy is regulated at 80 percent. Households are, however, allowed to take on loans of up to 100 percent of the value of the house, as long as they post collateral beyond the house; the maximum LTV is thus 80 percent of the value of the house plus other collateral.

The Wall Street Journal,[6] in a nice post about Italian mortgages, wrote

The carefree attitude embodied by the Italians is one of the main attractions for those looking to buy a second home in the country. Unfortunately, the country's property laws aren't quite as carefree as its residents.

There are four ways in which Italian lending is stringent: (1) although the LTV ceiling is regulated to be 80 percent, in practice lenders require higher down payments; (2) pay-off periods for Italian mortgages tend to be relatively short (10–15 years); (3) lenders will require borrowers to pay off loans before

---

6. See http://online.wsj.com/article/SB10001424052702304410504575559510518468670.html

reaching a certain age (say 65 or 70); (4) payment-to-income ratios above 1/3 are not permitted.

At the same time, because Italy has a relatively small number of mortgage lenders (see Casolaro 2006), the mortgage market is not competitive there, so fees are quite high. All of this helps explain the relatively small size of Italy's mortgage market.

Hong Kong

Mortgage terms in Hong Kong change across time—in particular, when the housing market is strong, banks lower the maximum allowable loan-to-value ratio on first-lien mortgages, and when it is weak, banks raise the maximum LTV. Borrowers in Hong Kong can get piggy-back loans (with mortgage insurance) to get to a cumulative LTV of 90 percent.

Banks in Hong Kong offer 3-, 5-, and 7-year fixed rates mortgages, but the take-up rate on these mortgages is low. As in the United Kingdom, borrowers in Hong Kong prefer the lower cost of the variable rate mortgage.

Hong Kong has a mortgage interest deduction,[7] and mortgages are recourse loans. Because loans are overwhelmingly variable rate mortgages, the loans rarely come with prepayment penalties.

Japan

According to Lea (2010), Japan has the most even division in the take-up rates of mortgage duration types; there are substantial borrowers with variable, short-term fixed, medium-term fixed, and long-term fixed rates. Japan also has convertible mortgages, which allow borrowers the option to switch from one type of loan to another at various points in the life of the loan. Japanese mortgages do not generally have prepayment penalties, perhaps because interest rates in that country have been so low for so long, the financial incentive to prepay has been very small.

Japan is famous for having 100-year mortgages,[8] reflecting the combination of very low interest rates and very high house prices. Although house prices are still 65 percent lower than they were in 1990, they remain very high by world standards: newly constructed condominiums cost $8800 per square foot.[9] Japanese mortgages come with recourse. Mortgage interest is not deductible in Japan.

---

7. http://www.gov.hk/en/residents/taxes/salaries/allowances/deductions/homeloan.htm
8. See Chang (1996) et al.
9. See http://www.reinet.or.jp/en/pdf/2013/Six-Large-City-Areas2013.pdf

Republic of Korea

Mortgages in South Korea not only have variable rates, they have short maturities (as is the case in Canada); the typical loan has a term of only three years.[10] The Korean mortgage market is also relatively new—as recently as 20 years ago, mortgage-debt outstanding to GDP in Korea was less than 10 percent.

Korea faces the problem that it only has short-to-medium term capital markets available to it, because investors worry about whether the threat from North Korea could lead to a cataclysmic event in the not-too-distant future. Korean loans come with recourse.

Maximum LTVs are set through government policy. For example, in response to a run-up in house prices in 2002, the maximum LTV for Korea was established at 60 percent. Given how often Korean loans must rollover, banks have a strong incentive to keep LTV loans.

More generically, Korea has used LTV as a tool of macro-prudential policy, a phenomenon we will discuss a little later in this chapter.

SOURCES OF FUNDING

Different countries have very different sources of mortgage funding, which is why the characteristics of mortgages vary so much. As discussed in Chapters 2 and 12, banks and other depositories are better suited to funding fixed rate mortgages, as fixed-rate mortgages create balance sheet risk arising from a mismatch of short-term liabilities and long-term assets.

Countries where mortgages are financed principally by banks—which include Canada, the United Kingdom, Ireland, and Italy—are also countries that rely on variable-rate mortgages.[11] On the other hand, countries that have fixed-rate mortgages, such as the United States, Denmark, and Germany, rely on capital markets for funding.

Capital market funding can take one of three forms: mortgage-backed pass-through securities, long-term bonds where the issuer is a financial institution, and covered bonds, which are a mixture of long-term bonds and mortgage-backed securities.

The pass-through model is currently dominant in the United States: in 2012, roughly 90 percent of mortgages where financed by agency issued mortgage-backed securities.[12] The mortgage-backed security model, which is described in depth elsewhere in this book, was undeniably successful between the early 1980s and the late 1990s. Indeed, it was so successful that some other countries, such as Japan and South Korea, saw it as a model worth attempting to emulate for their mortgage markets.

---

10. http://www.reuters.com/article/2013/01/16/korea-economy-debt-idUSL4N0AL0BO20130116
11. Although France and Japan rely on banks for finance and have large fixed-rate markets.
12. See Flow of Funds data, Table F218.

Nevertheless, much went wrong with the MBS model starting in the late 1990s. Specifically, the underwriting on the underlying mortgages for MBS deteriorated, both for agency-backed MBS and especially for private-label MBS, where issuers tried to tranche their way to creating high-quality credit out of low-quality mortgages.

A legitimate (and to this point unsatisfactorily answered) question is whether poor lending standards are an inherent feature of MBS. In particular, it is a worthwhile question to ask whether the chain between originators to investors (i.e., broker to lender to securities underwriter to securities holder) has too many links in it for investors to be well-informed about what they are buying, and whether those links have too many built-in perverse incentives for the model to be sustainable.

In light of the unraveling of MBS during the financial crisis, covered bonds have been advanced as an alternative capital market method for financing mortgages. Covered bonds have been issued in Denmark since 1795, with performance that has been characterized as "unblemished."[13] A number of analysts think covered bonds are the best way for capital markets to fund mortgages.[14]

According to the European Covered Bond Council web site, the salient features of a covered bond are:[15]

- The bond is issued by—or bondholders otherwise have full recourse to—a credit institution that is subject to public supervision and regulation.
- Bondholders have a claim against a cover pool of financial assets in priority to the unsecured creditors of the credit institution.
- The credit institution has the ongoing obligation to maintain sufficient assets in the cover pool to satisfy the claims of covered bondholders at all times.
- The obligations of the credit institution with respect to the cover pool are supervised by public or other independent bodies.

So how does a covered bond work? It is a form of debt that is issued by a financial institution (typically a bank), and is very senior, in the sense that it is bankruptcy remote. It is "covered" because its cash flows are covered by another asset, such as a mortgage. Typically, when a mortgage that contributes to covering a bond fails, it is removed from supporting the bond and is replaced with another mortgage. In the event that the financial institution issuing the covered bond fails, holders of covered bonds are still protected, because by their very design, covered bonds have priority over all other creditors.

It is this seniority that makes it difficult for covered bonds to establish a large presence in the United States. In particular, the Federal Deposit Insurance Corporation (FDIC) has indicated concern about the priority of covered bonds over

---

13. See http://danskebank.com/da-dk/ir/Documents/Other/Danish-Covered-Bond-Handbook-2012.pdf, page 3
14. See Lucas et al. (2008).
15. See http://ecbc.hypo.org/Content/default.asp?PageID=503

other credit holders in the event that a bank becomes subject to FDIC receivership or conservatorship.[16]

But more generically, it is hard to understand why covered bonds are inherently superior to MBS. The key to the success of covered bonds in Denmark (and in Germany) has been tight underwriting. If we look at the characteristics of covered bonds extolled by the European Covered Bond Council, two of the four refer quite specifically to regulatory oversight. This oversight could apply to MBS as easily as it could to covered bonds. Alas, as we shall discuss later, we have little reason to think such oversight will actually happen.

DIFFERENCES IN GOVERNMENT INTERVENTION IN MORTGAGES

Lea (2010) and Jaffe (2010) argue that the United States is unusual, if not unique, in its level of government intervention in mortgage markets. Min (2013), on the other hand, argues that many countries have their governments intertwined in mortgage markets. We might think such an issue would be a matter of fact, rather than interpretation, but this is not correct.

Lea (2010) compares countries in three dimensions: whether they have a government mortgage insurer, whether they provide security guarantees, and whether they have government-sponsored enterprises for mortgages. As it happens, the number of countries with such features outside of the United States is small (Table 8.1).

But Min (2012) makes an important distinction between countries with explicit and implicit guarantees. In particular, he notes that many countries have deposit insurance. If banks issue mortgages are funded with deposits, and deposits are insured by the government, then it is hard to argue that government is not involved in mortgage finance. We could respond that in this instance, mortgage finance is no more favored than any other type of bank finance, except that under the Basel rules that regulated bank capital, banks were required to hold less capital against mortgages than other types of capital. We will discuss this further in the section on macro-prudential supervision (Table 8.2).

More interesting is the fact that throughout Europe, governments did intervene with financial institutions that were under stress in 2008. As Min (2012) notes in Table 4 of his publication, the Canadian government went beyond its insurance role and purchased mortgages to bring liquidity to the mortgage market, the Danish government provided blanket guarantees for all obligations of Danish banks (including covered bonds), the Irish government instituted a blanket guarantee for all its banks, the ECB created a covered bond purchase program, Ireland and the United Kingdom nationalized some of their banks, and so on. It is one thing for a

---

16. For obvious reasons, FDIC is jealous of its seniority over other investors in the event of bank failure.

TABLE 8.1 Direct Government Intervention in Mortgage Markets

Countries with Government Mortgage Insurer	Countries with Mortgage Security Guarantees	Countries with Government-Sponsored Enterprises
United States, The Netherlands, Canada	United States, Canada, Japan	United States, Korea, Japan (possible)

Source: Lea (2011).

TABLE 8.2 Countries with Indirect Intervention in Mortgage Markets

Countries with Deposit Insurance	Countries That Guarantee Covered Bonds	Countries That Bailed Out Financial Institutions
United States, Canada, Denmark, France, Ireland, Spain, United Kingdom, Korea, Sweden, Germany, Austria, Italy, Iceland, Belgium	United States,* Canada,* France,* Denmark,* Ireland,* Spain,* United Kingdom*	United States, Belgium, France, Luxembourg, The Netherlands, Canada, Denmark, ECB, France, Germany, Ireland, United Kingdom

*Implicit guarantee.
Source: Min (2012) and Demirgüç-Kunt and Kane (2008).

country to claim that it has no government involvement in its mortgage system; it is something else for them to act in a manner consistent with that claim.

Beyond these considerations, mortgages are heavily regulated in many countries outside the United States. For example, German mortgages must meet government-specified underwriting criteria before they are permitted to be placed into covered bonds. As we have discussed in our review of countries, some governments regulate maximum LTV ratios. Moreover, many countries that have arguably less intervention in the mortgage market than the United States have far more intervention in other aspects of the housing market. For example, tenants have much stronger rights in Germany and Italy than in the United States; the United Kingdom has far more social housing than the United States.

HOW CONSUMER-FRIENDLY IS THE US MORTGAGE?

The US mortgage is unique in that it favors consumers in all major characteristics: borrowers can get loans with small down payments (even in the aftermath of the crisis with FHA), long terms (30 years), a fixed interest rate, free prepayment, and in many states, no recourse. This would make the United States appear to be the most consumer-friendly mortgage market in the world.

But in two ways it is not. The first is perhaps not that important—for the United States as a whole, the average time for the foreclosure process to move from start to finish is a little more than a year, whereas in Europe it is about two years.[17] More important on a day-to-day basis is that mortgages in the United States cost more than they do in other countries.

Jaffee (2010) ranks 17 countries by average mortgage interest rate. In the comparison, the United States has the highest average interest cost of any country. Of course, the US mortgage is more likely to be a fixed rate mortgage, and so is priced off the long end of the yield curve, and this will tend to push up its cost. Given that Americans have long had the choice of a variable rate mortgage, and that they choose not to use it, it is hard to say that comparing the average US rate to the average rate in countries with other terms is fair.

But Lea (2010) shows that when we compare adjustable rate mortgages in the United States to other countries, the spreads required from a US borrower are considerably higher than in other countries. Most European Indexed ARMs have a margin between one and two percentage points, whereas in the United States they are typically 275 basis points. Canadians, Danes, and the Swiss can get mortgages with margins as low as 50 basis points!

The question we might ask is why. One answer might be that US mortgages have a free prepayment option, but this option is not so valuable for adjustable rate mortgages. Another is the absence of recourse, although the United States has states that have recourse for residential mortgages; mortgages in these states do not feature the sorts of spreads we see in Europe. Perhaps the answer arises from underwriting. Outside of the United Kingdom, the United States has looser underwriting than any other country in the world, particularly with respect to the ability of lenders to originate loans with layers of risk. Large numbers of risky mortgages place the housing market at risk, which in turn needs to be priced.

Ironically, one of the least consumer-friendly aspects of the European mortgage market—the preponderance of adjustable rate mortgages—may have helped save much of Europe from poor mortgage performance. Default and foreclosure rates in Europe have remained low relative to the United States, even as that continent's economic recovery has been exceptionally weak. Duebel (2011) shows that the rates paid by borrowers with adjustable rate mortgages fell dramatically from 2008 to 2010 in the United Kingdom, Spain, and Ireland. This allowed mortgage payments to fall, and took pressure off of households that were facing other economic difficulties. Moreover, to the extent that rates are indexed to an international benchmark, such as LIBOR, adjustable rate mortgages can insulate borrowers from risks associated with poor credit conditions in their own country. Differences in mortgage performance are depicted in Figure 8.1.

---

17. See Lea (2010) and http://www.nolo.com/legal-encyclopedia/states-with-long-foreclosure-timelines.html. There is a lot of variation within Europe and the United States.

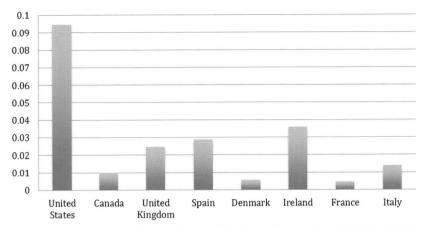

FIGURE 8.1   90-day deliqunicy rates by country, Dec 2009. *Sources: Lea (2010), Jaffee (2010), European Commission (2011). Japan, S. Korea and Hong Kong are not listed because default in those countries is "rare." See White (2010), BIS (2012), and Lim (2012).*

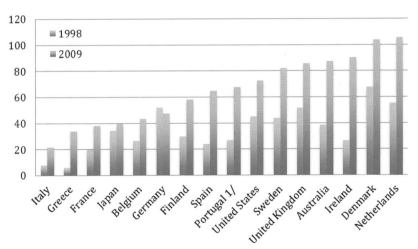

FIGURE 8.2   Mortage debt outstanding to GPD ratios: 1998–2009. *Source: IMF (2011). Table 3.6.* http://www.imf.org/external/pubs/ft/gfsr/2011/01/.

SIZE OF MORTGAGE MARKETS

The combination of house prices, underwriting incentives, and tax policies explains a great deal of differences in mortgage market sizes across countries. The most common metric for comparing mortgage market sizes across countries is the Mortgage-Debt Outstanding (MDO) to GDP ratio. The International Monetary Fund (2011) collects statistics on MDO to GDP for a number of countries, shown in Figure 8.2.

An interesting thing to note is that among PIIGS (Portugal, Italy, Ireland, Greece and Spain), the countries that have been under the most economic stress since the financial crisis, there was substantial variation in the size of mortgage markets: they were very small in Greece and Italy, average in Spain and Portugal, and large in Ireland. This implies that as much as we have reason to believe the US mortgage crisis was a major source of the US financial crisis, mortgages had little to do with the disasters we have seen overseas.

MORTGAGES AND MACRO-PRUDENTIAL SUPERVISION

The word "macro-prudential" barely existed at the beginning of the last decade (the 2000s; Galati and Moessner, 2012). To some extent, monetary policy is supposed to perform the function of macro-prudential supervision; when the economy is overheated, it is traditional for monetary policy-makers to slow the money supply; when it is underperforming, monetary authorities should increase the money supply. One mechanism for doing so is bank capital rules: when the economy is strong, central banks can raise capital standards (which is a mechanism for reeling in money) for banks, and can do the converse when the economy is weak.

Two important things conspired to undermine the ability of bank capital rules to lean against economic conditions: Basel I[18] and the shadow banking system.

Basel I was a set of risk-based capital rules that determined whether banks were or were not sufficiently capitalized. There were two basic rules; Tier 1 capital (which consists of paid up capital and retained earnings) under Basel I has to be greater than 8 percent of risk weighted assets. Lower risk weights mean that a bank needs to put up less capital. For example, if a bank has Tier I capital of $100, and has $1000 of assets with a risk-weight of 50 percent, its capital to risk-weighted asset ratio is $100/($1000 * 0.5), or 20 percent.

Risk weights that were assigned to different assets are presented in Table 8.3. Residential mortgages receive preference over other types of loans, and GSE-backed mortgage-backed securities receive preference over whole mortgages. This gave lenders a strong regulatory incentive to (1) finance homes and (2) sell mortgages of their balance sheet to Fannie Mae and Freddie Mac, and then buy back the securities issued by the GSEs.

Beyond the question of whether the risk weights are correct, they have the fundamental problem of being static. In a period such as 2006, it was becoming quite clear that mortgages were becoming dangerous, not just in the United States, but also in Spain, Ireland, and the United Kingdom, as house prices rose to a point where only a small number of people could afford them. Had there

---

18. Basel I was the first set of rules that came out of the Basel Committee on Bank Supervision, an international advisory body created to create a framework that would place the world's banks on an equal regulatory footing.

TABLE 8.3 Basel I Risk Weights for Real Estate

Risk Weight	Types of Asset
20%	GSE-backed mortgage-backed securities
50%	Residential mortgages
100%	Commercial mortgages

been a mechanism in place through which lenders would have been able to post more capital, it would have been helpful.

To some extent, this idea was supposed to be part of Basel II, which was supposed to add new supervisory and disclosure requirements to the capital requirements, and have more sophisticated capital requirements. But Basel II put into place model based capital rules; other parts of this book have demonstrated the limits of models with respect to risk management. As it happens, it also took a very long time to implement Basel II, and so it was not relevant to the development of the financial crisis.

Beyond the issue of bank capital, though, is the lack of regulation of the shadow banking sector and off-balance sheet investment vehicles. Shadow banks are institutions that are financial intermediaries that do not have access to central bank funding; in exchange for not getting that privilege, they have operated without regulatory oversight. The Financial Stability Board, an international body with representatives from the G20, has proposed regulating the shadow banking sector. The framework for such regulations were released on August 29, 2013.[19]

More prosaically, some countries employed macro-prudential supervision through LTV ratio rules. South Korea, Hong Kong, Singapore, and China all reduced maximum LTV standards in the midst of housing booms in order to attempt to keep the booms from creating debt overhangs. Kim (2012) and Wong et al. (2011) provide evidence that using LTV maximums to lean against housing booms and busts can be an effective policy.

REFERENCES

Biasin, Massimo, Smith, Halbert, C. CRE EMERITUS, 2010. The Valuation of Mortgage Security by Italian Banks. Real Estate Issues 35.2, 28.

Casolaro, Luca, Gambacorta, Leonardo, Guiso, Luigi, 2006. "Regulation, Formal and Informal Enforcement and the Development of Household Loan Market: lessons from Italy". The Economics of Consumer Credit. MIT Press, Boston 93–134.

Dübel, Hans-Joachim, 2005. Fixed-rate Mortgages and Prepayment in Europe. mimeo.

19. See http://www.financialstabilityboard.org/publications/r_130829b.pdf

Galati, Gabriele, Moessner, Richhild, 2012. Macroprudential policy–A literature review. Journal of Economic Surveys.

Ghent, Andra C., Kudlyak, Marianna, 2011. Recourse and residential mortgage default: Evidence from US states. Review of Financial Studies 24.9, 3139–3186.

Green, Richard K., Wachter, Susan M., 2007. The Housing Finance Revolution. The Blackwell companion to the economics of housing: The housing wealth of nations, 414–445.

Jaffee, Dwight M., 2011. Reforming the US mortgage market through private market incentives. Fisher Center for Real Estate and Urban Economics.

Kim, In-June, 2012. The global financial crisis and the challenges of the Korean economy. Seoul Journal of Economics 25.3, 339–366.

Lea, Michael, 2010. International comparison of mortgage product offerings. Research Institute for Housing America.

Lim, Kyung-Mook, 2012. 11. Structural fundamentals of Korean corporations: This time was different. Global Economic Crisis: Impacts, Transmission and Recovery, 250.

Lucas, Douglas J., et al., 2008. Covered Bonds: A New Source of US Mortgage Loan Funding? The Journal of Structured Finance 14.3, 44–48.

Miles, David, 2004. The UK mortgage market: Taking a longer-term view. Final Report and Recommendations.

Min, David, 2013. How Government Guarantees in Housing Finance Promote Stability. Harvard Journal on Legislation.

White, Brent T., 2010. Underwater and not walking away: Shame, fear and the social management of the housing crisis.

Wong, Tak-Chuen, et al., 2011. Loan-to-Value Ratio as a Macroprudential Tool-Hong Kong's Experience and Cross-Country Evidence. Systemic Risk, Basel III, Financial Stability and Regulation.

The Subprime Crisis

The meltdown of the mortgage market was a precipitating event of the financial crisis—this is not controversial. The causes behind the meltdown are, however, controversial.

This chapter will not make a statement about the most important cause of the meltdown, but rather will lay out the varying views of the crisis. It will do so in three ways. First, we will look at people's views pre-crisis. There are some people who saw it coming, and others who didn't—it is worth exploring why. Second, we will look at research that has taken place post-crisis whose intent is to explain the crisis.

THOSE WHO SAW IT COMING

Shiller

Robert Shiller distinguished himself by calling the housing bubble, and having a coherent argument for why there was, in fact, a bubble. The implications of a

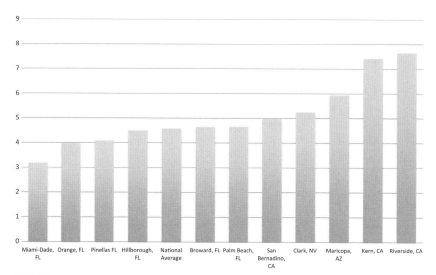

FIGURE 9.1 Share of employment in construction: selected counties. *Source: County Business Patterns 2011.*

bubble about to burst on housing finance and therefore on the broader economy were pretty straightforward—as owners with leverage found themselves underwater, they would have incentives to default. Defaults would put further downward pressure on housing, which in turn would lead to more defaults.

Many of the cities that appeared bubbly also relied heavily on housing construction (Phoenix, Las Vegas, The Inland Empire of California, and Florida cities are examples; see Figure 9.1). With a fall in house prices came a fall in construction jobs, which led to unemployment, which led to mode default, and so on. Even now, Las Vegas and the Inland Empire have among the highest rates of unemployment of any regions of the country (see Figure 9.2).

Shiller's views on bubbles were informed by an influential paper he wrote in 1981,[1] where he tested the efficiency of the stock market. His test was both simple and powerful.

He begins with a simple relationship from finance: that the value of an asset is equal to the expected present value of its cash flows. In the case of stock, this means:

$$p_t = \frac{E(d_t)}{1+r} + \frac{E(d_{t+1})}{1+r^2}$$

This is the price comes from the *ex ante* forecast of future dividends. Now let's suppose we could know the future with certainty. This is equivalent to deriving a price from an *ex post* forecast.

---

1. Robert J. Shiller. Do stock prices move too much to be justified by subsequent changes in dividends? American Economic Review, 71(3):421–436, June 1981.

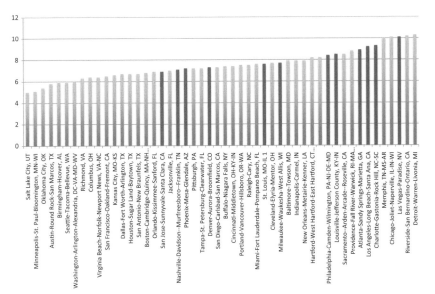

FIGURE 9.2   Unemployment by MSA, 50 Most Populus.

$$p_t^* = \frac{(d_t)}{1+r} + \frac{(d_{t+1})}{1+r^2}$$

The difference between p_t and P_t^* is just a forecast error, so that

$$p_t^* = p_t + \mu_t$$

It markets are efficient, then p_t and μ_t are independent, which implies

$$\sigma_{p*}^2 = \sigma_p^2 + \sigma_\mu^2$$

because

$$\sigma_\mu^2 \geq 0, \ \sigma_{p*}^2 \geq \sigma_p^2$$

We compare the variance of P_t^* and p_t, where CPI owner's equivalent rent is used as a proxy for rent (or d), the 10-year Treasury rate is used for r, and house prices are based on the Case-Shiller house price index. To standardize the two series, we compute a coefficient of variation for both of them. The dates run from 1987 through 2013, and are monthly. The coefficient of variation for p_t is 0.22, and for P_t^* it is 0.27. It is quite evident that house prices are far more volatile than those an efficient market would produce. The fact that the housing market is inefficient means that it is predictable, which also means there are times when we can know that it is overvalued, and that lending secured by housing is vulnerable. During these times, lenders should be pulling back; in 2005 to 2006 lenders instead went full speed ahead.

Shiller tried to put his views into practice, by creating a futures market in housing based on the house price index he created with Karl Case. By allowing homeowners to buy put options in a housing futures market, they could hedge their long positions in housing. Alas, very few trades actually took place, yet those that did trade showed foresight.

Gramlich

Federal Reserve Governor Ned Gramlich was arguably the Federal Reserve System's leading expert on subprime mortgages. He was also a voice in the wilderness.

Gramlich was the governor who was placed in charge of consumer lending issues. Early on in the development of the rise of subprime mortgages, he began raising concerns about the sustainability of the mortgages. In particular, he worried about deterioration in underwriting standards. He also worried about predatory lending.

In a speech in 2004, Gramlich laid out the benefits and problems with subprime lending. The principal benefit of subprime lending was that it made capital available to people who could not get capital previously. This led to what proved to be a short-lived rise in the national homeownership rate. Of course, these new entrants to the housing market pay higher interest rates and otherwise receive less favorable terms than traditional prime borrowers.

Gramlich asked a fundamental question, which is whether the increase in homeownership was a sufficiently large benefit to offset the pain people bore when they were foreclosed upon. He noted that subprime loans had substantially higher rates of delinquency and foreclosure, even in 2004, and that therefore the question of benefits and costs was germane. The fact that subprime loans did not perform well even in a period where house prices were rising was a powerful indicator that the underwriting of subprime loans was poor.

One of the most important things Gramlich noted was that many institutions that made subprime loans did not receive regular examinations from federal regulators on their financial health. Forty-three percent of subprime loans were made by finance companies that were affiliated with banks, and 12 percent were made by unregulated brokers. As such, Gramlich identified the importance of the "shadow banking" system to subprime lending, and the vulnerability created by the lack of supervision over it. He argued for the need for supervision of all parts of the mortgage system, so that lenders could not get around regulation. He was famously dismissed by Federal Reserve Chair Alan Greenspan,[2] about whom we will say more later.

Roubini

On September 6, 2006, Noriel Roubini gave a famous speech to an International Monetary Fund conference where we predicted a collapse in housing, and that

---

2. www.nytimes.com/2007/12/18/business/18subprime.html?pagewanted=all

the collapse would have a profound impact on the macroeconomy. Specifically, he noted:

The direct effects of a fall in residential investment I argue are going to be similar or larger than the fall in tech goods investment in 2000–2001. At the rates we are observing right now, you could have residential investment falling between this year and next year by about 2 percent of GDP. That is similar to the direct fall in investment in tech goods during the 2 years before the previous recession.

Of course, people say housing is only 6 percent of GDP while consumption is 70 percent. So a recession call has to be based not just on the direct effect from the housing bust but also the indirect effects. Let me mention three.

First, the indirect effects I think are important because the wealth effects of housing are larger because, unlike tech stocks, housing is a significant fraction of a household's wealth. In 2000 you had the big bubble in tech stocks. These stocks were held by a bunch of people in Silicon Valley, day traders and some households, but they were not widely held by the average household. But, as we know, about 50 percent of household wealth today is housing.

Second, the other point that is relevant here is that, savings have been negative, and the only way you can consume more than your income is that either you run down your assets or you increase your liabilities. There are not that many liquid assets to run down for U.S. households because half of wealth is locked into long-term savings plans, and the other half is essentially illiquid in housing. Therefore, the only way you can liquefy your wealth is by using your home as your ATM machine, and that is exactly what has happened in the last few years. Last year we had almost $800 billion of home equity withdrawal or extraction. Of that, almost $200 billion went to consumption, another $100 billion went into home improvements, and the rest essentially to essentially financial balances — reducing credit card debt and so on. It has been crucial to have home equity withdrawal as a way to sustain this excessive spending and consumption over income. If this effect is going to disappear because house prices are going to now flatten and then fall, then you are going to have a significant problem in sustaining consumption.

The third reason I think the housing bust is going to be more important than the tech bust is that the tech sector was not very labor-intensive. You had high-skilled, high value-added kinds of jobs in the tech sector, while employment growth in housing has been much more important. I have estimated that about 30 to 40 percent of the increase in employment since 2001 has been due to housing either directly or indirectly. So the fall of housing is going to have a much more meaningful effect on employment.

The nice thing about this prediction is that it gave a mechanism through which a collapse in housing would have an impact on the broader economy. But Roubini is also criticized for being a perma-bear—a critique that has some merit. More importantly, however, while Roubini saw that a collapse in housing could have broad implications for the economy, he didn't emphasize THE mechanism that would lead to such a spectacular implosion. That insight would come from the Oracle of Omaha.

Warren Buffet and Counterparty Risk[3]

I worked for a short time for Freddie Mac. One of the issues occasionally discussed at lunch was the company's vulnerabilities. I think it is fair to say that those of us who were worker bees wanted to be sure that the taxpayer would never be on the hook for Freddie Mac debt and/or guarantees.

This was 2002 and 2003, so default risk was not a great worry: the company's underwriting practices at the time were sound, and mortgages were protected either by 20 percent down payments or mortgage insurance, and property values were still rising, but not yet at a bubble-like pace in places like Las Vegas and Florida. As for interest rate risk, the company purchased hedges so that its balance sheet would always have duration of less than a month, and so that duration risk was quite small too—although while hedging duration is pretty straightforward, convexity is more complicated (as we note in Chapter 12, duration is basically the first derivative in how capital value changes with respect to interest rates; convexity is the second derivative). I personally thought the people who executed risk management at Freddie at that time were very good at their jobs. In these discussions, we failed to predict the principal reason the company got into trouble; we had no idea that senior management would recklessly gamble the charter through accounting that was both misleading and, as it turned out, incompetent. I have arguments with William Poole, who was an early critic of Fannie Mae and Freddie Mac, but when he said that management risk was a huge problem with having institutions like Fannie and Freddie, he was right.

But one among us (whose name I will reveal if he/she gives me permission to do so) did predict a major source of the current problem: counterparty risk. For example, Freddie Mac would buy instruments called swaptions, which would give the company the option to swap floating rate debt for fixed rate debt, and vice versa. These swaptions would allow Freddie to manage its balance sheet when interest rates changed in the future. Suppose, for instance, Freddie borrowed long-term in order to finance fixed-rate mortgages. Now interest rates fall and borrowers refinance. Swaptions allowed Freddie to trade its expensive fixed rate debt into less expensive floating rate debt to match the lower return on its portfolio (and the converse when interest rates rise). But of course, swaptions would be useless if the institution with which Freddie contracted could not make good on its part of the bargain when interest rates changed.

In 2003, Warren Buffett called derivatives (such as swaptions) weapons of mass financial destruction. Like everyone else, I have long admired Buffett, but I thought he got this one wrong. Derivatives allowed institutions to hedge and therefore reduce risk! Or at least I thought this was the purpose of derivatives.

---

3. A version of this discussion was in my blog, real-estate-and-urban-blogpost.com, on September 28, 2008.

But of course, investors can also use derivatives to speculate, and when they do so (and particularly when they do so using leverage), derivatives become very dangerous. AIG, for instance, guaranteed against mortgage default. This meant that when defaults rose to levels not seen since the Great Depression, it didn't have enough capital to meet its responsibility to its counterparties. So the counterparties who thought they had hedged their risk found themselves exposed, which in turn ate into their capital position, and so a cascade was on.

Buffett had and has no objection to straightforward derivatives—Berkshire Hathaway uses them all the time. But he made a particularly important point in his 2002 letter to shareholders:[4]

Unless derivatives contracts are collateralized or guaranteed, their ultimate value also depends on the creditworthiness of the counter-parties to them. But before a contract is settled, the counter-parties record profits and losses – often huge in amount – in their current earnings statements without so much as a penny changing hands. Reported earnings on derivatives are often wildly overstated. That's because today's earnings are in a significant way based on estimates whose inaccuracy may not be exposed for many years.

The errors usually reflect the human tendency to take an optimistic view of one's commitments. But the parties to derivatives also have enormous incentives to cheat in accounting for them. Those who trade derivatives are usually paid, in whole or part, on "earnings" calculated by mark-to-market accounting. But often there is no real market, and "mark-to-model" is utilized. This substitution can bring on large-scale mischief. As a general rule, contracts involving multiple reference items and distant settlement dates increase the opportunities for counter-parties to use fanciful assumptions. The two parties to the contract might well use differing models allowing both to show substantial profits for many years. In extreme cases, mark-to-model degenerates into what I would call mark-to-myth.

I can assure you that the marking errors in the derivatives business have not been symmetrical. Almost invariably, they have favored either the trader who was eyeing a multi-million dollar bonus or the CEO who wanted to report impressive "earnings" (or both). The bonuses were paid, and the CEO profited from his options. Only much later did shareholders learn that the reported earnings were a sham.

Another problem about derivatives is that they can exacerbate trouble that a corporation has run into for completely unrelated reasons. This pile-on effect occurs because many derivatives contracts require that a company suffering a credit downgrade immediately supply collateral to counter-parties.

Imagine then that a company is downgraded because of general adversity and that its derivatives instantly kick in with their requirement, imposing an unexpected and enormous demand for cash collateral on the company. The need to meet this demand

---

4. See http://www.fintools.com/docs/Warren%20Buffet%20on%20Derivatives.pdf

can then throw the company into a liquidity crisis that may, in some cases, trigger still more downgrades. It all becomes a spiral that can lead to a corporate meltdown.

Derivatives also create a daisy-chain risk that is akin to the risk run by insurers or reinsurers that lay off much of their business with others. In both cases, huge receivables from many counter-parties tend to build up over time. A participant may see himself as prudent, believing his large credit exposures to be diversified and therefore not dangerous. However under certain circumstances, an exogenous event that causes the receivable from Company A to go bad will also affect those from Companies B through Z.

It is worth quoting this passage at length because I don't know of anyone else who foresaw the implications of derivatives as well as Buffett. He was particularly insightful about the daisy chain effect, which meant that the subprime crisis had a particularly profound impact on the rest of the economy.

When the Resolution Trust Corporation was created in 1989 to resolve the Savings and Loan Problem, nominal GDP was about 40 percent of what it was in 2008. That RTC took over about $400 billion in assets; the total balance on all subprime loans at that time was about $1 trillion. Thus is appears that the subprime crisis should have been no worse than the Savings and Loan crisis, which created a mild, short-lived recession.

But of course we have instead had the worst economic performance since the Great Depression—as of 2013, the US economy had failed to recover all the jobs it lost from 2007 to 2009 (see Figure 9.3). The severity came about because of Buffett's insight—positions in the derivatives market were not really

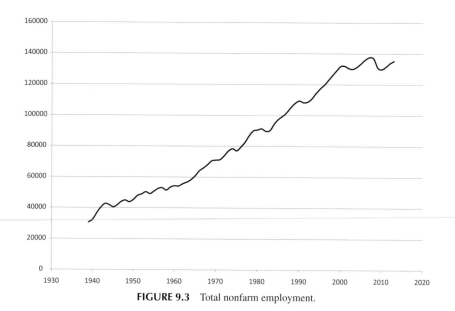

FIGURE 9.3 Total nonfarm employment.

symmetric, and as a result of that, a cascade nearly brought about the end of the US housing finance system.

Michael Burry and John Paulson

Michael Burry and John Paulson were the protagonists in two books about the financial crisis: *The Big Short* See Lewis (2011) and *The Greatest Trade Ever* Zuckerman (2010), respectively. Both Burry and Paulson decided as early as 2006 that housing was overvalued, and so wanted to take short positions on the market.

Finding a method for shorting housing proved difficult. The most obvious method for shorting the housing market seemed to be to short homebuilder stocks, but while homebuilder stocks are correlated with the housing market, they seem to move with a lag, and are much less than perfectly correlated.

The instrument Burry and Paulson used was the CDS, or credit default swap. The instrument essentially was an insurance policy against failing mortgages: if mortgages lost value, the counterparty (insurer) on a CDS would owe money to the owner (insured). This allowed Burry and Paulson to take what were essentially naked shorts.

The downside to those who shorted the market was that they had to pay premiums month after month in exchange for getting nothing in the event that mortgage values did not fall. Burry decided this was a good play, because "In 2003, something curious had happened. The interest-only mortgage was reintroduced. That spurred me to write a section in my letter called Basis for Concern."[5]

This was actually not quite true—interest-only mortgages have been around for some time. But his more generic insight *was* true—mortgage underwriting was getting worse, and so the mortgage market was becoming increasingly vulnerable. This made the premiums on CDS look very cheap, and therefore Burry and Paulson were willing to accept the drip, drip, drip of paying premiums in exchange for a large future payoff when the mortgage market collapsed.

Amazingly, despite the rapid increase in loan value, there were not enough loans outstanding to meet the hunger for Collateralized Debt Obligations (CDOs). Consequently, there were not just Collateralized Mortgage Obligations (CMOs) and CDOs backed by actual mortgages, but also synthetic CDOs that referred to a reference set of mortgages. The cash flows for these CDOs came from the CDS premiums. Principal actually didn't trade hands in these deals—only coupon payments. The "notional value" of the securities was thus $\frac{CF}{r}$, where r was a capitalization rate. Thus the "notional value" of mortgage derivatives was much larger than all the mortgage debt outstanding. The shorters, beyond profiting from the collapse of the mortgage market, may well have exacerbated the crisis.

---

5. http://www.zerohedge.com/article/profiling-big-shorts-michael-burry

THOSE WHO SAID HOUSE PRICES WOULD RISE FOREVER

Very few people foresaw the housing calamity—those named earlier are rare for their clairvoyance, and in some cases, may have just been outliers who got a "lucky," if that is the word, draw.

But a few people really got things wrong.

David Lereah

David Lereah was the Chief Economist of the National Association of Realtors. In 2005, he wrote a book with the unfortunate title, *Are You Missing the Real Estate Boom?*, which became subject to considerable ridicule. But he actually made some reasonable arguments:

- That mortgage rates had steadily retreated over 25 years, and were getting capitalized into prices
- The age-profile of the population, which had echo-boomers at the threshold of their home-buying years, suggested that housing demand would increase
- Returns on other assets had been disappointing
- Minorities, who had been underserved, would demand increasing amounts of housing

The largest criticisms one could levy at Lereah were that he was working for a group that had an interest in having people take long positions in housing, and that he encouraged people to take on leverage (he discouraged people from paying off their mortgages).

Because his position as an employee of NAR was transparent, it is not clear why people would expect him to do anything other than advocate for people to buy houses. But the criticism about his enthusiasm for leverage has some merit: he pointed out how leverage improves expected return while failing to emphasize that it also places people at greater risk.

Greenspan

Alan Greenspan was leery about the state of housing markets. There is a famous quote from him from June 9, 2005:

That said, there can be little doubt that exceptionally low interest rates on ten-year Treasury notes, and hence on home mortgages, have been a major factor in the recent surge of homebuilding and home turnover, and especially in the steep climb in home prices. Although a 'bubble' in home prices for the nation as a whole does not appear likely, there do appear to be, at a minimum, signs of froth in some local markets where home prices seem to have risen to unsustainable levels.

So Greenspan did a reasonably good job of understanding there was a problem. However, he received substantial criticism for his unwillingness to respond to the problem.

Specifically, Greenspan thought (and continues to think) markets were self-regulating—that firms cared too much about their reputation to do anything that caused long-term damage. He did admit in 2009 that "Those of us who have looked to the self-interest of lending institutions to protect shareholder's equity—myself especially—are in a state of shocked disbelief."[6]

EX POST VIEWS ON CAUSES OF THE FINANCIAL CRISIS

The Financial Crisis Inquiry Commission

Congress created The Financial Crisis Inquiry Commission to "examine the causes, domestic and global, of the current financial and economic crisis in the United States." The Commission's statutory instructions set out 22 specific topics for inquiry and called for the examination of the collapse of major financial institutions that failed or would have failed if not for exceptional assistance from the government.[7]

The Commission issued a report, which really was three reports: one by the Democrats, who were majority of commissioners, one by three Republicans, and one by a lone Republican, Peter Wallison.

The majority report listed a set of conclusions:

- The crisis was avoidable.
- There were widespread failures in financial regulation and supervision that proved devastating to the stability of the nation's financial markets.
- There were dramatic failures of corporate governance and risk management at many systemically important financial institutions that were a key cause of the crisis.
- A combination of excessive borrowing, risky investments, and lack of transparency put the financial system on a collision course with crisis.
- The government was ill-prepared for the crisis, and its inconsistent response added to the uncertainty and panic in financial markets.
- There was a systematic breakdown in accountability and ethics.
- Collapsing mortgage-lending standards and the mortgage securitization pipeline lit and spread the flame of contagion and crisis.
- Over-the-counter derivatives contributed significantly to this crisis.
- Failures of credit rating agencies were essential cogs in the wheel of financial destruction.

The Republican minority report listed the following set of causes:

- A credit bubble
- A housing bubble

---

6. http://www.independent.co.uk/news/business/analysis-and-features/quotes-of-2008-we-are-in-a-state-of-shocked-disbelief-1220057.html
7. The list is at http://fcic.law.stanford.edu/about/history

- Nontraditional mortgages
- Credit ratings and securitization
- Financial institutions concentrated correlated risk
- Leverage and liquidity risk
- Contagion
- Common shock
- Financial shock and panic
- Financial crisis causing economic crisis

To some extent, these explanations overlap. The one issue the minority report mentions that goes unmentioned in the majority report is the possibility of a credit bubble—that there was simply too much cash sloshing around the world chasing too few investment opportunities. In the chase for yield, investors made questionable bets.

Although all of these explanations have some plausibility, only some have been subject to rigorous academic analysis. We discuss some of those issues here.

Government

There was a report written by a lone dissenter—Peter Wallison, who placed nearly all the blame for the financial crisis on government institutions and government programs that encouraged lending to low income people and low income neighborhoods. The best known of the programs were the Community Reinvestment Act and the GSE Affordable Housing Goals.

The Community Reinvestment Act encouraged banks to make loans to underserved communities. These communities were defined as census-tracts with low-to-moderate incomes, which in turn were defined as tracts whose median incomes were at or below 80 percent of area median income. Banks with strong CRA ratings were in a stronger position to be granted mergers.

The Affordable Housing Goals similarly encouraged Fannie Mae and Freddie Mac to purchase mortgages in low, moderate, and even middle-income census tracts; tracts with median household incomes less than 100 percent of AMI qualified.

There is now a reasonably long literature on the impact of CRA on the financial crisis, and it overwhelmingly finds that CRA had little, if any. Andra C. Ghent, Ruben Hernandez-Murillo, and Michael T. Owyangy (2012) show that neighborhoods that nearly qualified for CRA status were no different in the quality of the loans they received from the neighborhoods that just qualified for such status. This is probably the most convincing empirical strategy for finding that CRA did not lead to dangerous lending. Avery and Brevoort (2011) and Laderman and Reid (2008) found that tracts that qualified for CRA targets were no more likely to have subprime loans than those that did not qualify.

The one outlier in this literature is Agarwal, Benmelech, Bergman, and Seru (2012), whose paper has been quoted approvingly by think tanks that are seeking to pin the blame for the mortgage meltdown on CRA. But Reid (2013) argues that Agarwal et al. is flawed because they demonstrate a lack of understanding about how CRA bank examinations work. This is important, because the result Agarwal et al. try to demonstrate is that banks facing CRA examinations generate riskier mortgages than those that don't.

Perhaps the most important fact relating to the culpability of the CRA is that the majority of subprime loans were made by institutions not covered by the CRA.

Fannie Mae and Freddie Mac

As noted in Chapter 1, Fannie Mae and Freddie Mac's management did not always behave in the best interest of taxpayers. Nevertheless, they were followers rather than leaders into the crisis.

Some of the important facts about Fannie and Freddie: their loan portfolios performed better than the general mortgage market, and in fact the default rates on Fannie and Freddie MBS were considerably lower than PLS default rates (see Thomas and Van Order, 2010).

Two other facts are worth noting: Fannie and Freddie were losing market share as the subprime market expanded, and while they did begin investing in PLS, they invested in AAA tranches. For the subprime market to grow, lenders needed investors that were willing to take on the subordinate pieces of the capita structure. Fannie and Freddie did not feed the machine.

SECURITIZATION

One of the fiercest debates about causes of the crisis involved securitization. A literature has developed around whether those that originated loans did so knowing that they could easily shed their bad ones—particularly those that had poor unmeasured, or soft, characteristics.

This is a classic asymmetric information—or lemons—problem. Lenders that initially fund a loan know more about it than the investors who purchase securities, which in turn undermines the existence of a market.

To understand why this is true, suppose that the value of a mortgage is the sum of its observables and its unobservables.

$$V_m = V_o + V_u$$

Observables are underwriting standards that are easy to measure, such as FICO score, debt-to-income ratio, and loan-to-value ratio. An unobservable might be something like the quality of a borrower's employer. Buyers know the distribution of unobservables, and that the mean of the unobservables is zero, and that the maximum value of V_u is V_o, and that the minimum value is $-V_o$, and that V_o is uniformly distributed.

Now the buyers of the mortgage with a certain set of observables assumes that it has the average set of unobservables. What happens? Lenders who hold high above-average mortgages refuse to sell them, because the price isn't high enough. This means that the only mortgages available for sale are worse-than-average mortgages. This in turn means that the average mortgage in the market now becomes $V_o - 1/2V_o$. This process continues until no mortgages are available for sale: economic theory predicts that in the market for lemons, we will observe no transactions.

And yet we did, in fact, observe transactions—the question is why. Is it more than a lemons issue? Did lenders pull something over on purchasers of MBS? Two papers have very different takes on the issue.

Keys (2010), Mukherjee, Seru, Vig

Keys et al. rely on an exogenous cut-off rule to identify the impact of securitization on screening. Specifically, they argue that it was easier for lenders to sell loans into private label securities when borrower FICO scores were above 620, meaning that they had to keep loans with lower scores on their own books. They argue that lenders will underwrite their borrowers more carefully if they know they are unlikely to sell mortgages, and therefore collect more information about borrowers.

The finding of the paper that is interesting is that mortgages with borrowers just below the 620 FICO cut-off performed better than those above the cut-off. They use this as evidence that lenders care more about what they eat than what others eat.

There are two problems with this finding. First, it contradicts the markets for lemon theory. Second, one of the things that sunk many lenders (Countrywide, WAMU, IndyMac) is that when times got even a little tough, they couldn't really get loans off their balance sheets.

Bubb and Kaufman

Bubb and Kaufman (2009) have a different interpretation of why we might observe discontinuities at loan cut-offs:

We offer an alternative rational theory for credit score cutoff rules and refer to our theory as the lender-first theory. When lenders face a fixed per-applicant cost to acquire additional information about each prospective borrower, cutoff rules in screening arise endogenously. Under the natural assumption that the benefit to lenders of collecting additional information is greater for higher default risk applicants, lenders will only collect additional information about applicants whose credit scores are below some cutoff (and hence the benefit of investigating outweighs the fixed cost). This additional information allows lenders to screen out more high-risk loan applicants.

The lender-first theory thus predicts that the number of loans made and their de-fault rate will be discontinuously lower for borrowers with credit scores just below the endogenous cutoff.

This interpretation seems more consistent with economics of information theory. They back it up by looking at loan-level data from both the conforming and low-documentation loan markets; in these markets, they find the same discontinuity in performance at the 620 FICO cut-off as Keys et al., but find no discontinuity in propensity to securitize. This suggests that the securitization market disciplined lenders into gathering more information about borrowers when FICO scores deteriorated past a certain level; this is inconsistent with the notion that securitization per se created a deterioration in lending.

Sufi and Mian

Perhaps the most important (and certainly the most cited) paper on the impact of securitization on the collapse of housing is by Amir Sufi and Atif Mian (2009). They point out that zip codes that had large numbers of subprime loans (1) saw credit rise dramatically while incomes in these same zip codes was falling and (2) had elevated levels of default once the default crisis began to hit in 2007.

Most germane, they point out that the prevalence of increased lending in falling income zip codes was associated with an increase in securitization. They use a wide variety of specifications to support their conclusion, and their results are robust.

RATING AGENCIES

The Ratings Agencies—Moody's, Standard and Poors, and Fitch—have come under considerable criticism as being responsible for the subprime crisis. The argument is that they too freely rated mortgage-backed securities as AAA, and thus gave dangerous investments the illusion of being safe.[8]

There are two thrusts to the criticism. First, bond raters are paid by bond issuers; if issuers don't like the rating they receive, they can simply go unrated and not pay (White, 2010). The criticism is similar to those advanced about appraisers, who tried to avoid assigning low values to houses in order to avoid stopping deals from happening.

The more substantive criticism is that the rating agencies didn't have the know-how to rate complicated securities accurately. A more accurate criticism is likely that no one had the know-how to truly rate securities that were filled up with exotic

---

8. On July 31, 2013, The New York Times ran an article alleging that even now, Standard and Poors is giving out favorable bond ratings into order to generate business. See http://dealbook.nytimes.com/2013/07/31/an-analysis-finds-a-bias-for-banks-in-s-p-ratings/?hp&_r=0

mortgages. As it is, the models used by the rating agencies were almost laughable in their precision. A model might say that for something to be rated AAA, it needed to have a subordination level of, say, 15.46 percent (which is to say the agency thought losses could be no higher than 15.46 percent). This faux precision reflected a slavish reliance on model coefficients—coefficients that almost certainly produced estimates that had large confidence intervals around them.

MODELS

Sampling

There is a very real sense in which subprime mortgages were a good idea. Before subprime, the mortgage market operated through rationing. Prices were pretty uniform, and a borrower either qualified for a mortgage at a particular price, or a borrower didn't. The idea behind subprime lending was to make credit available to more borrowers, and then to charge these borrowers extra to compensate for the extra potential default costs.

But in order to price mortgages, we must estimate default likelihood. Before the development of the subprime market, default models were estimated using prime borrowers. Thus, the sample of borrowers used to calibrate models was fundamentally different from the population of borrowers using the subprime market. This seems like an obvious point, but it did nothing to prevent some lenders from using underwriting models based on prime borrower characteristics for underwriting nonprime borrowers.

Calibration

Risk-based pricing became widespread in the subprime market in the late 1990s along with the development of private-label securitization of nonconforming mortgages. But while the algorithms for rationing credit became sophisticated, the algorithms for pricing subprime mortgages (to the extent such things even exist) faced a serious identification problem. From 1997 to 2005, the period in which the subprime market grew dramatically, nominal home prices in the United States rose rapidly and nearly ubiquitously. This meant that the incentive to default was extremely low—households had a strong incentive to sell their houses and preserve their equity rather than default. Capital allocation models calibrated to data from periods with rising house prices could not possibly inform risk managers about how much capital they would need to set aside for mortgages.

Beyond that, the subprime market expanded the use of products whose features had never faced a severe test. In particular, lenders marketed 2/28 and 3/27 ARMs with prepayment penalties. These mortgages would have introductory teaser rates (for two or three years) that would reset to London interbank offered rate (LIBOR) or one-year Treasuries with a large spread. Borrowers would qualify for the loan based on the initial teaser rate, and then would be locked into the higher rate after the teaser expired. Pavlov and Wachter (2007) show how prices increased specifically in markets where the subprime's market share grew, so that a portion of the price increases were credit-induced rather than based on fundamentals.

Past research on teaser-rate ARMs originated in the 1980s showed that borrowers had a strong propensity to prepay when rates adjusted to a market rate of interest plus a large margin (see Green and Shilling 1997). These ARMs did not have prepayment penalties, but research suggests that borrowers as a group understood the product they were getting themselves into; they would take advantage of the teaser and then exit the mortgage at the moment when it became profitable for the lender.

Gaussian Copula

The Gaussian Copula became notorious as the model that caused mortgage-backed securities to blow up.[9] This is an exaggeration, but the way the function was used was symptomatic of the problems with how Wall Street treated mortgage-backed securities.

Let us start with a simple security that contains two mortgages, and divide that security into two pieces—a senior piece and a subordinated piece. Let's also have a simple setup where if neither loan defaults, both the senior and the subpieces get fully paid, if one loan defaults, the senior gets paid and the sub doesn't, and if both loans default, neither gets paid.

Now let's turn to the formula for a bivariate Gaussian-Copula: Salmon (2009)

$$C_p = \Phi\left(\Phi^{-1}(u), \Phi^{-1}(v), \rho\right)$$

What does this give? It essentially says the following: suppose we estimate the probability of mortgage u defaulting and of mortgage v defaulting. We will now take the normal inverse of those probabilities and combine them with a correlation between the two mortgages to get a probability that both mortgages default.

Under this set-up, from the perspective of the holder of the sub-holder, all that matters is the probability that either one of the mortgages defaults. From the perspective of the senior-holder, what matters is that both default.

There are two crucial assumptions here: (1) default probabilities are distributed randomly and (2) correlations remain stable across time, and can be estimated. Neither one of these assumptions has ever been true. This is why senior pieces of the security structure were not as safe as investors thought they were.

SUPPLY CHAIN

One thing that is still not well understood—or understood at all—is how the supply chain for mortgages might have led the mortgage market to lose discipline.

---

9. See http://www.wired.com/techbiz/it/magazine/17-03/wp_quant?currentPage=all.

A notorious, funny, profane, and perhaps accurate depiction of this comes from the "subprime primer," which circulated on the World Wide Web.

It begins with a borrower at a mortgage broker. The borrower asks for a no-money down loan that will have high payments. The broker assures the borrower that this is fine, because house prices always go up. The broker also offers a teaser-rate loan; the borrower asks if he needs to have his employer verify his employment; the broker says no. The broker also notes that his compensation is independent of loan performance.

The cartoon then moves onto the bank that funds the loan. The bank wants to off-load its mortgages, so calls a Wall Street investment bank to package them into a mortgage-backed security. The investment bank creates CDOs, relies on diversification and rising housing prices to underwrite loans, tranches them, gets the senior pieces rated by rating agencies, sells the senior pieces, and keeps the most junior piece.

The junior piece is then placed in an off-shore special-purpose vehicle, where it is hard for the shareholders of the investment bank to find them. The end investor (both shareholders in the investment bank and investors in senior tranche CDOs) are now far removed from the original loan, which makes it very hard to judge the loan's quality.

Here is where transparency in the market completely fell apart. The number of steps in the process, combined with the complexity of the deals, made it nearly impossible for end investors to evaluate their investments. But finding an empirical method that tries to identify how the collective steps in the mortgage process may have contributed more mischief than the individual steps is probably, well, too complicated.

REFERENCES

Agarwal, Sumit, et al., 2012. Did the Community Reinvestment Act (CRA) Lead to Risky Lending?. No. w18609. National Bureau of Economic Research.

Avery, Robert B., Brevoort, Kenneth P., 2011. The subprime crisis: Is government housing policy to blame?

Bubb, Ryan, Kaufman, Alex, 2009. Securitization and moral hazard: Evidence from a lender cutoff rule. No. 09, 5. Public policy Discussion Papers. Federal Reserve Bank of Boston.

Green, Richard K., Shilling, James D., 1997. The Impact of Initial–Year Discounts on ARM Prepayments. Real Estate Economics 25.3, 373–385.

Hernández-Murillo, Rubén, Ghent, Andra, Owyang, Michael, 2012. Did affordable housing legislation contribute to the subprime securities boom? Available at SSRN 2022461.

Keys, Benjamin J., et al., 2010. Did securitization lead to lax screening? Evidence from subprime loans. The Quarterly Journal of Economics 125.1, 307–362.

Laderman, Elizabeth, Reid, Carolina, 2008. Lending in low-and moderate-income neighborhoods in California: the performance of CRA lending during the subprime meltdown. Federal Reserve Bank of San Francisco.

Lewis, Michael, 2011. The big short: Inside the doomsday machine. WW Norton & Company.

Mian, Atif, Sufi, Amir, 2009. The consequences of mortgage credit expansion: Evidence from the US mortgage default crisis. The Quarterly Journal of Economics 124.4, 1449–1496.

Pavlov, Andrey, Wachter, Susan, 2007. Aggressive Lending and Real Estate Markets. Samuel Zell and Robert Lurie Real Estate Center at Wharton Working Paper 566.

Reid, Carolina, Seidman, Ellen, Willis, Mark, Ding, Lei, Sliver, Josh, Ratcliffe, Janneke, 2013. Debunking the CRA Myth–Again. UNC Center for Community Capital.

Salmon, F., 2009. Recipe for Disaster: The Formula That Killed Wall Street (2009). Wired Magazine February 23, 2009.

Thomas, Jason, Van Order, Robert, 2010. Housing Policy, Subprime Markets and Fannie Mae and Freddie Mac: What We Know, What We Think We Know and What We Don't Know. St. Louis FRB Conference.

White, Lawrence J., 2010. Markets: The credit rating agencies. The Journal of Economic Perspectives 24.2, 211–226.

Zuckerman, Gregory, 2010. The greatest trade ever: The behind-the-scenes story of how John Paulson defied Wall Street and made financial history. Random House Digital, Inc.

Chapter 10

Consumers in Mortgage Markets

Vanessa G. Perry

The GW School of Business, Washington, DC, USA

The largest asset in the portfolio of the typical American household is a house, which is most often financed through a residential mortgage contract. According to the most recent decennial Census (2010), 69.7 percent of US owner-occupied households have been purchased with a mortgage loan. Thus, the choice of a mortgage loan has significant implications for wealth-generation and other long-term financial outcomes. This choice is a complex one because it involves many interrelated choices. The first decisions, and perhaps the most prominent in the consumer's mind, are whether to buy a house in the first place, and which house to buy. Evidence suggests that consumers spend more time shopping for a home than searching for a mortgage loan (Talaga and Buch 1998). Favorable interest rates and house prices may lead consumers into the mortgage market and thus may be tied to these initial decisions to search for and/or purchase a home. The prospective homebuyer must decide how much he or she is willing to pay for the

Introduction to Mortgages & Mortgage Backed Securities.
http://dx.doi.org/10.1016/B978-0-12-401743-6.00010-X

house (this may differ from a lender's underwriting affordability requirements), and how to finance and how much to put toward a down payment.

Next, the homebuyer must select a lender or broker, and then choose within an array of mortgage loan types (e.g., conventional, FHA or VA, or jumbo). Within these loan types, the prospective borrower has to choose a particular product—either a fixed- or adjustable-rate loan, and each of these options include several possible variations in repayment requirements, such as whether to pay upfront points in exchange for a lower rate, loan term (e.g., 30-year, 20-year, or 15-year fixed, 5/1 versus 10/1 ARMS), and the type of payment structure (e.g., balloon, interest only payments, or hybrids). In addition, after origination, the borrower has an option to prepay, refinance, or default.

These are complex decisions, and require that the borrower evaluate factors influencing quality of the investment, as would any other investor. These factors include the costs of the loan, the property and transactions, and the probability of default. There are also implications related to household factors, such as the likelihood of moving, liquidity constraints, and taxes (Basciano et al. 2008). Thus, in order to make informed decisions, consumers must react to uncertainty in inflation, interest rates, income, cash-flow, house prices, borrowing ability, as well as other potential social and financial constraints (Campbell and Cocco 2003).

In this chapter, we will begin with an examination of mortgage decisions from a rational, economic perspective. Next, we will consider the role of psychological factors such as knowledge and decision-making heuristics and biases. The third section presents contextual influences on mortgage decisions, including lender marketing activities and public policy.

ECONOMIC MODELS OF MORTGAGE LOAN CHOICE

Why do borrowers select adjustable-rate mortgages (ARMs) versus fixed-rate mortgages (FRMs)? Figure 10.1 includes a fixed-rate versus adjustable-rate mortgage choice model in which the authors assume that these two types of

$$\Psi i = \gamma(RF, RA, M', \theta i) + \varepsilon,$$

where Ψi is the preference of borrower i, RF and RA are the initial interest rates of the FRM and ARM contracts, respectively; M is a vector of macroeconomic variables; θ is a vector of borrower characteristics; and ε an error term.

FIGURE 10.1 Model of fixed-rate versus adjustable-rate mortgage choice. *Source: Coulibaly and Li (2009).*

mortgage contracts are identical in terms of maturity, points, and other loan features. These mortgages differ only in terms of the initial interest rates, which will typically be highest for the FRM. These authors also assume that borrowers have heterogeneous preferences and financial circumstances. Thus, the borrower's decision problem is as follows in Figure 10.1.

$$\Psi_i = \gamma \, (\text{RF}, \text{RA}, \text{M}', \theta i) + \varepsilon,$$

where Ψ_i is the preference of borrower i, RF and RA are the initial interest rates of the FRM and ARM contracts, respectively; M is a vector of macroeconomic variables; θ is a vector of borrower characteristics; and ε an error term.

According to studies of ARM versus FRM choice, consumers are more likely to select ARMS when the spread between ARM and FRM rates increases, particularly in the market for conventional (conforming and jumbo) loans. In addition, borrowers with lower incomes or borrowers who are in the market for higher priced homes are more likely to seek the lower initial financing costs that the ARM product typically provides. Borrowers with smaller or less expensive houses relative to income, more stable incomes, co-borrowers or married couples also more likely to choose adjustable rate mortgages (Campbell and Cocco 2003). Other groups who lean toward ARMs include those with lower risk aversion or a higher probability of moving. Conversely, borrowers who expect short-term rates to increase in the future will be more likely to select a FRM (Berkovec et al. 2001).

There are important differences in the case of borrowers in the subprime market. Fixed rates are more common when the LTV is low. However, as LTV increases, borrowers become more likely to choose ARMs up to a certain point, at which they revert to a preference for FRMs. Evidence suggests that for subprime borrowers, when the LTV is low, a "term structure effect" occurs in which increasing LTV ratios render ARMs less costly. However, when LTVs are high, the "interest volatility effect" comes into play and FRMs again become attractive (Elliehausen and Hwang 2010).

Borrowers attempt to maximize expected wealth, and therefore select mortgage products based on their expected mobility, particularly in the ARM market. Borrowers will for example choose an ARM with a fixed-rate period that is directly related to their probability of moving. Fortowsky et al. (2011) found that mobility hazards of 3/1, 5/1, and 7/1 ARMs were 20 percent, 14 percent, and 11 percent higher than that of a 30-year FRM. Asymmetric information with respect to borrowers' mobility also plays a role in the choice of FRMs—there is evidence that borrowers who pay fewer points prepay (and thus feel free to move) more quickly than borrowers who pay more points(Stanton and Wallace 1995). Expected mobility even affects refinancing: borrowers who are planning to move in the short term are less likely to refinance (Fortowski et al. 2011).

Borrowers seeking FRMs must choose between 15-year and 30-year loan terms. In the case of the 15-year, a borrower makes higher monthly mortgage payments. Record-low rates have increased the popularity of the 15-year mortgage, especially for refinance borrowers. For example, in 2007, 8.5 percent of refinance loans were 15-year mortgages compared to 35 percent of refinance originations in 2012 (MacDonald 2013). Borrowers who are interested in diversifying their financial portfolio via alternative investments may prefer the 30-year mortgage loan, and evidence suggests that the 30-year loan benefits individuals who face higher marginal tax rates. Tax benefits often influence borrowers to choose 30-year loans because they are able to qualify for larger loans due to the lower monthly payments Basciano and Grayson 2007).

PREPAYMENT AND DEFAULT DECISIONS

Based on an option-theoretic approach, borrowers have two ways to terminate their loans before the end of their contract term, either by refinancing (call option) or defaulting (put option). Defaults are more common in the case of high LTVs and house price volatility, as seen in the recent mortgage crisis. Most models of rational borrower prepayment behavior assume that borrowers will default as soon as the value of the house falls below the value of the loan (a.k.a., "underwater" mortgage). In addition, this approach assumes that borrowers will prepay as soon as the value of the mortgage exceeds the par value of the loan (Kau and Keenan 1995; LaCour-Little 2008). However, there are other reasons for prepayment, and these are often due to differences in borrower characteristics. For example, borrowers in high income areas are more likely to refinance when rates drop, while lower income households are less likely to refinance, and more likely to move or default (Pavlov 2000).

The actual incidences of default and prepayment are far less frequent than what options theory would predict. There may be any number of circumstances that might lead a borrower to prepay at an economic disadvantage, such as a divorce or sale of the house. In addition, there are a number of circumstances in which a borrower might defer prepayment. For example, depending on how long the borrower plans to keep the house, as well as transaction costs, the rational decision may be to keep the existing mortgage (LaCour-Little 2008). Borrowers with credit problems or income uncertainty also might not want to attempt a refinance; at the same time, borrowers worried about reputational effects—their credit profile, social stigma, and so on—might incur substantial costs to avoid default.

According to standard option-pricing models of refinancing, there is an optimal interest-rate differential above which borrowers should refinance, as well as an optimal time to refinance. However, borrower behavior often fails to correspond to these predictions of the model, even after accounting for transactions costs. For example, a recent study found evidence that borrowers refinance at mortgage rates that are approximately 60 basis points higher than the optimal rate; 52 percent of borrowers are off by 50 basis points. Thus, borrowers lose money by refinancing at too small an interest rate differential. In addition, borrowers often wait too long to refinance. The average borrower waits 2.7 months too long to refinance, and 17 percent of borrowers wait at least six months too long (Agarwal et al. 2012).

According to early versions of the option-based view of "ruthless default," ruthlessness occurs when the borrower defaults as soon as the value of the home falls below the value of the mortgage loan. A seminal study on this issue (Foster and Van Order 1984) found that only 4.2 percent of borrowers with LTVs of 110 percent or more defaulted, which the authors attributed to transactions costs. According to the "ruthless" or "strategic default" hypothesis, default occurs when a borrower's equity falls below some threshold and the expected costs of maintaining the mortgage exceed the expected benefits (Deng et al. 2000; Experian Oliver Wyman 2009). This issue has received considerable attention in the popular media as well as in the public policy arena (Christie 2011). There is also evidence to support the "double trigger" hypothesis, which suggests that strategic default occurs when equity is negative and the borrower is faced with a negative income shock.

CONSUMER KNOWLEDGE AND MORTGAGE DECISIONS

The factors described in the previous sections are based on models of rational economic behavior. For example, the model in Figure 10.1 as well as other economic models of mortgage choice assume perfect information. In addition, the vector of borrower characteristics does not include factors that affect a homebuyer's ability to mentally evaluate mortgage choices. These include financial knowledge as well as considerations that affect a buyer's ability to process information—such as the amount of time and attention a buyer can devote to choosing her mortgage. In practice, there are a number of additional influences on consumer behavior in mortgage markets.

Economic theory would suggest that consumers in the mortgage market would search for the optimal mortgage contract as long as the expected returns to search exceeded costs (Stigler 1961). However, there is evidence to the contrary. According to one study of mortgage search behavior, 23% of purchase mortgage borrowers and 14% of refinance borrowers contacted only one lender when searching for a loan. It turns out that searching can have significant benefits. For example, refinance borrowers who searched a great deal obtained an APR that was 11 percent smaller than those who did no shopping, and 5.5 percent smaller than those who did a moderate amount of shopping (Lee and Hogarth 1999). Evidence suggests that borrowers sacrifice at least $1,000 by shopping from too few brokers. At the same time, borrowers who shop may not get the best deal because of a failure to understand the tradeoff between rates and points (Woodward and Hall 2010b).

Many other accounts in the scholarly, policy, and popular media suggest that the product alternatives available in the mortgage market are far too complex for even sophisticated consumers, and there is considerable evidence that consumers do not understand many of the intricacies of the financial marketplace.

Many consumers are confused about the price of a home mortgage loan as measured by the difference between the contract interest rate and the APR (Lee and Hogarth 1999). The study of the compensation that borrowers pay to mortgage brokers by Woodward and Hall (2010) found that confused borrowers overpay brokers for their services.

Information overload refers to a state in which an individual is presented with communication inputs that exceed his or her cognitive capacity for processing or utilization. It has been well-documented by psychologists that human capacity to process information in short-term, active memory is limited to an average of seven "chunks" of information. While evidence is mixed on the effects of information overload on decision quality, the general consensus is that "less is more" (Malhotra 1984). Research by Perry and Blumenthal (2012) on mortgage disclosures has found that although consumers often report a preference for more information, their ability to comprehend or integrate this information is questionable.

BEHAVIORAL DECISION-MAKING PERSPECTIVES AND MORTGAGE BORROWERS

Several decision-making principles may affect borrowers' attention to and evaluation of these charges, including cognitive miserliness, heuristics, and biases in decision-making.

Cognitive Misers

When individuals are highly motivated, as in the case of high-risk decisions, they will devote substantial effort in searching for, integrating, and evaluating information. However, in many decision situations, individuals prefer to avoid expending cognitive effort, and defer to simple decision-making shortcuts (i.e., heuristics), which are more efficient. Many studies have found that judgments based on these heuristics can be inaccurate (Fiske and Taylor 1984). Given the circumstances, uncertainty, and time pressures associated with the mortgage origination process, borrowers may act as "cognitive misers," thereby reserving their abilities to make deliberate, informed judgments for those decisions they perceive as most important (Simon 1955). Thus, efforts to improve borrowers' decision-making ability should (1) increase motivation to process information (e.g., increase perceived risk), and (2) reduce the need for intense cognitive effort.

Framing and Reference Pricing

Individuals are highly sensitive to how choices are presented or "framed." In other words, they determine whether a given course of action will result in a gain or loss compared to the status quo (or some other salient reference point). Research shows that subjective price judgments rely on a comparison of market prices to a reference price or range of reference prices. This reference price can be internal, based on memory or experience with the product category, or external—based on explicit or implicit cues provided by the seller, retailer, or competitor. In the case of an interest rate offer, for example, a prospective borrower might recall the rate they paid for another loan as an internal reference point. An external reference price could be a "teaser" rate, a competitor's interest rate offer, or the prime rate. There is considerable evidence in the literature on consumer decision-making and price perceptions that a consumer's evaluation of a price as fair as well as his or her willingness to pay is a function of the salient reference point. Consumers often lack internal reference prices, or rely on incorrect reference prices when judging services like loan products. In the absence of an explicit reference point, the consumer may have difficulty making accurate judgments. This is particularly problematic in the mortgage market, since a given product may have many different prices associated with it.

Mental Accounting

Individuals often engage in mental accounting to plan and organize their personal finances. This principle suggests that people "frame" or organize their expenses into mental categories, or accounts, based on purpose, source, or time frame. Thus, if there is a mental category for mortgage payments, other routine monthly expenses, or savings, an individual will budget and spend accordingly. Often, the most important time horizon for budgeting is the month, since many regular payments are monthly ones. Individuals rely on mental accounting to develop rules-of-thumb in order to manage their cash flows. One generalization from the literature on mental accounting is that mental accounts tend to be inflexible, and lead to violations of assumptions of traditional economic theory, such as the fungibility of money (Thaler 1985, 1990). There is evidence that mental budgeting affects borrowing behavior (Perry 2000). Mortgage borrowers who use mental accounts will be more likely to make decisions based on the affordability of monthly housing expenses rather than considering or comparing costs such as points, fees, or itemized charges.

Intertemporal Choice

Short-term-oriented individuals psychologically discount future events exponentially. In the case of short-term orientation, negative future outcomes will be steeply discounted, while present gains will enjoy disproportionately greater psychic value. These individuals have an incentive to minimize their monthly payments while deferring increases in principle and interest payments into the future, as found in many mortgage products that feature adjustable rates, interest-only payments, or balloon payments. Many studies have shown that the constant discount factor assumed in exponential discounting does not reflect actual behavior; instead, individuals often engage in hyperbolic or time-inconsistent discounting. In hyperbolic discounting, the discount factor changes over time, such that individuals are impatient in the short-run but more patient in the long-run (Frederick et al. 2002). Under hyperbolic discounting, mortgage borrowers might be willing to draw down their home equity or accumulate high unsecured debt balances in the short term while simultaneously investing in retirement plans.

Cognitive Resource Depletion

The principle of cognitive resource depletion suggests that acts requiring high cognitive effort, such as the exercise of willpower or self-restraint, may temporarily reduce or deplete mental energy, and will in turn affect subsequent decision-making capabilities. According to an experimental study by Sichelman (2010), after the house shopping experience, consumers devoted less attention to the mortgage-choice process, and were more likely to rely on faulty decision heuristics that resulted in a higher propensity to select higher-risk mortgage products (Perry and Lee 2012).

Biases in Decision Making

According to research in the psychology of decision-making under risk and uncertainty, individuals are subject to bias when making decisions. These biases are systematic anomalies in the decision process that cause individuals to base decisions on cognitive factors that are not consistent with evidence. Cognitive biases can thus result in judgment errors and are not solely a function of lack of knowledge. One widely studied cognitive bias is loss aversion, which suggests that the disutility of giving up an object is greater that the utility associated with acquiring it (Kahneman et al. 1991). As a result, individuals may incur additional costs to avoid losses relative to experiencing gains. In the mortgage market, borrowers may fail to default ruthlessly or strategically because of loss aversion, leading them to be overly optimistic about house price appreciation (Bhutta et al. 2010).

One implication of loss aversion is a bias toward the status quo (also known as consumer inertia). Per economic theory, individuals choose among alternatives based on well-defined preferences. However, evidence suggests individuals often exhibit a significant status quo bias: the more options available, the stronger the bias for the status quo; the stronger an individual's preference for a selected alternative, the weaker said bias (Samuelson and Zeckhauser 1988). These biases may explain borrowers who fail to refinance higher-rate mortgages, despite favorable interest rates, credit quality, or equity advantages. According to one estimate, approximately 17 percent of borrowers miss out on the optimal time to refinance. And, consistent with the notion that strong preferences will weaken a status quo bias, there is evidence that inattentive borrowers will pay more attention to refinancing opportunities when there is more to gain (Agarwal et al. 2012).

Another bias that relates to mortgage decisions is known as *anchoring and adjustment*. Decision makers often focus on or "anchor on" the information that they perceive to be the most important, and then adjust this evaluation when they encounter less important information (Hogarth and Einhorn 1992). Thus, many consumers will anchor on an initial value, such as a monthly PITI payment, and then devote less effort to processing additional charges. In most cases, consumers fail to adequately account for the additional charges, or they ignore them all together (Bertini and Wathieu 2008; Morwitz et al. 1998). There is evidence that mortgage borrowers focus on the monthly payment and pay less attention to additional points and fees (ICF Macro 2009).

Previous research on biases in judgment and decision-making has also shown that individuals tend to display overconfidence about their knowledge and ability (Kahneman and Tversky 1996; Lichtenstein and Fischoff 1977). Due to overconfidence, people often believe that they know more than they actually do, and this can have negative consequences. For example, people who do not know their credit rating are more likely to overestimate than to underestimate their credit quality. This tendency toward overestimation may lead consumers to be less cautious in their financial decision-making (Perry 2008).

Mortgage lenders have been criticized for taking advantage of these biases by featuring monthly payments, obscuring charges and fees, emphasizing short-term benefits versus long-term costs or risks, imposing time constraints, and creating barriers to comparison shopping (Retsinas and Belsky 2008).

EXTERNAL INFLUENCES ON MORTGAGE DECISIONS

As shown in Figure 10.2, there are a number of factors that contribute to what is treated as borrower heterogeneity in economic models. These influences include disclosures, lender marketing, word-of-mouth, the media, prior knowledge, and advice from professionals like real estate agents or mortgage brokers. In addition, these decisions are affected by macroeconomic conditions, such as house prices, tax and interest rates; financial regulations, including those designed for consumer protection in mortgage markets; and demographic characteristics, such as income, level of education, geographic location, gender, race, and ethnicity. Any or all of these influences can affect the choice of a loan or the choice of a lender, as well as the home purchase decision.

THE HOME PURCHASE DECISION

Decisions about financing may not always be an integral part of the home purchase process, and because the home purchase is the ultimate goal, influences on the choice of a home may outweigh influences on the choice of a mortgage loan. There is some evidence, for example, that when consumers are asked to make mortgage decisions immediately after shopping for a home, they are more likely to rely on heuristics and less likely to process detailed information about

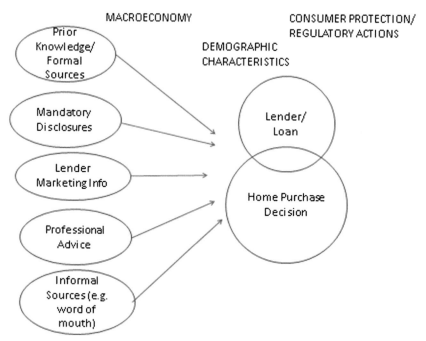

FIGURE 10.2 Influences on home purchase and financing decisions. *Adapted from Perry and Blumenthal (2012).*

loan features (Perry and Lee 2012). Individual differences, economic and marketplace conditions, and other contextual variables are also likely to affect all of these influences and outcomes.

Mortgage Advertising

There is evidence that advertising content has a significant and positive effect on demand for new loans. One experimental study found that ads that included a female photograph as well as ads that did not specify a loan purpose resulted in an increase in demand that was similar to that which would occur from a 200 basis point reduction in interest rate (Bertrand et al. 2010). Other research underscores the difficulty for consumers not well-versed in mortgage market tactics to make valid price comparisons across mortgage loan offerings. For example, information provided in mortgage loan ads often do not contain cues related to specific product and service attributes. Perry and Motley's (2009) study of advertising messages for mortgage loan products found that the prominent elements of many of these ads are slogans and taglines that do not specifically provide loan offer details. Another study additionally found that although subprime borrowers face the highest complexity and variability in product offerings, they were the least likely to be presented with loan term information. Subprime borrowers were more likely to be presented with negatively-framed advertising messages about mortgage products while prime borrowers were more likely to be exposed to positively-framed messages that included more specific information about pricing and loan terms (Perry and Motley).

CONSUMER PROTECTION IN MORTGAGE MARKETS

Several researchers have argued that the mortgage crisis was a function of informational asymmetries, which could have been prevented if borrowers were given more information about the costs and risks of their loans (Green 2008). Others suggest that these disclosures confuse borrowers, and lead to market inefficiencies including excessive charges for loans (Woodward and Hall 2010a). Some mortgage market analysts and researchers have suggested that clearer, simpler mortgage disclosures could help prevent defaults, and that improving the mandatory Truth in Lending Act (TILA) and Real Estate Settlement Procedures Act (RESPA) disclosures will help to standardize prices and facilitate comparison shopping (McCoy 2007).

Lenders in the subprime market have been criticized for irresponsible practices, such as including unfair or deceptive pricing, as well as targeting less financially-sophisticated consumers—including lower-income, minority, and elderly borrowers—with high-risk products. There have also been a number of widely publicized lawsuits resulting in substantial damages paid to borrowers by lenders. The Federal Trade Commission (FTC) indicates that predatory mortgage lending practices hide information from consumers that is essential for making decisions about "their single greatest asset—their home" (Engel and McCoy 2002) Hill and Kozup's (2007) study of subprime borrowers' experiences in the origination process found that these lenders often presented a "friendly veneer," along with promises of "courtesy, availability, and speed"; however, borrowers experienced a "lack of full disclosure" in these transactions. Another study based on a survey comparing prime and subprime borrowers found that subprime borrowers had significantly higher levels of dissatisfaction with their loan and the origination process. There is also evidence that risk-related underwriting factors did not fully explain why borrowers took out subprime loans; financial knowledge, information search, and demographic variables were also predictive (Courchane et al. 2004). The Consumer Financial Protection Bureau (CFPB) reports that loose underwriting practices, such as failure to verify the consumer's income or debts and qualifying consumers for mortgages based on short-term "teaser" rates contributed to the mortgage crisis and ultimately the current economic recession (http://files.consumerfinance. gov/f/201301_cfpb_ability-to-repay-summary.pdf).

This discussion highlights a number of areas that warrant public policy interventions. One concern stems from the availability of high-risk loan product alternatives, such as loans with interest-only payments and low borrower documentation requirements (http://www.cbsnews.com/8301-505144_162-57563203/new-rules-aim-to-shield-consumers-mortgage-lenders/). Another issue is whether

consumers are able to make informed decisions due to the complexity of the informational environment as well as a lack of financial literacy. Other problems result
from the structure of the market, such as the oft-cited lack of "skin in the game,"
in which misaligned incentives result because lenders who plan to sell loans to
the secondary market have little motivation to engage in responsible underwriting
(Zandi and Deritis 2011). There are also widespread allegations of irresponsible,
deceptive and predatory practices.

The Dodd-Frank Wall Street Reform and Consumer Protection Act of 2010
established the CFPB. Before the CFPB, jurisdiction over consumer protection regulation and policy was spread across seven different federal agencies.
In response to the mortgage market crisis that began in 2008, federal lawmak-
ers with the support of the Obama administration created a single agency that
would provide oversight for the entire financial marketplace. The CFPB mission
is as follows:

*Our mission is to make markets for consumer financial products and services
work for Americans—whether they are applying for a mortgage, choosing among
credit cards, or using any number of other consumer financial products…Above
all, this means ensuring that consumers get the information they need to make the
financial decisions they believe are best for themselves and their families—that
prices are clear up front, that risks are visible, and that nothing is buried in fine
print. In a market that works, consumers should be able to make direct comparisons
among products and no provider should be able to use unfair, deceptive, or abusive
practices. (http://www.consumerfinance.gov/the-bureau/*

Several major consumer protection regulations subject to CFPB enforcement are summarized in Table 10.1.

One of the first and most publicized of the CFPB's initiatives was to develop
new mortgage loan disclosure documents intended to integrate and streamline
this information. The new documents would replace existing disclosures including the Good Faith Estimate designed by the Department of Housing and Urban
Development (HUD) under RESPA, as well as the Truth in Lending disclosure
designed by the Board of Governors of the Federal Reserve System (FRB) under
TILA. The first new disclosure was intended to be a simple "mortgage shopping
sheet," provided by the lender, that includes the costs, risks, and features of
the loan offer. By law, the lender cannot charge consumers any fees until after
the consumers have been given this sheet, known as the Loan Estimate form,
and communicated their intention to proceed with the transaction. Prospective
homebuyers would be able to use this sheet to compare offers across lenders.

Another document, known as the Closing Disclosure Form, was designed
to replace the HUD-1 form (created by HUD under RESPA) and combine it
with the Truth in Lending disclosure. Lenders are required to give prospective borrowers their Closing Disclosure form at least three business days before
the scheduled closing date. If any changes occur during the interim three-day
period, the consumer must be given a new form another three days in advance

TABLE 10.1 Selected Key Federal Consumer Protection Regulations[1]

Regulation	Purpose
Regulation B—Equal Credit Opportunity	• To promote the availability of credit to all creditworthy applicants without regard to race, color, religion, national origin, sex, marital status, or age (provided the applicant has the capacity to contract); to the fact that all or part of the applicant's income derives from a public assistance program; or to the fact that the applicant has in good faith exercised any right under the Consumer Credit Protection Act. • The regulation prohibits creditor practices that discriminate on the basis of any of these factors. • The regulation also requires creditors to notify applicants of action taken on their applications; to report credit history in the names of both spouses on an account; to retain records of credit applications; to collect information about the applicant's race and other personal characteristics in applications for certain dwelling-related loans; and to provide applicants with copies of appraisal reports used in connection with credit transactions.

Regulation C—Home Mortgage Disclosure	(1) To provide the public with loan data that can be used:
	  (i) To help determine whether financial institutions are serving the housing needs of their communities;
	  (ii) To assist public officials in distributing public-sector investment so as to attract private investment to areas where it is needed; and
	  (iii) To assist in identifying possible discriminatory lending patterns and enforcing antidiscrimination statutes.
	(2) Neither the act nor this part is intended to encourage unsound lending practices or the allocation of credit.

Regulation G—S.A.F.E. Mortgage Licensing Act – Federal Registration of Residential Mortgage Loan Originators	• Aggregating and improving the flow of information to and between regulators; • Providing increased accountability and tracking of mortgage loan originators; • Enhancing consumer protections; • Supporting anti-fraud measures; • Providing consumers with easily accessible information at no charge regarding the employment history of, and publicly adjudicated disciplinary and enforcement actions against, mortgage loan originators.
Regulation N—Mortgage Acts and Practices-Advertising	To seek civil penalties for deceptive mortgage advertising, and clarifies and provides examples of what constitutes deceptive mortgage advertising. In addition, it institutes record-keeping requirements on mortgage advertisers.

Continued

TABLE 10.1 Selected Key Federal Consumer Protection Regulations[1]—cont'd

Regulation	Purpose
Regulation O—Mortgage Assistance Relief Services	Prohibits "Mortgage Assistance Relief Services" ("MARS") providers from making false or misleading claims about the services they provide. MARS providers are broadly defined to include providers of any of the following services, if such service is provided in exchange for consideration: (1) Stopping, preventing or postponing foreclosure; (2) Negotiating a loan modification, foreclosure or extension; and/or (3) Negotiating a short sale or deed in lieu arrangement. The Rule also covers sale-leaseback transactions marketed as a way to save a consumer's home from foreclosure.
Regulation P—Privacy of Consumer Financial Information	(1) Requires a financial institution to provide notice to customers about its privacy policies and practices; (2) Describes the conditions under which a financial institution may disclose nonpublic personal information about consumers to nonaffiliated third parties; and (3) Provides a method for consumers to prevent a financial institution from disclosing that information to most nonaffiliated third parties by "opting out" of that disclosure
Regulation V—Fair Credit Reporting	Requires that persons that obtain and use information about consumers to determine the consumer's eligibility for products, services, or employment: • share such information among affiliates, and • furnish information to consumer reporting agencies.
Regulation X—Real Estate Settlement Procedures Act	To further the national housing goal of encouraging homeownership by regulating certain lending practices and closing and settlement procedures in federally related mortgage transactions to the end that unnecessary costs and difficulties of purchasing housing are minimized, and for other purposes.
Regulation Z—Truth in Lending	• To promote the informed use of consumer credit by requiring disclosures about its terms and costs • Gives consumers the right to cancel certain credit transactions that involve a lien on a consumer's principal dwelling, and provides a means for fair and timely resolution of credit billing disputes. • It also imposes limitations on home-equity plans

TABLE 10.1 Selected Key Federal Consumer Protection Regulations[1]—cont'd

Regulation	Purpose
	• Prohibits a creditor from making a mortgage loan unless the creditor determines that the consumer will have the ability to repay the loan • Requires that lenders collect 8 required underwriting factors from reliable third-party records • For adjustable-rate mortgages, the monthly payment must be calculated using the fully indexed rate or an introductory rate, whichever is higher. • Establishes special payment calculation rules for loans with balloon payments, interest-only payments, or negative amortization. • Sets higher underwriting standards for "non-Qualified Mortgages," also known as higher-cost or subprime loans.

[1]Adapted from http://www.consumerfinance.gov/regulations/#ecfr

of closing. As it stands, the lender is responsible for the provision and accuracy of the Closing Disclosure Form, although the CFPB is considering alternative proposals for the appropriate roles and responsibilities of the settlement agent (http://files.consumerfinance.gov/f/201207_cfpb_detailed-summary_proposed-rule-to-improve-mortgage-disclosure.pdf).

The evidence on the effects of mandatory mortgage disclosures on borrowing decisions is mixed. Previous research on mortgage loan disclosures has found that consumers focus on monthly payment and often misunderstand other terms such as the annual percentage rate (ICF Macro 2009). A study conducted in the United Kingdom found that consumers viewed financial information as complicated, confusing, and of limited interest, and that a few key messages were more effective than more cluttered disclosures documents (Financial Services Authority 2005). In a controlled experimental study, simplified disclosures significantly increased consumer knowledge and recall of key loan features such as interest rate, settlement charges, or whether or not a balloon payment or prepayment penalty was required (Lacko and Pappalardo 2010). However, there is very little conclusive evidence that disclosure content improves decisions or has any other significant impact on behavior. One study found that disclosures about mortgage broker compensation significantly increased the likelihood that consumers chose more expensive loans by mistake (Lacko and Pappalardo 2004). It is important to note, however, that despite these limitations, disclosures can serve more broadly as educational tools, and can motivate consumers to seek additional information (Perry and Blumenthal 2010).

CONCLUSION: WHAT'S THE OPTIMAL MORTGAGE FOR A BORROWER?

Many mortgage loan products have been demonized in the popular media and in the public policy arena, including ARMs and interest-only payments or balloon payments (Der Hovanesian 2006). Many of these characterizations, such as "toxic mortgages," have been oversimplified or exaggerated. A key challenge for public policy makers, lenders, and consumer advocates is to identify the optimal mortgage product for borrowers, given the overwhelming variation in household financial and personal circumstances and macroeconomic scenarios. Some products carry higher default risk and are more sensitive to economic shocks, but may be optimal choices for some consumers given expected mobility, income, or house price growth. Borrowers with good credit might be worse off for choosing FRMs when they could have lower interest rates in the near term. Also, decisions about down payment size, how to finance closing costs, and home improvement expenditures must be balanced against a family's resources, risk preferences, and expectations about their future. As a result, there has yet to be developed a model that fully incorporates all the economic, behavioral, and situational variables that are relevant to actual mortgage borrowing decisions.

REFERENCES

Agarwal, Sumit, Rosen, Richard J., Yao, Vincent, Why Do Borrowers Make Mortgage Refinancing Mistakes? (November 2, 2012). FRB of Chicago Working Paper No. 2013-02. Available at: http://ssrn.com/abstract=2259715.

Basciano, P., Grayson, J., 2007. Is the 30-year Mortgage Preferable to a 15-year Mortgage? Financial Counseling and Planning 17 (1), 14–21.

Basciano, Peter M., Jackson, Pamela Z., Grayson, James M., 2008. Mortgage choice: A review of the literature. Journal of Personal Finance 7 (1), 42–67.

Berkovec, James A., Kogut, David J., Nothaft, Frank E., 2001. Determinants of the ARM Share of FHA and Conventional Lending. Journal of Real Estate and Economics 22 (1), 23–41.

Bertini, Marco, Wathieu, Luc, 2008. Attention Arousal Through Price Partitioning. Marketing Science 27 (2), 236–246.

Bertrand, Marianne, Dean, Karlan, Sendhil, Mullainathan, Eldar, Shafir, Jonathan, Zinman, 2010. What's Advertising Content Worth? Evidence from a Consumer Credit Marketing Field Experiment. Quarterly Journal of Economics 125 (1), 263–305.

Bhutta, Neil, Dokko, Jane, Shan, Hui, 2010. The Depth of Negative Equity and Mortgage Default Decisions, Washington, DC Div. of Research & Statistics and Monetary Affairs. Federal Reserve Board.

Campbell, John Y., Cocco, Joao F., 2003. Household risk management and optimal mortgage choice. The Quarterly Journal of Economics November, 1449–1494.

Christie, Les, June 7, 2011. Walk away from your mortgage? Time to get 'ruthless,' Les Christie, CNNMoney. http://money.cnn.com/2011/06/07/real_estate/walk_away_mortgage/index.htm.

Coulibaly, B., Li, G., 2009. Choice of mortgage contracts: Evidence from the survey of consumer finances. Real Estate Economics 37 (4), 659–673.

Courchane, M.J., Surette, B.J., Zorn, P.M., 2004. Subprime Borrowers: Mortgage Transitions and Outcomes. Journal of Real Estate and Finance.

Deng, Yongheng, Quigley, John M., Van Order, Robert, 2000. Mortgage Terminations, Heterogeneity, and the Exercise of Mortgage Options. Econometrica 68 (2), 275–307.

Der Hovanesian, 2006. How Toxic is Your Mortgage? Business Week. September 11. Available from: http://www.businessweek.com/magazine/content/06_37/b4000001.htm.

Elliehausen, Gregory, Hwang, Min, 2010. Mortgage Contract Choice in Subprime Mortgage Markets. Federal Reserve Board Finance and Economics Discussion Series 2010-53.

Engel, Kathleen C., McCoy, Patricia A., 2002. A Tale Of Three Markets: The Law And Economics Of Predatory Lending. Texas Law Review 80 (May), 1257–1381.

Experian-Oliver Wyman, 2009. Understanding Strategic Default in Mortgages Part I. Experian-Oliver Wyman Market Intelligence Report 2009 Topical Report Series.

Financial Services Authority, 2005. Key Facts Quick Guide: Research Findings. Financial Services Authority, Consumer Research 41, July. Available from: http://www.fsa.gov.uk/pubs/consumer-research/crpr41.pdf.

Fiske, S.T., Taylor, S.E., 1984. Social Cognition. Addison-Wesley Pub. Co, Reading, MA.

Fortowsky, Elain, LaCour-Little, Michael, Rosenblatt, Eric, Yao, Vincent, 2011. Housing Tenure and Mortgage Choice. J Real Estate Finan Econ 42, 162–180.

Foster, Chester, Van Order, Robert, 1984. An Option-Based Model of Mortgage Default. Housing Finance Review 3, 351–372.

Frederick, S., Loewenstein, G., O'Donoghue, T., 2002. Time Discounting and Time Preference: A Critical Review. Journal of Economic Literature 40 (2), 351–401.

Green Richard, K., 2008. Imperfect Information and the Housing Finance Crisis: A Descriptive Overview. Journal of Housing Economics 17 (4), 262–271.

Hogarth, Robin M., Einhorn, Hillel, 1992. Order Effects in Belief Updating: The Belief Adjustment Model. Cognitive Psychology 24 (1), 1–55.

ICF Macro, 2009. Design and Testing of Truth in Lending Disclosures for Closed-End Mortgages. Federal Reserve Board of Governors, July 16. Available from: http://www.federalreserve.gov/boarddocs/meetings/2009/20090723/Full%20Macro%20CE%20Report.pdf.

Kahneman, Daniel, Knetsch, Jack L., Thaler, Richard H., 1991. Anomalies: The Endowment Effect, Loss Aversion, and Status Quo Bias. The Journal of Economic Perspectives 5 (1), 193–206, Winter 1991.

Kahneman, Daniel, Tversky, Amos, 1996. On the Reality of Cognitive Illusions. Psychological Review 103 (3), 582–591.

Kau, J.B., Keenan, D., 1995. An Overview of Option-Theoretic Pricing of Mortgages. Journal of Housing Research 6, 217–244.

LaCour-Little, Michael, 2008. Review articles: Mortgage termination risk: A review of the recent literature. Journal of Real Estate Literature 16 (3), 297–326.

LaCour-Little, Michael, 2008. Mortgage termination risk: A review of the recent literature. Journal of Real Estate Literature 16 (3), 297–326.

Lacko, James M., Pappalardo, Janis K., 2004. The Effect of Mortgage Broker Compensation Disclosures on Consumers and Competition: A Controlled Experiment. Federal Trade Commission Bureau of Economics Staff Report, Federal Trade Commission, Washington: February.

Lacko, James M., Pappalardo, Janis K., 2010. The failure and promise of mandated consumer mortgage disclosures: Evidence from qualitative interviews and a controlled experiment with mortgage borrowers. The American Economic Review 100 (2), 516–521.

Lee, Jinkook, Hogarth, Jeanne M., 1999. Returns to information search: Consumer mortgage shopping decisions. Journal of Financial Counseling and Planning 10 (1), 49–67.

Lichtenstein, Sarah, Fischhoff, Baruch, 1977. Do Those Who Know More Also Know More about How Much They Know? Organizational Behavior and Human Performance 20, 159–183.

MacDonald, Jeffrey, 2013. Americans now love 15-year fixed mortgages, The Christian Science.

McCoy, Patricia A., 2007. Rethinking Disclosure in a World of Risk-Based Pricing. Harvard Journal on Legislation 44, 123.

Monitor, January 28, http://www.csmonitor.com/Business/2013/0128/Americans-now-love-15-year-fixed-mortgages

Malhotra, Naresh K., 1984. Reflections on the Information Overload Paradigm in Consumer Decision Making. Journal of Consumer Research 10 (March), 436–440.

Morwitz, Vicki G., Greenleaf, Eric A., Johnson, Eric J., 1998. Divide and Prosper: Consumers' Reactions to Partitioned Prices. Journal of Marketing Research (November), 453–463.

Pavlov, A.D., 2000. Competing Risks of Mortgage Prepayments: Who Refinances, Who Moves, and Who Defaults? Journal of Real Estate Finance and Economics 23 (2), 185–212.

Perry, Vanessa, 2000. Antecedents of Consumer Financing Decisions: A Mental Accounting Model of Revolving Credit Usage. UMI Dissertation, Vanessa Gail Perry.

Perry, Vanessa G., 2008. Is Ignorance Bliss? Consumer Accuracy in Judgments About Credit Ratings. Journal of Consumer Affairs 42 (2) Summer, 189–205.

Perry, Vanessa G., Blumenthal, Pamela M., 2012. Understanding the Fine Print: The Need for Effective Testing of Mandatory Mortgage Loan Disclosures. Journal of Public Policy & Marketing 31 (2), 305–312.

Perry, Vanessa G., Lee, J.D., 2012. Shopping for a Home vs a Loan: The Role of Cognitive Resource Depletion. International Journal of Consumer Studies 36 (5), 580–587.

Retsinas, Nicolas P., Belsky, Eric S., 2008. Borrowing to Live: Consumer and Mortgage Credit Revisited. Brookings Institution Press and Joint Center for Housing Studies at Harvard University.

Samuelson, William, Zeckhauser, Richard, 1988. Status Quo Bias in Decision Making. Journal of Risk and Uncertainty 1, 7–59.

Sichelman, Lew, June 06, 2010. After shopping for a home, tired buyers often make poor mortgage choices. Los Angeles Times.

Simon, Herbert A., 1955. A Behavioral Model of Rational Choice. Quarterly Journal of Economics 69, 7–19.

Stanton, Richard H., Wallace, Nancy E., 1995. Mortgage Choice: What's the Point?, working paper. Available at SSRN: http://ssrn.com/abstract=15163 or http://dx.doi.org/10.2139/ssrn.15163.

Stigler, George, 1961. The Economics of Information. Journal of Political Economy 69, 213–225.

Talaga, J., Buch, J., 1998. Consumer trade-offs among mortgage instrument variables. International Journal of Bank Marketing 16 (6), 264–270.

Thaler, Richard, 1985. Mental Accounting and Consumer Choice. Marketing Science 4 (Summer), 199–214.

Thaler, Richard, 1990. Anomalies: Saving, Fungibility, and Mental Accounts. Journal of Economic Perspectives 4 (1), 193–205.

Woodward, S.E., Hall, R.E., 2010a. Consumer confusion in the mortgage market: Evidence of less than a perfectly transparent and competitive market. The American Economic Review 100 (2), 511–515.

Woodward Susan, E., Hall, Robert E., 2010b. Diagnosing Consumer Confusion and Sub-Optimal Shopping Effort: Theory and Mortgage-Market Evidence. NBER Working Paper Series, vol. w16007.

Zandi, Mark, Deritis, Cristian, 2011. The Skinny on Skin in the Game, Moody's Analytics. March 11, 2011 http://www.economy.com/mark-zandi/documents/QRM_030911.pdf.

Chapter 11

The Yield Curve, Monte Carlo Methods, and the Option-Adjusted Spread

Mortgages, because they are self-amortizing, are strange creatures. When we invest in a zero-coupon bond, all the cash flows arrive at maturity, and it is easy to know how to discount the cash flows. For a Treasury security, we need only read the interest rate off the constant maturity yield curve for the appropriate maturity, and then discount the cash flow received by $1/(1 + r)^T$, where r is the spot rate for the maturity and T is the maturity. For zero-coupon corporate bonds, we can easily interpret the spread between the corporate bond rate and the Treasury rate for a given maturity as a risk premium.

But mortgages have even cash flows throughout their lives, which means that they are a mixture of short-term, medium-term, and long-term maturities. While we can to some extent use the difference in yield between a mortgage of, say, 10-year expected duration and a 10-year Constant Maturity Treasury rate (CMT) to characterize the risk associated with mortgages, this is a weak approximation.

Instead, when we look at mortgages, we need to consider the option-adjusted spread (OAS) between the yield curve and the times that mortgages pay cash flows.

Krause (2007) discusses the three types of spread we can use to determine the cost of embedded risks to investors in mortgages: the nominal spread, the zero- or z-spread, and the option-adjusted spread.

The nominal spread compares the yield on a non-Treasury security to a Treasury security of equal maturity. It is just one number: if, for example, a corporate zero-coupon bond has a maturity of 10 years, we just subtract its yield from

Introduction to Mortgages & Mortgage Backed Securities.
http://dx.doi.org/10.1016/B978-0-12-401743-6.00011-1

Introduction to Mortgages & Mortgage Backed Securities

a zero-coupon Treasury security for 10 years; the difference between the two numbers reflects how the market is pricing the various risks associated with the corporate bond.

This obviously creates a problem when evaluating mortgages, because even in the absence of prepayment issues, mortgages have lots of maturities. We could deal with this problem by comparing mortgage and Treasury rates for securities of equal durations, and in practice, investors do this. In fact, Bloomberg screens are set up to allow investors to do just that (see Figure 11.1).

But there are more complete ways to measure the difference in risk between mortgages. We start with the z-spread.

Let's start with a simple example. Suppose we had a four-year, fixed payment $100 mortgage. Let's assume that the interest rate on the mortgage is 7 percent, and the yield curve is on the particular day we are evaluating the mortgage is the curve presented in tab 1 of Spreadsheet 11.1.

The underlying assumptions of the mortgage produce payments of $29.52 for four years. Let us also say the market is valuing the mortgage at par. Then the z-spread is the spread such that:

$$
Value = \frac{29.52}{(1+r_1+Zspread)} + \frac{29.52}{(1+r_2+Zspread)^2} + \frac{29.52}{(1+r_3+Zspread)^3}
+ \frac{29.52}{(1+r_4+Zspread)^4}
$$

```
<HELP> for explanation, <MENU> for similar functions.

3/15 15:20       TBA  ANALYSIS: FNCL                     Page 2 of 4
   FNCL  30-year             For Month: APR          <BACKPAGE> for MAR   1 - MAR
                                                         21<Go>            3 - MAY
                                                                          4 - JUN
  BGN   ASK              B.Median          -BMK-  -Sprd-        May  Apr  May
  Cpn 15:19 Cpn Chg   Yld Prepay WAM  WAL Sprd-Chg WAL  7  OAS Roll% May  Jun
 1) 2½   98-20  4-04 + 13  2.68 149P 357  8.5 69/10 -2 100  78  28. 0.09 7    7
 2) 3   102-24  2-18 + 10  2.51 228P 358  6.6 168/5 -1 125  89  15.-0.24 9    8
 3) 3½  105-10  1-05 + 06  2.13 368P 352  4.3 130/5 +0 144  93  19.-0.08 9    8
 4) 4   106-15  1-05 + 01  2.01 390P 338  3.6 118/5 +3 149  90  49. 0.89 5    5
 5) 4½  107-20  0-20 + 00  2.02 405P 327  3.4 177/2 +1 154  95  73. 0.93 4    4
 6) 5   108-08  0-22 - 01  1.73 499P 319  2.7 148/2 +3 137  84 114. 1.63 1    2
 7) 5½  108-30  0-23 + 00  1.85 510P 303  2.7 160/2 +1 151 100 121. 1.78 1    1
 8) 6   109-21  1-10 + 00  2.24 484P 304  2.8 199/2 +1 187 134 156. 1.56 3    3
 9) 6½  110-31  3-29 + 01  2.64 435P 299  3.2 239/2 +1 220 164 172. 2.58 1    0
10) 7   114-28 -6-20 + 00  1.93 434P 299  3.2 168/2 +2 149  91 139.-0.72 10  10
11) 7½  108-08      + 00  4.86 364P 297  3.8 403/5 +4 428 377 362. 3.76 4    4

Australia 61 2 9777 8600 Brazil 5511 3048 4500 Europe 44 20 7330 7500 Germany 49 69 9204 1210 Hong Kong 852 2977 6000
Japan 81 3 3201 8900    Singapore 65 6212 1000   U.S. 1 212 318 2000   Copyright 2013 Bloomberg Finance L.P.
                                                SN 614110 PDT GMT-7:00 G576-1358-1 15-Mar-2013 12:21:10
```

FIGURE 11.1 Sample Bloomberg Screen of Mortgage Pricing, Coupons, and Weighted Average Life.

The $r_i s$ are the interest rates for maturities 1, 2, 3, and 4. We can calculate this spread using solver or goal seek—we merely need to tell Excel that we want it to find the value in cell B5 in the tab labeled z-spread that produces a value of 0 in cell B14.

This z-spread is just the average spread over the yield curve that values a mortgage where all payments are made on schedule. However, in the United States, borrowers often prepay their mortgages, which means that they will not return the cash flows at the schedule depicted in the amortization schedule. As interest rates go up and down, or as mobility rates change, so does the timing of mortgage cash flows. We need to take this into account—our method for doing so is the calculation of the option-adjusted spread.

The procedure for figuring out option-adjusted spread is as follows: We model forward one period interest rates in an interest rate tree. We care about one-period forward rates because we are going to work backward from the last period of the life of a mortgage-backed security. If a mortgage (or part of a mortgage) survives until the last scheduled period, which we will call T, its value at that point will be par. At period T-1, borrowers are going to look forward to determine whether they prepay their outstanding balance or wait one period to repay their mortgage on schedule. In order to make this decision, they look at the present value of keeping the mortgage versus the present value of repaying it. Because this is a one-period decision, the forward one period rate is the relevant rate for analytical consideration.

Before doing our work, then, we need to model the evolution of one year interest rates.

INTEREST RATE MODELS[1]

The first thing we need to do in calculating an option-adjusted spread is develop a model that allows interest rates to change. We can do this by using a structural model of interest rates, or we can use Monte Carlo methods. We shall discuss each.

Our ultimate goal is to develop an interest rate tree that takes the form:

$$
\begin{array}{ccccc}
 & & & & r_{hhhh} \\
 & & & r_{hhh} & \\
 & & r_{hh} & & r_{lhhh} \\
 & r_h & & r_{lhh} & \\
r & & r_{hl} & & r_{llhh} \\
 & r_l & & r_{llh} & \\
 & & r_{ll} & & r_{lllh} \\
 & & & r_{lll} & \\
 & & & & r_{llll}
\end{array}
$$

1. Excellent explanations of how to calculate option-adjusted spread using spreadsheets include Liu (see http://www.public.asu.edu/~chliu1/recapmarkets_dese/Docs/recm_mbs_CMO2008.pdf) and Spindt (see elvis.sob.tulane.edu/Documents/Finc774/BondPrice.xls).

The node r_h contains the rate for an up movement in period 1; r_l contains the rate for a down movement. The node r_{hh} is two up movements, rhl is one up, one down or one down, one up, and so on.

A commonly used interest rate model is the Black-Derman-Toy (BDT) (1990) model. This model has the virtue of being straightforward, and, using numerical methods, may create an interest rate tree that is consistent with any yield curve.

The underpinning of the model is the equation:

$$dln\,(r) = \left(\theta\,(t) + \frac{d\sigma\,(t)}{\sigma\,(t)} \ln\,(r) \right) dt + \sigma\,(t)\,dV$$

where r is the short rate, $\sigma\,(t)$ is the volatility of short rates at time t, and θ is an adjustment speed parameter. Wang, Halifu, and Shao[2] show that we can use forward recursion to create an interest rate tree consistent with the process given earlier.

Suppose we have the information from Table 11.1 on the yield curve at a particular point in time.

Now let's consider the value of a tree one period from now. It is (0.5Su + 0.5Sd)/(1 + r), which is the discounted value of the security one period from now, assuming there is a 50 percent chance of drawing an "up" state of nature and a 50 percent chance of drawing a "down" state.

From a time zero perspective, the value of the two period bond is 0.971. We discount the first period at 1 percent. Hence, we need to find a down rate and an up rate such that:

$$\frac{\dfrac{0.5}{1+r_d} + \dfrac{0.5}{1+r_u}}{1+0.01} = 0.971$$

TABLE 11.1 Assumptions for Developing Interest Rate Tree[*]

Maturity	Rate	Z-Price	Z-Sigma
1	0.01	0.990	0.24
2	0.015	0.971	0.22
3	0.02	0.942	0.20
4	0.03	0.888	0.18
5	0.04	0.822	0.16

[*]Other interest rate models are Brennan and Schwartz (1980), Cox, Ingersoll, and Ross (1985), Dothan (1978), Merton (1973), and Vasicek (1977). We use the BDT model for illustrative purposes here.

2. http://prosoftware.se/stud/II2008/BDT.pdf

Of course, there are infinite combinations of r_d and r_u that solve the equation. To pin down the rates, we impose the condition that:

$$r_u = r_d e^{2\sigma\sqrt{\Delta t}}$$

This gives us two equations and two unknowns. Because they are nonlinear, we can use solver or goal-seek in Excel to solve the equations. Spreadsheet 11.1, with the tab on OAS for ordinary bonds, shows how an interest rate tree spins out given the assumptions in Table 11.1.

We start by looking at the option-adjusted spread on a noncallable bond. We begin in the final period, period 4, where no matter the interest rate, the present value of the bond will be its par value plus the coupon owed to it. Now let's look at how a bond holder would value it at the end of period three. By construction, the interest rate tree is set up to rise or fall with 50 percent probability each. If the bond-holder is at the r_{lll} node, the valuation will be the coupon owed plus the present value at the realization of the r_{llll} node, multiplied by 50 percent, plus the valuation will be the coupon owed plus the present value at the realization of the r_{lllh} node, multiplied by 50 percent. In other words:

$$V_{lll} = .5 \frac{V_{llll}}{(1 + r_{llll} + OAS)} + .5 \frac{V_{lllh}}{(1 + r_{lllh} + OAS)} + coupon$$

We work through each node until we get to period zero, where we get the theoretical price of the bond.

We once again use solver to find the spread at which the market price of the bond is equal to the theoretical price. Because this bond is not callable, we interpret the OAS as a reflection of the cost of the put option of the bond—the cost of default.

Now let's move to a traditional callable bond. Let's suppose that borrowers are ruthless, and exercise the option to call the bond whenever it is in the money. Once again, the value of the bond that is held until the last period is just the face value of the bond plus the coupon. But let us consider node V_{lll} of the bond is callable. It will be:

$$V_{lll} = IN \left[.5 \frac{V_{llll}}{(1 + r_{llll} + OAS)} + .5 \frac{V_{lllh}}{(1 + r_{lllh} + OAS)} + coupon, Par + coupon \right]$$

In other words, if the borrower has the option of paying off its bond at a lower value than the present value, it will do so. We populate the value nodes accordingly, get a value tree, and once again use solver to equilibrate the market price to the theoretical price. In environments with falling interest rates, the value of the nodes on the tree on the callable will always be lower than on the noncallable, which in turn implies a higher discount rate. The difference in the OAS reflects the cost of the call option.

Now let us move on from traditional bonds to mortgages. For now, to make things easy, suppose that borrowers prepay ruthlessly—if the market rate on a mortgage falls from one period to the next, they prepay the mortgage (we will adjust this extreme assumption later). The exercise works as before, except now the mortgage is amortizing, so its value is falling each period because of a pay-off of principal. The borrower is making a decision by comparing the present value of waiting to repay the mortgage against the value of the remaining loan balance.

But we also see the problem here. When the yield curve is upward sloping (which is the case most of the time), the "down" node of the tree populated by the yield curve is going to generally produce rates at which there will not be an incentive to refinance—after all, an upward sloping yield curve is one that predicts rising interest rates.

MONTE CARLO METHODS

Consider another possible method of looking at how the prepayment option should be priced. Borrowers make mortgage decisions based on a long rate: if the 30-year fixed rate mortgage rate falls, borrowers have an incentive to refinance. If it rises, borrowers lose the incentive. Because 30 years is the end of the yield curve, we have no mechanism for determining forward 30-year rates. Consequently, when modeling mortgages, we might want to consider looking at potential 30-year paths.

With no other information to go on, we might consider the possibility that the best mean forecast for a period ahead 30-year rate is 0 percent. We can then get a measure of volatility by looking at the history of 30-year rates.

If we go to the tab in Spreadsheet 11.1 labeled Monte Carlo spreadsheet, we may see how this can work. We assume a seven-year, fixed payment mortgage, with an initial rate of 7 percent. We assume long-term rates change with a mean (drift) of zero and a standard deviation of 0.2. We also assume rates are normally distributed. We may then use the formula G11*EXP(NORMINV(RAND(),0,B$4)) to simulate a 30-year mortgage rate evolution from period 1 to period 2. The random number generator generates numbers from a uniform distribution between 0 and 1; the inverse random function gives the values associated with each probability from 0 to 1 based on the specified mean and standard deviation.

To calculate an option adjusted spread, we generally run Monte Carlo simulations of thousands of interest rate paths. In our case, we will demonstrate using three. We will also associate a prepayment speed as a percent of PSA with each interest rate spread: the difference between the coupon rate on the loan and the simulated path of market interest rates. This gives us different sets of cash flows for each interest rate path.

Notice that the interest rate paths change with each change in the spreadsheet—this is because the random number generator in Excel is "seeded" by the internal clock in the computer at any point in time. Excel in Windows, through the Analysis Toolpack, allows us to seed a set of random numbers, which means that they are reproducible. The iOS version of Excel does not have an Analysis Toolpack module, and so does not have the nice feature that allows for reproducible results. As a result, I have taken a randomly generated set of interest rates and copied and pasted them into the tab "Fixed Monte Carlo Spreadsheet." As before, we find the OAS that produces the margin above future one-year spot rates that equalizes the price of a mortgage in the market and the present value of its cash flows.

CONTROVERSY

Calculating OAS for mortgages requires a large number of heroic assumptions: that we can model interest rates well, and that we can specify a prepayment model that reliably characterizes the relationship between market-coupon spreads and prepayment behavior. Both of these are subject to criticism, and can make us wonder whether the exercise has value. Lacour-Little, Green, and Yun (2009) showed how unreliable prepayment models are: the coefficients on any prepayment model are highly unstable.

One of the most successful mortgage traders[3] of the past 10 years claims that he does not use OAS—he simply looks at the price-yield relationship for mortgages and compares the contemporaneous price of mortgages against rates against the historic relationship between price and rates. If for a given yield, prices seem low, he buys; if for a given yield, prices seem high, he sells.

REFERENCES

Black, Fischer, Derman, Emanuel, Toy, William, 1990. A one-factor model of interest rates and its application to treasury bond options. Financial Analysts Journal, 33–39.

Brennan, M.J., Schwartz, E.S., 1980. Conditional predictions of bond prices and returns. The Journal of Finance 35 (2), 405–417.

Cox, John C., Ingersoll Jr., Jonathan E., Ross, Stephen A., 1985. A theory of the term structure of interest rates. Econometrica: Journal of the Econometric Society, 385–407.

Dothan, L. Uri, 1978. On the term structure of interest rates. Journal of Financial Economics 6.1, 59–69.

Krause, David, 2007. Valuing Bonds with Embedded Options. Powerpoint.

Merton, Robert C., 1973. An intertemporal capital asset pricing model. Econometrica: Journal of the Econometric Society, 867–887.

Vasicek, Oldrich, 1977. An equilibrium characterization of the term structure. Journal of Financial Economics 5.2, 177–188.

Wang, Wei, Halifu, Maierdan, Shao, Yankai, Black-Dermon-Toy Model with Forward Induction. Available at http://prosoftware.se/stud/II2008/BDT.pdf.

3. Who spoke to me on the condition of anonymity.

A Brief Discussion of Duration and Convexity[1]

INTRODUCTION

For mortgage investors, duration and convexity risk are as important as default risk. In fact, under normal circumstances, duration and convexity risk are more important than default risk. This chapter explains issues of duration and convexity with respect to fixed-rate mortgages.

Let us begin with the premise that the value of an asset is equal to the present value of its expected cash flows. One of the nice aspects of most fixed income instruments is that at the time of investment, investors know both expected cash flows and market discount rates.

To illustrate the point, let us consider a newly issued one-year treasury security. For the purposes of this example, we shall assume that a newly issued one-year treasury security is issued with a coupon rate of 2 percent. Treasury securities pay coupons every six months and then the full par value, or face value, of the security at the security's maturity date.

In the case of a $100 security, and investor will receive one dollar after six months and $101 after 12 months (or one year). Now let's suppose, the day after an investor purchases a one-year treasury security with a coupon rate of 2 percent, a market shock drives the interest rate on one-year treasury securities

---

1. A book-length treatment of this topic may be found in Fabozzi (1999). Conroy (2008) has excellent teaching notes.

to 4 percent. So now we need to calculate the present value of this treasury security. We use the simple present value formula to do so and find:

$$PV = \frac{1}{1.02} + \frac{101}{1.02^2}$$

Note that treasuries compound every six months and that the discount rate has risen from 2 to 4 percent on the day after the investor bought the security. We will ignore the impact of one day of discounting for the purposes of this example.

When we solve the present value we find that the value of the security has dropped from $100 to $98.06. Let's ignore the six cents for a minute and focus on the $98. The value of this one-year treasury security has dropped by about 2 percent, or by about the same amount that the interest rate required for investors to invest in treasury securities has risen. This is not a coincidence. Notice that nearly all the cash flows going to the Treasury security happen at the end of one year. This means that the approximate *duration* for a one-year treasury is one. When market rates for security of duration T increase by percentage point, the value of that security falls by roughly 1 percent, and vice versa.

Consider Figures 12.1 and 12.2, which map out the relationship between interest rates and value for a one-year treasury security with a coupon rate of 2 percent and for a 10-year treasury security with a coupon rate of 4 percent. Note that an X percentage point change in the one year treasury rate leads to approximately a 2 percent change in the value of the one-year treasury, while an X percentage point change in the 10-year treasury rate leads to approximately a 10X percent change in the value of the 10-year treasury.

But note that this is only an approximation. Three things prevent the relationship from being exact. First, and easiest to deal with, is the fact that not all cash flows are going to investors in one- and 10-year treasuries, respectively, at time one and time 10. The fact that there are intermediate cash flows shortens duration of the securities a little bit. We can adjust for this by looking at

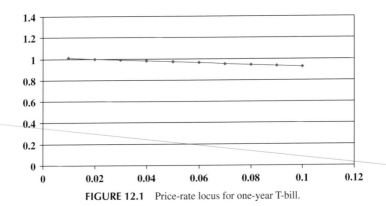

FIGURE 12.1   Price-rate locus for one-year T-bill.

the relationship between rates and values for zero coupon bonds. These bonds accrue but do not pay out interest until maturity. Figure 12.3 shows the relationship between rates and values for a 4 percent 10-year zero coupon bond. Note that the slope of this line is a little more negative than the slope in Figure 12.2. This reflects the fact for the z-bond, the investor is receiving all cash flows at maturity. Nevertheless, we can see that the duration approximation is just that, an approximation.

To understand the second reason why the rule-of-thumb method for calculating the change in value with respect to a change in interest rates doesn't quite work, we need to now become more formal in our treatment of the relationship between rates and values. We began with the general present value formula:

$$PV = \sum_{t=1}^{T} \frac{CF_t}{(1+r)^t}$$

where PV is present value, CF_t is cash flow at time t, T is the terminal cash flow period, and r is the discount rate.

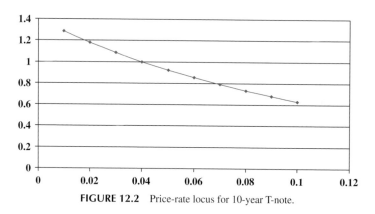

FIGURE 12.2   Price-rate locus for 10-year T-note.

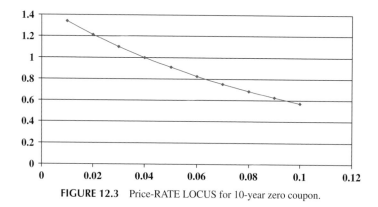

FIGURE 12.3   Price-RATE LOCUS for 10-year zero coupon.

To find how the present value of a security changes with a change in the discount rate, we assume the discount rate is the market rate of interest, and take a first derivative:

$$\frac{dPV}{dr} = \sum_{t=1}^{T} \frac{-tCF_t}{(1+r)^{t+1}}$$

Because we want to standardize sensitivity, we actually want to look at the percentage change in value with respect to a percentage point change in interest rates. To do so, we divide both sides of the previous equation by PV, and get:

$$\frac{dPV}{dr}\frac{1}{PV} = \sum_{t=1}^{T} \frac{-tCF_t}{(1+r)^{t+1}}\frac{1}{PV}$$

This expression is known as the modified duration formula, and gives, for small changes in r, the sensitivity of bond prices in percent with respect to a percentage point change in interest rates.

Let's consider that zero coupon bond for a moment. I receive all my cash flows at time T. This means that for a zero coupon bond with a maturity of 10 years, the "modified" duration is:

$$\frac{dPV}{dr}\frac{1}{PV} = \frac{-20CF_{20}}{(1+r)^{21}}\frac{1}{PV}$$

What are the cash flows at time T, or 20 (remember that there will be 20 semiannual payments over 10 years)? The amount initially invested (PV) compounded for 10 years at interest rate r, or $PV(1+0.02)^{20}$. Substituting, we find:

$$\frac{dPV}{dr}\frac{1}{PV} = \frac{-20(1+0.02)^{20}}{(1+r)^{21}}\frac{PV}{PV}$$

or

$$\frac{dPV}{dr}\frac{1}{PV} = \frac{-20}{(1+0.02)}$$

so when interest rates are small, the duration is approximately equal to 20 half-years, or 10 years, when all the cash flows are paid out. More generally, the time weighted average present value of cash flows, which is:

$$\frac{dPV}{dr}\frac{1+r}{PV} = \sum_{t=1}^{T} \frac{-tCF_t}{(1+r)^{t}}\frac{1}{PV}$$

and is known as MacCauley Duration, reflects the sensitivity of a fixed income cash flow to interest rates, multiplied by one plus the discount rate.

But let's go back to our graph, which gives the locus of prices and rates for a 10-year zero coupon rate treasury security. Modified duration predicts that a two-percentage point change in interest rates should produce a $20/(1.02)^2$

percent, or 19.22 percent change in value, but our graph shows that value falls by only 17.4 percent. The reason for this is the curvature of the locus, or convexity.

First derivatives are useful approximations of how the value of a function changes with respect to a change in one of its arguments. But they are just that—approximations. Derivatives give the slope of a tangent line to a point on a curve. If a function has lots of curvature, and/or interest rates change a lot, the approximation inferred from duration will become less and less accurate.

People in the bond trading business thus take things one derivative further, and measure convexity as:

$$\frac{d^2PV}{dr^2}\frac{1}{PV} = \sum_{t=1}^{T} \frac{t(t+1)\,CF_t}{(1+r)^{t+2}}\frac{1}{PV}$$

Notice that this is a positive expression. This is because as interest rates rise, their negative effect on value gets smaller. In the case of our previous example, the convexity is:

$$\frac{d^2PV}{dr^2}\frac{1}{PV} = \frac{110}{1+r^2}$$

We put duration and convexity together in a formula to get a more accurate approximation of the impact of an interest rate change on value:

$$dPV = -\,duration * dr + \frac{1}{2}convexity * dr^2$$

PROBLEMS CREATED BY DURATION-CONVEXITY

For those who purchase mortgages with equity—those who have no outstanding liabilities—duration is more an annoyance than a problem. But for those whose investment money is borrowed from others, duration is a large problem.

With American mortgages, the duration problem runs in both directions. On the one hand, in a world of rising interest rates, fixed-rate mortgages have lengthening duration.[2] This means that two things drive their value down: increasing discount rate and the lengthening period of principal repayment. On the other hand, in a world of falling interest rates, fixed-rate mortgages shorten their duration, so the benefit of the lower discount rate is somewhat offset by the decreasing sensitivity to interest rate movements.

---

2. A mortgage with a 30-year amortization period still had a shorter duration than 30-year Treasury securities. The reasons for this are (1) mortgages amortize, which means they pay principal throughout their lives, whereas Treasuries pay interest (if that) only until they mature; (2) even in rising rate environments, people move, which means they prepay their mortgage and thus bring forward cash flows—which in turn shortens duration.

Consider for a moment what happens to loans when interest rates fall below the coupon rate. The value of the loan when the market rate is equal to the coupon rate is par. If the loan did not have a prepayment feature, the value of the loan would rise similarly to a Treasury security of comparable duration. But because of the prepayment feature, borrowers can buy their loans back at par, which means that the value of the mortgage is a weighted average:

$$V = w_r V_N + (1 - w_r) V_*$$

where w_r is the share of mortgages that don't prepay at a particular interest rate, r; V_N is the value of the mortgages they never prepaid; and V_* is the par value of the mortgage. Note that because V_* is fixed, there may be a point at which rising prepayment speed leads to a reduction in value when interest rates are falling. In particular, because both w_r and V_N are functions of r, we can see that:

$$\frac{dV}{dr} = \frac{dw_r}{dr} V_N + w_r \frac{dV_N}{dr} - \frac{dw_r}{dr} V_*$$

or

$$\frac{dV}{dr} = \frac{dw_r}{dr} (V_N - V_*) + w_r \frac{dV_N}{dr}$$

We know

$$\frac{dw_r}{dr} > 0$$

and

$$\frac{dV_N}{dr} < 0$$

and for periods when market rates are lower than coupon rates:

$$V_N - V_* > 0$$

So if

$$\frac{dw_r}{dr} (V_N - V_*) > w_r \frac{dV_N}{dr}$$

then

$$\frac{dV}{dr} > 0$$

which is the same thing as saying there is negative duration. This is illustrated in Figure 12.4.

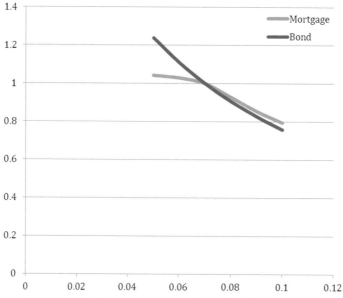

FIGURE 12.4   Mortgage vs treasury pricing: illustration of convexity.

This means levered investors that own mortgages face a problem. For those with short-term liabilities, interest rates rising are dangerous because a small increase in interest rates can lead to a large diminution in asset value, while the value of liabilities remain constant. This is what led to the insolvency of Savings and Loans (S&Ls) in the late 1970s and early 1980s—the value of the mortgages on their balance sheets dropped precipitously, as interest rates rose, while the value of their liabilities (which barely had any duration at all) fell. If mortgages have a duration of, say, 10 years, and S&Ls start with capital of 10 percent, and interest rates rise by two percentage points, the value of assets will fall to around 90 percent of liabilities, rendering the S&L insolvent.

On the other hand, consider what happens to investors with long-term liabilities, such as insurance companies and pension funds, when interest rates fall. Now the present value of liabilities rises, but the present value of assets doesn't rise as much, or might even fall, because of negative duration. Once again, a firm that relies on mortgages as an investment might find itself insolvent as a result of interest rate risk.

There is one more issue: duration itself is not an adequate measure of interest rate risk. Because duration arises from a derivative, it only gives an approximation of value change for a small change in interest rates. As interest rate movements become larger, the accuracy of the duration approximation gets worse.

It is therefore exceptionally tricky to manage the interest rate risk attached to mortgages. We discuss some methods for doing so next.

METHODS FOR MANAGING MORTGAGE INTEREST RATE RISK

There are at least three methods for managing mortgage interest rate risk: mimicking the yield curve, callable debt, and hedging through derivatives.

The first method essentially requires investors to distribute the debt they owe across maturities. Owing debt with long maturities alleviates the risk associated with increasing interest rates, and owing debt with short maturities helps with the risk associated with decreasing interest rates. A bank could do this by funding mortgages through a blend of deposits, short-term, medium-term, and long-term bonds.

The second method matches callable mortgages on the asset side of the balance sheet with callable debt on the liabilities side of the balance sheet. This way, when a mortgage borrower repays a mortgage before it is due, the institution holding the mortgage can use the funds to pay its creditors early.

The third method for managing the interest rate risk is through derivative products, including and especially swaptions.[3] Investors who purchase a swaption purchase the right to either swap fixed-rate debt for floating debt (by paying a fixed rate and receiving a floating rate), or floating debt for fixed-rate debt (by paying a floating rate and receiving a fixed rate).

Let's think about a bank. The deposits they hold are floating rate debt, so the bank may wish to purchase a swaption that will allow it to pay a fixed rate in exchange for receiving a floating rate. This allows them to effectively assure that their debt costs cannot rise above a certain ceiling.

Fannie Mae and Freddie Mac use all three methods for hedging their interest rate risk. The more they hedge, the less likely they are to get in trouble because of interest rate movements. But hedges also cost money, and therefore diminish profits.

The government-sponsored enterprises (GSEs) attempt to disclose their interest rate risk in their monthly volume summary.[4] Table 12.1 displays the interest rate sensitivity disclosure for June 2013 for Freddie Mac. Note that the GSE's duration gap (or net duration) is always one month or less—Freddie Mac as a matter of business aims for zero duration.

They also run simulations to see what would happen to portfolio values if all interest rates move by 50 basis points, or if the slope of the yield curve changes by 25 basis points. When we consider that Freddie's portfolio is roughly $2 trillion, movements in value of $300 million are very small.

But the GSEs have been criticized by Dwight Jaffee (2003) and others for disclosing only conservative assumptions. This criticism has some merit—over the summer of 2013, for example, mortgage rates moved by 100 basis points in

---

3. Recent papers on swaptions include Fan, Gupta, and Ritchken (2003) and Driessen, Klaasen, and Melenberg (2003).
4. An example of a Monthly Volume Summary for Freddie Mac may be found at http://www.freddiemac.com/investors/volsum/pdf/0613mvs.pdf.

TABLE 12.1 Example of Freddie Mac Monthly Volume Summary Interest Rate Sensitivity Disclosure

TABLE 8 - INTEREST - RATE RISK SENSITIVITY DISCLOSURES[17]

	Portfolio Market Value Level (PMVS-L) (50 bp) (dollars in millions)		Portfolio Market Value Yield Curve (PMVS-YC) (25 bp) (dollars in millions)		Duration Gap (Rounded to Nearest Month)	
	Monthly Average	Quarterly Average	Monthly Average	Quarterly Average	Monthly Average	Quarterly Average
Jun 2012	$115	$156	$14	$18	0	0
Jul	33	–	21	–	0	–
Aug	253	–	60	–	(1)	–
Sep	371	215	77	52	(1)	(1)
Oct	204	–	84	–	0	–
Nov	205	–	20	–	(1)	–
Dec	363	256	67	58	0	0
Full-Year 2012	212	–	36	–	0	–
Jan 2013	203	–	35	–	0	–
Feb	255	–	15	–	0	–
Mar	301	252	15	22	0	0
Apr	355	–	15	–	(1)	–
May	359	–	33	–	1	–
Jun	286	335	21	23	0	0
YTD 2013	$295	–	$23	–	0	–

less than a month. Another, related, issue is that hedged positions are valued with models—models that have proven unreliable in extreme conditions. It is probably safe to say that it is impossible to know how well hedged enterprises such as Fannie Mae, Freddie Mac, and large national banks really are.

OPTION ADJUSTED SPREAD[5]

Prepayment gives borrowers a call option—the ability to repurchase their mortgage at any time. Investors need to be compensated for this option. This is why Ginnie Mae securities, which do have default risk, pay higher coupons than comparable duration Treasuries.

There are three types of spreads: the nominal spread, the zero-volatility or z-spread, and the option adjusted spread.

The nominal spread is simply the difference in coupon between a mortgage-backed security and a Treasury security. This spread is generally not considered appropriate for capturing the cost of the prepayment option to the borrower, because with Treasuries principal is returned to investors at maturity, whereas with mortgages investors receive principal every month.

The second type of spread, the z-spread, attempts to deal with this issue by inferring forward interest rates from the yield curve. Forward rates reflect the market's current pricing of future spot rates. We discuss how we implement this issue in Chapter 11. Then, using trial and error, analysts will find some constant spread to add to forward Treasury rates until the present value of the future cash flows equals the current price of the mortgage.

The final type of spread is called the option adjusted spread. The option adjusted spread is calculated by doing simulations of various Treasury rate paths, and then finding the spread at which the present value of cash flows equals the market value. This captures the fact that stochastic movements in interest rates have asymmetric effects on values via discounting (think about convexity again). The difference between the z-spread and the option adjusted spread is called the option cost. We discussed the specifics of OAS models in Chapter 11.

HOW INVESTORS THINK THEY CAN MAKE MONEY USING CONVEXITY

PIMCO is the best-known bond fund in the United States. In 2008 it acquired large positions in agency securities,[6] and it profited handsomely on those securities. There is a fairly widespread view that Gross believed that explicit government backing of Fannie and Freddie was on the way, and that he took advantage of that belief.

---

5. A nice discussion of spreads is in Chapter 14.43 of the CFA level 1 course.
6. PIMCO Chairman Bill Gross referred to Fannie and Freddie securities as "excellent buys," on July 22, 2008. See http://bigpicture.typepad.com/comments/2008/07/pimcos-gross-fa.html

But PIMCO benefited from something else. Many traders thought that economic calamity would bring about a substantial reduction in interest rates. In this they were correct. They also assumed that the drop in interest rates would lead to waves of refinances. Essentially, many traders thought Fannie and Freddie securities' greatest upside potential was slightly above par.

This was a mistake. Along with falling interest rates, house prices fell at an unprecedented level. This placed one-quarter of US borrowers underwater on their homes, and homeowners without equity are in no position to refinance. This made agency MBS a great investment: their credit was protected by the government, and their coupons were paying substantial premiums relative to market rates. PIMCO benefited not only from government backing, but from prepayment speeds that were smaller than those projected by the market.

This, in a nutshell, is how traders try to make money off of convexity. When MBS are trading at a premium, those who think prepayments will be slower than what the market thinks will be buyers of MBS, while those who think prepayments will be faster will be sellers. The converse is true when MBS are trading at a discount.

REFERENCES

Conroy, Robert M., 2008. Duration and Convexity. Darden Case No. UVA-F.-1238.

Driessen, Joost, Klaassen, Pieter, Melenberg, Bertrand, 2003. The performance of multi-factor term structure models for pricing and hedging caps and swaptions. Journal of Financial and Quantitative Analysis 38.3, 635–672.

Fabozzi, Frank J., 1999. Duration, Convexity, and Other Bond Risk Measures, Vol. 58. John Wiley & Sons.

Fan, Rong, Gupta, Anurag, Ritchken, Peter, 2003. Hedging in the possible presence of unspanned stochastic volatility: Evidence from swaption markets. The Journal of Finance 58.5, 2219–2248.

Jaffee, Dwight, 2003. The interest rate risk of Fannie Mae and Freddie Mac. Journal of Financial Services Research 24.1, 5–29.

Chapter 13

The Rise and Fall of Fannie Mae and Freddie Mac: Lessons Learned and Options for Reform

Richard K. Green and Ann B. Schnare

AB Schnare Associates LLC, Washington, DC, USA

Introduction to Mortgages & Mortgage Backed Securities.
http://dx.doi.org/10.1016/B978-0-12-401743-6.00013-5
181

INTRODUCTION

Not so long ago, the US housing finance system was arguably the best in the world. Consumers had access to products—most notably, the 30-year fixed-rate, freely prepayable mortgage—that were not available elsewhere, and the market was able to sustain major economic disruptions—including the 1998 financial crisis and the 9-11 terrorist attack—with relatively little impact on either the cost or availability of mortgage credit. Fannie Mae and Freddie Mac (hereafter the GSEs[1]) provided the cornerstone of the mortgage market and deserve much of the credit for its success.

Despite their many accomplishments, the two government-sponsored enterprises (GSEs) have fallen into widespread disfavor as a result of perceived abuses of market power, accounting scandals, deteriorating underwriting standards, and ultimately, the need for government conservatorship. Most academics and policymakers have now concluded that their quasi-governmental model is no longer viable and that an alternative structure must be devised (e.g., Jaffee and Quigley 2007). Viewed in terms of a continuum of government involvement ranging from "purely private" to "purely public," the "purely public" solution seems to be winning out.

In our view, however, much would be lost if we moved to *either* end of the support continuum. The purely private model has clearly failed in the past two years. Almost no mortgage lending occurs today without the implicit or explicit backing of the federal government, and private institutions that once competed with the Fannie Mae and Freddie Mac have either failed or are now reliant on government funding. Even before the financial crisis, Freddie Mac's former Chief Economist, Robert Van Order, argued that banks' reliance on FDIC insurance made them another form of GSE. These similarities are more apparent than ever today. In the end, there is relatively little difference between the

---

1. For ease of exposition, we use the term GSE to refer only to Fannie Mae and Freddie Mac. Our comments do not include references to the Federal Home Loan Banks, which are another form of GSE.

government's treatment of Fannie Mae and Freddie Mac and its treatment of private companies such as Citigroup and AIG that were deemed too big to fail.

At the same time, it is difficult to argue that a purely governmental approach would be a good alternative to Fannie Mae and Freddie Mac. FHA's ability to serve the market has long been hampered by management, political, and resource constraints. The current crisis, which has generated an explosive growth in FHA lending, has further contributed to these problems. FHA's regulatory capital is rapidly running out (Goldberg and Schnare 2008, 2009), and a recent report by HUD's Inspector General cites numerous examples of the Agency's lax underwriting standards, failure to monitor lenders, and vulnerability to fraud (HUD 2009). Even if reformed, it is doubtful that FHA could ever produce the range of benefits heretofore provided by the GSEs.

This chapter attempts to establish a case for GSE reform that retains a market-driven approach but addresses acknowledged problems through better regulation and charter revisions. Our core assumption is that reform is possible without abandoning key aspects of the original GSE model, including access to a government guarantee and a reliance on profit incentives to set priorities and allocate resources.

The next section describes the basic business model that Fannie Mae and Freddie Mac have used for the past two decades. The third section presents a brief history of the rise and eventual fall of the GSEs. The fourth section discusses the benefits that have been produced by the GSE model, as well as its major drawbacks. The fifth section proposes several overarching principles that should be the basis of any reform, and the final section evaluates several alternative models on the basis of these principles. Although our analysis inevitably reflects our own opinions and experiences, we have drawn on empirical evidence whenever possible to develop and support our case.

HOW FANNIE MAE AND FREDDIE MAC SUPPORT THE MORTGAGE MARKET

Fannie Mae and Freddie Mac have two basic lines of business: a mortgage "guarantee" business and a mortgage portfolio, or "investment" business. Both activities help to support a secondary market for residential mortgages.

The guarantee side of the business involves the securitization of mortgages. This includes purchasing mortgages from loan originators, bundling the mortgages into mortgage-backed securities (MBS), and selling the resulting securities to other investors through Wall Street firms. Fannie Mae and Freddie Mac assume the underlying credit risk on the mortgages that they securitize and are responsible for any losses that occur when a loan defaults. The fee that they charge for such insurance is known as the "guarantee fee." Profits are earned by charging a guarantee fee that is sufficient to cover the losses arising from default, as well as the associated administrative and capital costs.

The investment side of the GSEs' business involves their retained mortgage portfolios, which include both individual mortgages ("whole loans") as well as MBS and other types of asset-backed securities (ABS). While Fannie Mae and Freddie Mac retain some of the individual mortgages they acquire from loan originators, their primary holdings consist of MBS (or ABS) that are purchased in the capital market. The GSEs fund their mortgage holdings through the issuance of corporate debt. Profits from such activities are generated from the difference between the interest earned from their mortgage holdings and their funding and hedging costs.

There are four types of risks that are generally associated with Fannie Mae's and Freddie Mac's business: credit risk, interest rate risk, market risk, and management risk.

1. Credit risk arises from mortgage default. In general, it reflects both the probability that the borrower will default as well as the losses incurred upon default (i.e., the loss severity rate).

2. Interest rate risk arises from a change in interest rates. Since mortgages are fully prepayable, declining rates will cause the security to prepay at a faster rate, forcing the investor to reinvest the proceeds at a lower rate. Rising rates will have the opposite effect.

3. Market risk arises from external events that affect their major lines of business, for example, a decline in market demand that reduces the value of their portfolio holdings. Since securities have to be marked-to-market on a regular basis, any change in their market value will have an immediate impact on the GSEs' balance sheets.

4. Management (or operational) risk stems from operational breakdowns, or errors, that can affect a company's earnings.

While all of the GSEs' activities are susceptible to management risk, the risks associated with the guarantee and investment sides of their two business lines are distinctly different.

The guarantee (or securitization) side of their businesses primarily exposes the companies to credit risk—the risk that the loans will default. Since the MBS are sold into the capital market, the security's investors—as opposed to the GSEs—assume the "interest rate" risk. To manage their credit risk, the GSEs establish underwriting guidelines for the loans they are willing to buy, and conduct on-going quality control reviews to ensure that lenders are following the established guidelines. Loans that fail to meet established guidelines are subject to repurchase.

In contrast, the investment side of the business primarily exposes the GSEs to interest rate risk. Interest rate risk is managed through a variety of means, for example, by matching the maturity of the debt with the projected life of the loans or by purchasing an interest-rate hedge. Traditionally, most of the GSEs' mortgages holdings have consisted of their own securities (or other forms of guaranteed MBS). As a result, their investment portfolios did not expose them to additional credit risk. However, this has changed in recent years, since both agencies invested heavily in "private label" MBS and other types of asset-backed securities.[2]

While the bulk of the GSEs' activities involve single family residential mortgages, they also play an important role in financing multifamily housing. The majority of multifamily loans that are purchased by Fannie Mae and Freddie Mac are funded through their investment portfolios. Given the heterogeneous nature of multifamily mortgages, they are less suitable for securitization. As a result, while both GSEs have issued a certain amount of multifamily MBS over the years, the volume has typically been relatively low in comparison to their annual purchases of multifamily loans.[3]

A BRIEF HISTORY OF FANNIE MAE AND FREDDIE MAC

Fannie Mae and Freddie Mac were established to create a liquid and stable market for residential mortgages. Although their histories and original mandates differed, both companies were given substantially identical charters with the passage of the Financial Institutions Reform Recovery and Enforcement Act (FIRREA) in 1989. As shareholder-owned, federally-chartered entities with a public purpose and special privileges, Fannie Mae and Freddie Mac became increasingly dominant forces in the mortgage market over the ensuing years.

Fannie Mae was established as a federal agency in 1938 to provide a secondary market for FHA (and, shortly thereafter, VA) loans. Fannie Mae operated as an independent government agency for the next 30 years, but was restructured as a shareholder-owned corporation in 1968, largely to remove its liabilities from the federal government's books in the face of mounting deficits from the Viet Nam War. At the same time, Fannie Mae's mandate was expanded to include the purchase of conventional mortgages and a new government agency was formed—the Government National Mortgage Association, or Ginnie Mae. Ginnie Mae, which became part of the newly created US Department of Housing and Urban Development, established a securitization vehicle for securities backed by government-insured loans by guaranteeing the timely payment of interest and principle. The first Ginnie Mae security was issued in 1970.

Freddie Mac was created in the same year to provide a competitor for Fannie Mae and to further support a secondary market for conventional loans. While originally owned by the Federal Home Loan Banks, Freddie Mac issued 15 million shares of nonvoting stock to member thrifts in 1984, effectively becoming an industry-owned cooperative. Freddie Mac was transformed into a

---

2. Since their security holdings are required to be marked-to-market, these investments also exposed the GSEs to massive write-offs following the collapse of the subprime market. Whether or not these write-offs are accurate reflections of the losses that will ultimately be incurred is difficult to determine at this stage.

3. See 2008 Annual Report, Federal Housing Finance Agency, Tables 1, 2, 10, and 11.

shareholder-owned company five years later following the passage of FIRREA. In fact, the proceeds from its sale helped offset the massive losses experienced by the thrifts as a result of the S&L crisis in the late 1980s.

For the purpose of this discussion, we have divided the histories of Fannie Mae and Freddie Mac from 1970 into five distinct periods: 1970 through 1989, which began with privatization of Fannie Mae and the creation of Freddie Mac and ended with the passage of FIRREA; 1990 through 1998, when Fannie Mae and Freddie Mac came into their own as shareholder-owned companies and began to consolidate their market power; 1998 to 2003, which witnessed the explosive growth of the two companies and their increasing market dominance; 2004 through mid-2007, which saw the ascendance of private conduits and the explosion of subprime lending; and mid-2007 through today, which encompassed the meltdown of the private mortgage market, the creation of a new regulatory agency—the Federal Housing Finance Agency (FHFA)—and the government takeover of both Fannie Mae and Freddie Mac.

The Formative Years: 1970 to 1989

Most of the GSEs' activities in these early years involved establishing the basic infrastructure required to support a robust secondary mortgage market for conventional mortgages. One of their first and most important accomplishments was to standardize the origination and underwriting process. At the time, conventional underwriting guidelines varied from lender to lender, as did application procedures, documentation requirements, and closing and servicing protocols. In order to facilitate the development of a secondary market for these loans, Fannie Mae and Freddie Mac had to develop a wide array of standardized forms and legal documents that governed the closing, funding, and subsequent sale of any loan. They also developed a comprehensive set of underwriting guidelines that specified the terms and conditions of the loans they would buy. Such standardization enabled otherwise heterogeneous loans to be pooled and transformed into mortgage-backed securities without requiring detailed reviews of each underlying loan.

Other major milestones of this period involved the development and refinement of conventional mortgage-backed securities. In 1971, Freddie Mac issued the first conventional mortgage-backed security, known as the Mortgage Participation Certificate, or PC. Like the original Ginnie Mae securities, PCs were mortgage "pass-throughs," that is, they distributed the cash flows from a mortgage pool on a simple pro rata basis. Owing to the long duration of many mortgages, these instruments primarily appealed to long-term investors. Twelve years later, Freddie Mac greatly expanded the pool of potential investors by issuing the first Collateralized Mortgage Obligation, or CMO. Unlike a mortgage pass-through, a CMO structures the cash flows from a mortgage pool into separate bonds, or tranches, with different payment schedules. By creating bonds with shorter durations, this innovation significantly broadened the market for mortgage-backed securities.

In contrast to Freddie Mac, Fannie Mae continued to hold most of its mortgages on its books in these early years, following the approach it had used since its creation in 1938. As interest rates moved into double-digit territory in the mid-to-late 1970s, Fannie Mae's practice of funding long-term mortgages with short-term debt put it in the same precarious position as many S&Ls. By 1981 Fannie Mae was technically insolvent as its interest payments exceeded its interest costs, so the present value of its assets were less than the present value of its liabilities.[4] While it was able to survive largely as a result of its government ties, Fannie Mae remained in a weakened financial condition until 1985, when interest rates finally dropped from their historic highs.

Fannie Mae issued its first mortgage-backed security, or MBS, in 1981. Like Freddie Mac's Participation Certificates, Fannie Mae MBS were mortgage pass-throughs. Fannie Mae issued its first structured security in 1987 in the form of a Real Estate Mortgage Investment Conduit, or REMIC. Although the legal structure of a REMIC is different from a CMO, they are similar in their treatment of cash flows from a mortgage pool. While somewhat late to the securitization game, Fannie Mae entered the MBS market aggressively. By the end of the decade, Fannie Mae issuances of mortgage-backed securities exceeded those of Freddie Mac.[5]

The period came to an end with the passage of FIRREA, which changed the ownership structure of Freddie Mac into a shareholder-owned company with a charter comparable to that of Fannie Mae. By the time that FIRREA was passed, the securitization market for conventional mortgages was well-established and comparatively large. The GSEs' issuances of mortgage-backed securities (i.e., PCs and MBS) totaled about $170.5 billion in 1990, up from just $62.4 billion five years earlier.[6] Issuances of GSE multiclass securities (i.e., CMO/REMIC) were at $111.7 billion. By 1990, the total volume of outstanding GSE-backed securities was over $611 billion, 50 percent higher than GNMA MBS ($401 million).[7] While there was a small emerging market for private-label securities, the outstanding volume of nonagency MBS was just $55 billion in that year.

The Golden Years: 1990 to 2003

For Fannie Mae and Freddie Mac, the 13-year period following the passage of FIRREA can generally be characterized as one of consolidation and market innovation, followed by explosive growth and increasing market power.

Both GSEs emerged from FIRREA in positions of strength. Fannie Mae had largely recovered from its near financial collapse, and Freddie Mac had been

---

4. See http://www.fhfa.gov/webfiles/2335/FHFA_ReportToCongress2008508.pdf, p. 110. Accessed August 12, 2009.
5. Inside Mortgage Finance, Mortgage Yearbook for 2007, p. 21.
6. Ibid, p. 21.
7. Ibid, p. 33. Calculations exclude CMO/REMIC to avoid double-counting.

transformed from an industry-controlled cooperative into a shareholder-owned firm. As a result, both companies were poised to take advantage of the special privileges provided by their federal charters. These included a $2.5 billion line of credit with the US Treasury, exemptions from SEC registration requirements and state and local income taxes, and the classification of the GSEs' securities as "Tier 1" capital for reserving purposes. Since these charter privileges were generally interpreted as "implicit" guarantees on the part of the US government, the GSEs' debt and securities traded at favorable rates, making it difficult for other entities to compete.

The regulatory framework that would govern the companies for the next 15 years was put into place in 1992 with the passage of The Federal Housing Enterprise Financial Safety and Soundness Act. The legislation established a dedicated federal regulator—known as the Office of Federal Housing Enterprise Oversight, or OFHEO—and called for the development of risk-based capital standards and Affordable Housing Goals. While risk-based capital standards were designed to be an alternative to minimum capital requirements, for a variety of reasons, they proved to be less binding than the capital standards already in place. The net effect was that both GSEs were able to leverage their capital to a high degree in order to support their rapidly growing guarantee and investment activities.

Growing Market Share

The GSEs guarantee business grew dramatically over the 13-year period. Their combined market share (defined as the ratio of their new single-family business to total originations) rose from about 41.5 percent of the overall market in 1990 to 57.0 percent in 2003 (see Table 13.1). Excluding jumbo mortgages, their overall market share went from 54.4 to 73.2 percent. Over the same period of time, the outstanding volume of mortgage-backed securities issued by the GSEs (i.e., PCs and MBS) more than quadrupled, from about $610 billion in 1990 to some $2.8 trillion in 2003 (see Table 13.2).

The investment-side of the GSEs' businesses also grew dramatically, particularly between 1998 and 2003 (see Table 13.3). Freddie Mac did not hold a mortgage portfolio until the early 1990s, and the initial growth of its holdings was relatively slow. However, from 1998 to 2003, Freddie Mac's retained portfolio grew at an annual average rate of about 21 percent. Over the same period of time, Fannie Mae's mortgage holdings increased by an annual average rate of 17 percent. By 2003, Freddie Mac's retained portfolio ($661 billion) was about 72 percent as large as Fannie Mae's ($920 billion).

The high rate of growth of the GSEs' retained portfolios from 1998 to 2003 reflected a variety of factors, including pressures on their guarantee fees. However, the collapse of the Russian bond market and Long Term Capital in 1998 provided the GSEs with a rare opportunity. On the one hand, the rising spreads that resulted from the turmoil in global financial markets made their portfolio investments extremely profitable; as investors fled to quality, the GSEs'

TABLE 13.1 Combined GSE Market Share: 1990–2008 ($ billions)

Year	Fannie/Freddie New Business	Total Originations	Market Share
1990	$190.33	$458.44	41.5%
1991	$242.90	$562.07	43.2%
1992	$452.26	$893.67	50.6%
1993	$524.77	$1,019.86	51.5%
1994	$288.27	$773.12	37.3%
1995	$230.99	$639.43	36.1%
1996	$300.36	$785.33	38.2%
1997	$290.26	$859.12	33.8%
1998	$657.39	$1,450.00	45.3%
1999	$640.82	$1,310.00	48.9%
2000	$467.27	$1,048.00	44.6%
2001	$1,089.88	$2,215.00	49.2%
2002	$1,491.30	$2,885.00	51.7%
2003	$2,249.48	$3,945.00	57.0%
2004	$1,219.97	$2,920.00	41.8%
2005	$1,164.06	$3,120.00	37.3%
2006	$1,115.84	$2,980.00	37.4%
2007	$1,323.81	$2,430.00	54.5%
2008	$1,078.11	$1,485.00	72.6%

Sources: Inside Mortgage Finance Yearbook for 2007, p. 3; 2008 data from "Stabilizing the Mortgage Market" by James B. Lockhart III, speech given before the Urban Land Institute Terwilliger Center Annual Forum, slide 5

comparative funding advantage increased. At the same time, the GSEs' investment and securitization activities helped to ensure a steady flow of mortgage credit, a clear demonstration of their public purpose. This win–win situation gave Fannie Mae and Freddie Mac considerable political cover as they locked in long-term profits. The problem, as we now know, is that the GSEs held insufficient capital; their implicit debt subsidy also encouraged them to finance their portfolios with excessive debt.

But even after the crisis passed, both GSEs continued to grow their portfolios at a rapid rate, reflecting the high rates of return that were being generated

			GSEs		
Year	Ginnie Mae MBS	Nonagency MBS	Freddie Mac 1-4 PCs	Fannie Mae 1-4 MBS	Total
1990	$401,278	$55,000	$320,959	$289,683	$610,642
1991	$425,241	$96,700	$364,163	$360,549	$724,712
1992	$419,516	$142,300	$412,808	$433,353	$846,161
1993	$414,066	$167,900	$453,276	$483,666	$936,942
1994	$450,934	$183,000	$489,176	$517,116	$1,006,292
1995	$472,283	$193,800	$512,376	$565,567	$1,077,943
1996	$506,340	$215,400	$551,070	$628,757	$1,179,827
1997	$536,810	$253,500	$575,665	$683,124	$1,258,789
1998	$537,431	$321,500	$642,209	$799,983	$1,442,192
1999	$582,263	$353,200	$744,339	$922,138	$1,666,477
2000	$611,553	$377,500	$816,302	$1,014,301	$1,830,603
2001	$591,368	$463,200	$954,054	$1,242,703	$2,196,757
2002	$537,888	$544,100	$1,062,016	$1,365,779	$2,427,795
2003	$473,738	$666,000	$1,129,150	$1,641,641	$2,770,791
2004	$441,235	$1,045,700	$1,193,422	$1,694,408	$2,887,830
2005	$405,246	$1,618,000	$1,321,021	$1,780,352	$3,101,373
2006	$410,196	$2,128,300	$1,468,608	$1,932,927	$3,401,535
2007	$449,705	$2,162,600	$1,727,275	$2,259,256	$3,986,531
2008	$597,206	$1,838,600	$1,812,409	$2,545,059	$4,357,468

TABLE 13.2 Outstanding Mortgage Securities: 1990–2008 ($ millions)

Source: The 2009 Mortgage Market Statistical Annual, Volume II, p. 10

through this side of their businesses. The nature of their mortgage holdings also began to change. Prior to 1997, Fannie Mae and Freddie Mac primarily invested in whole loans and MBS whose performance was well-understood and guaranteed. In most instances, they purchased their own securities or retained loans acquired through the guarantee side of their business.[8] However, after this time,

---

8. Both agencies also purchased limited amounts of Ginnie Mae securities, as well as securities issued by the other agency. See Tables 1b and 10b, Part 1. Federal Housing Finance Agency 2008 Annual Report.

TABLE 13.3 Fannie Mae and Freddie Mac Total Mortgage Assets: 1990–2009 ($ millions)

Year	Fannie Mae	Freddie Mac	Total
1990	$114,066	$21,520	$135,586
1991	$126,679	$26,667	$153,346
1992	$156,260	$33,629	$189,889
1993	$190,169	$55,938	$246,107
1994	$220,815	$73,171	$293,986
1995	$252,868	$107,706	$360,574
1996	$286,528	$137,826	$424,354
1997	$316,592	$164,543	$481,135
1998	$415,434	$255,670	$671,104
1999	$523,103	$322,914	$846,017
2000	$607,731	$385,451	$993,182
2001	$706,347	$503,769	$1,210,116
2002	$820,627	$589,899	$1,410,526
2003	$919,589	$660,531	$1,580,120
2004	$925,194	$664,582	$1,589,776
2005	$736,803	$709,503	$1,446,306
2006	$726,434	$700,002	$1,426,436
2007	$723,620	$710,042	$1,433,662
2008	$767,989	$748,746	$1,516,735
2009	$789,634	$823,431	$1,613,065

Sources: 2008 FHFA Annual Report to Congress, pp. 111, 128; Fannie Mae and Freddie Mac Investor Relations

both GSEs began to acquire significant volumes of private-label asset-backed securities (ABS), which introduced a new layer of credit risk into their traditional portfolio holdings.

Private label securities represented roughly 7 percent of Fannie Mae's aggregate mortgage-related purchases from 1998 through 2003, up from zero in the early 1990s (see Table 13.4). The figures for Freddie Mac show a more aggressive entry into this market, with private label securities averaging around 15 percent of its purchases over this period (i.e., 1998 through 2003). While more detailed breakdowns of the GSEs' purchases were not available until 2002

TABLE 13.4 GSE Mortgage-Related Security Purchases: 1990–2008 ($ millions)

	Fannie Mae			Freddie Mac		
Year	Total Private-Label	Total Mortgage-Related Securities	Private-to-Total Ratio	Total Private-Label	Total Mortgage-Related Securities	Private-to-Total Ratio
2008	$2,295	$77,523	3.0%	$10,316	$297,614	3.5%
2007	$37,435	$69,236	54.1%	$76,134	$231,039	33.0%
2006	$57,787	$102,666	56.3%	$122,230	$241,205	50.7%
2005	$41,369	$62,232	66.5%	$179,962	$325,575	55.3%
2004	$90,747	$176,385	51.4%	$121,082	$223,299	54.2%
2003	$34,032	$408,606	8.3%	$69,154	$385,078	18.0%
2002	$7,416	$268,574	2.8%	$59,376	$299,674	19.8%
2001	$3,513	$209,124	1.7%	$24,468	$248,466	9.8%
2000	$8,466	$129,716	6.5%	$10,304	$91,896	11.2%
1999	$16,511	$169,905	9.7%	$15,263	$101,898	15.0%
1998	$15,721	$147,260	10.7%	$15,711	$128,446	12.2%
1997	$4,188	$50,317	8.3%	$1,494	$35,385	4.2%
1996	$777	$46,743	1.7%			
1995	$752	$36,258	2.1%			
1994	$0	$25,905	0.0%			
1993	$0	$6,606	0.0%			
1992	$0	$5,428	0.0%			
1991	$0	$3,080	0.0%			
1990	$0	$1,451	0.0%			

Source: 2008 FHFA Annual Report to Congress, pp. 107, 124

or later,[9] their private label purchases evidently began with commercial mortgage-backed securities (CMBS) but later extended to include large numbers of securities backed by subprime and Alt-A loans.

---

9. Fannie Mae data is available beginning in 2002. Freddie Mac data begins in 2006. See Tables 1b and 10b from the Federal Housing Finance Agency 2008 Annual Report.

TABLE 13.5 Fannie Mae and Freddie Mac Debt Outstanding and US Treasuries Outstanding ($ millions)

Year	Fannie Debt Outstanding	Freddie Debt Outstanding	Total F/F Debt Outstanding	Treasuries Outstanding
1990	$123,403	$30,941	$154,344	$3,233,313
1991	$133,937	$30,262	$164,199	$3,665,303
1992	$166,300	$29,631	$195,931	$4,064,621
1993	$201,112	$49,993	$251,105	$4,411,489
1994	$257,230	$93,279	$350,509	$4,692,750
1995	$299,174	$119,961	$419,135	$4,973,983
1996	$331,270	$156,981	$488,251	$5,224,811
1997	$369,774	$172,842	$542,616	$5,413,146
1998	$460,291	$287,396	$747,687	$5,526,193
1999	$547,619	$360,711	$908,330	$5,656,271
2000	$642,682	$426,899	$1,069,581	$5,674,178
2001	$763,467	$578,368	$1,341,835	$5,807,463
2002	$841,293	$665,696	$1,506,989	$6,228,236
2003	$961,280	$739,613	$1,700,893	$6,783,231
2004	$953,111	$731,697	$1,684,808	$7,379,053
2005	$764,010	$748,792	$1,512,802	$7,932,710
2006	$767,046	$744,341	$1,511,387	$8,506,974
2007	$796,299	$738,557	$1,534,856	$9,007,653
2008	$870,393	$843,021	$1,713,414	$10,024,725

Sources: 2008 FHFA Annual Report to Congress, pp. 111, 128; TreasuryDirect Historical Debt Outstanding, available at http://www.treasurydirect.gov/govt/reports/pd/histdebt/histdebt_histo5.htm

By 2003, Fannie Mae and Freddie Mac's total debt outstanding stood at $1.7 trillion, or about 25 percent of total US Treasuries ($6.8 trillion; see Table 13.5). The total volume of the GSEs' outstanding mortgage-backed securities was $4.4 trillion. Not only had Fannie Mae and Freddie Mac become the dominant players in the US mortgage industry, their securities and debt had become intrinsic parts of the global capital market. Indeed, in the late 1990s, when the country was experiencing a budget surplus, there was even some talk that Fannie Mae and Freddie Mac debt would become the new global benchmark.

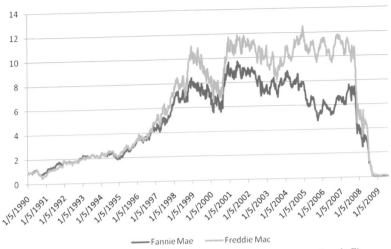

FIGURE 13.1 Fannie Mae and Freddie Mac Stock prices (1990 = 1). *Source: Google Finance*

Not surprisingly, both Fannie Mae and Freddie Mac were the darlings of Wall Street throughout much of this period. Both companies reported double-digit earnings growth year after year, with only one exception. And the stock of both companies soared, enriching management and shareholders alike. Most of the gains occurred between 1990 and 1999, when Fannie Mae and Freddie Mac share prices rose by 722 and 992 percent, respectively (see Figure 13.1).[10]

Introduction of Automated Underwriting

The rapid growth of the Agencies was accompanied by dramatic improvements in their ability to measure and manage their credit risk. Freddie Mac's introduction of credit scores to the underwriting process in 1996 had a revolutionary effect on the mortgage market. While initially resisted by the industry and many consumer groups, the use of credit scores rapidly became the norm, and is now an integral part of most lenders' underwriting, servicing, and risk management procedures.

The GSEs' concurrent development of automated underwriting systems (AUS) in the late 1990s also dramatically improved the loan origination process by making it faster, less expensive, and arguably fairer. One study by Freddie Mac found that moving from a manual to automated system expanded the market by increasing the number of qualified borrowers (Gates et al. 2003).

---

10. Calculations based on change between January 5, 1990 and January 1, 1999.

Whether or not we accept the broader applicability of these results, the GSEs' efforts to improve the underwriting process were clearly cutting edge and undoubtedly enhanced the industry's understanding of credit risk.[11] It also dramatically increased the ability of both the industry and the GSEs to handle the large volumes of loans that accompanied the refinancing booms of 1998 and 2002 to 2003.

Along with automated underwriting models, the GSEs developed automated capital allocation models, whose purpose was to map risks to prices. In principle, the GSEs could decide to purchase riskier mortgages in exchange for charging higher guarantee fees when the mortgages became securitized. It is not clear to us, however, whether the GSEs' risk was the principal determination of how they negotiated fees. Customer relationships likely had a large impact on the size of fees they charged.

However, some have argued that the movement to AUS, and the GSEs' dominance in this area, came at a cost—as the industry generally moved away from traditional underwriting and placed greater reliance on computerized scoring models, it helped to set the stage for the subsequent deterioration in underwriting standards. Looking back, this argument has some appeal. It is certainly the case that one of the drivers of the subprime crisis was the wholesale abandonment of underwriting standards and protocols that the GSEs had helped to develop and had previously imposed on the marketplace. It is also the case that as the housing market began to turn, scoring models based on more favorable economic conditions failed to perform.

Accounting Scandals

By the end of the 1990s, the growing market dominance of the GSEs was met with rising concerns among federal regulators and both the Clinton and Bush Administrations that the GSEs had become "too big to fail." Much of this concern surrounded the size of their investment portfolios and their exposure to interest rate risk. While both the Federal Reserve and the Treasury Department made numerous attempts to limit their investment holdings, these were invariably thwarted by sympathetic members of Congress from both sides of the aisle.[12]

Concerns over the potential exposure of the federal government were further heightened by separate accounting scandals that resulted in the ouster of senior management at both companies in 2003 and 2004. The problems began at Freddie Mac in the wake of the Enron scandal, which forced the company to replace its long-time auditor, Arthur Anderson. The new auditor concluded that certain

---

11. In a risk adverse environment such as today, more precision in underwriting should increase acceptance rates.

12. For a more detailed discussion, see McLean (2005).

accounting treatments in previous years had understated corporate earnings by about $5 billion. These findings ultimately led to ouster of Freddie Mac's long-time CEO and President in June 2003.

A similar scandal and management upheaval transpired a year and a half later at Fannie Mae. While the details are very different—Fannie Mae management was accused of overstating its earnings by $9 billion in order to maximize executive bonuses—the net results were essentially the same. Members of Fannie Mae senior management, including its CEO, were forced to resign in December 2004, and a new executive team was formed.

Some observers believe that the resulting turmoil at the two companies helped to pave the way for the rise of the private conduits and the explosion of nontraditional mortgage products, including subprime lending. In any event, new management teams at both GSEs were forced to devote a considerable amount of their time and resources to the complex task of restating earnings at a time when the market was changing rapidly. Over the next three years, Fannie Mae and Freddie Mac found themselves in the unfamiliar position of having to compete with private conduits on both price and product.

The Rise of Private Conduits and Subprime Lending: 2004 to Mid-2007

The market dominance of Fannie Mae and Freddie Mac began to erode in 2004 as a result of dramatic shifts in both the mortgage and capital markets. Record low mortgage rates and rapidly escalating housing prices triggered a massive refinancing boom in 2002 and 2003 that was followed by a 26 percent decline in originations in 2004. This decline was arrested in the following year by a dramatic increase in the origination of subprime mortgages and other nontraditional products such as "low doc" loans and "pay option ARMs" (collectively known as "Alt-A product"). The origination of subprime and Alt-A mortgages increased dramatically from 2005 through mid-2007, accounting for as much as 34 percent of the overall market (see Table 13.6). Most of these mortgages were packaged into private label securities and sold through Wall Street firms.

The underlying causes of these developments are well known and thoroughly documented, and stemmed from a deadly combination of rapidly accelerating housing prices, a global excess of capital, deteriorating underwriting standards, a private securitization model where the various entities involved in the transaction had little capital at risk, and an increased reliance on highly complex, financially-engineered products to manage the credit risk. The net result was to shift the mortgage market away from the relatively conservative and standardized underwriting practices that had been promulgated by the GSEs in favor of the significantly looser standards.

The decline in the relative importance of conventional, conforming mortgages—and the concurrent growth of subprime and Alt-A lending—had a dramatic impact on the guarantee side of the GSEs' businesses. In 2003,

TABLE 13.6 Mortgage Originations by Product Type: 1990–2008 ($ billions)

Year	FHA/VA	Conv/Conf	Jumbo	Subprime	Alt-A	Total
1990	$70	$240	$88	$37	$3	$438
1991	$62	$300	$113	$53	$6	$534
1992	$73	$530	$160	$80	$9	$852
1993	$119	$590	$175	$85	$11	$980
1994	$141	$356	$150	$75	$10	$732
1995	$75	$315	$135	$60	$10	$595
1996	$105	$380	$160	$70	$20	$735
1997	$100	$405	$190	$85	$25	$805
1998	$145	$705	$355	$135	$35	$1,375
1999	$172	$595	$315	$130	$40	$1,252
2000	$115	$495	$260	$100	$25	$995
2001	$175	$1,265	$460	$160	$40	$2,100
2002	$176	$1,706	$571	$200	$67	$2,720
2003	$220	$2,460	$650	$310	$85	$3,725
2004	$135	$1,210	$515	$540	$190	$2,590
2005	$90	$1,090	$570	$625	$380	$2,755
2006	$80	$990	$480	$600	$400	$2,550
2007	$116	$1,151	$348	$191	$275	$2,081
2008	$290	$920	$97	$23	$41	$1,371

Source: The 2009 Mortgage Market Statistical Annual, Volume I, p. 4

Fannie Mae and Freddie Mac accounted for roughly 71 percent of all single-family securitizations. By mid-2007, their share had dropped to 49 percent (see Table 13.7). Over the same period of time, the share of private-label securities backed by subprime and Alt-A loans increased from 46 to 68 percent. This development placed the GSEs in a difficult position—either they could accept a smaller, less profitable guarantee business or expand into these markets as well. Unfortunately, both companies chose the latter path.

At the same time, both Fannie Mae and Freddie Mac reduced their underwriting standards for their mainstream business by introducing "expanded" versions of their automated underwriting systems, DU and Loan Prospector. While essentially "black boxes" to the rest of the industry, the net result

TABLE 13.7 MBS Issuances by Type: 1995–2009 ($ millions)

| Year | GNMA | FHLMC | FNMA | Nonagency | | | | | Total |
				Prime	Subprime	Alt-A	Other	Total Nonagency	
1995	$72,763	$85,877	$110,456	$25,838	$17,771	$498	$4,818	$48,926	$318,022
1996	$100,880	$119,702	$149,849	$31,419	$30,769	$1,803	$55,903	$69,893	$440,324
1997	$103,743	$114,528	$149,429	$49,975	$56,921	$6,518	$5,719	$119,132	$486,832
1998	$149,112	$250,764	$326,148	$97,365	$75,830	$21,236	$8,780	$203,211	$929,234
1999	$151,410	$233,031	$300,689	$74,631	$55,852	$12,023	$5,394	$147,899	$833,029
2000	$103,251	$165,624	$210,205	$53,585	$52,467	$16,444	$13,463	$135,959	$615,039
2001	$172,708	$389,611	$525,321	$142,203	$87,053	$11,374	$26,691	$267,320	$1,354,965
2002	$172,135	$547,056	$723,299	$171,534	$122,681	$53,463	$66,277	$413,955	$1,856,893
2003	$217,716	$713,787	$1,198,616	$237,455	$194,959	$74,151	$79,652	$586,216	$2,717,133
2004	$124,388	$365,148	$527,145	$233,378	$362,549	$158,586	$109,639	$864,152	$1,882,836
2005	$85,766	$397,867	$481,260	$280,704	$465,036	$332,323	$109,388	$1,191,263	$2,155,987
2006	$82,275	$360,023	$456,857	$219,037	$448,600	$365,676	$112,139	$1,145,612	$2,045,420
2007	$95,511	$444,312	$617,707	$180,462	$201,547	$249,610	$75,394	$707,013	$1,867,676
2008	$269,046	$357,861	$541,960	$6,658	$2,261	$1,855	$47,358	$51,452	$1,168,867

Source: The 2009 Mortgage Market Statistical Annual, Volume II, pp. 9, 13

of these modifications—labeled "expanded authority" by Fannie Mae—was to extend the boundaries of conventional lending into territory previously occupied by subprime loans. Based on the recent performance of conventional loans insured by Genworth, subsequent versions of Fannie Mae's "Expanded Authority" program have led to increasingly higher rates of defaults.

Pressures on the guarantee side of the business were also accompanied by a dramatic slowdown in the growth of the GSEs' retained portfolios, their primary engines for earnings growth. Indeed, growth in their combined portfolios came to an end in 2004, and then began to decline. Several factors contributed to this development, including the 30 percent capital surcharge that OFHEO imposed in the wake of the companies' accounting scandals. More fundamentally, however, the market conditions that caused the explosion of subprime lending also affected the GSEs' comparative advantage on the investment side of their businesses by reducing the spreads they could earn on conventional mortgage-backed securities.

Like other investors at the time, both Fannie Mae and Freddie Mac became active investors in subprime securities in an effort to achieve higher yields and, some would assert, to meet their mandated affordable housing goals. Private label securities accounted for 56 percent of Fannie Mae's total mortgage-related security purchases from 2004 through 2006, and 54 percent for Freddie Mac (see Table 13.4). Most of these purchases involved securities backed by subprime or Alt-A mortgages (see Table 13.8). In 2006, the GSEs' purchases of such securities represented 9.8 percent of the total volume of subprime and Alt-A originations made within the year.

The Beginning of the End: Late-2007 to the Present

The mortgage market began to change again in mid- to late 2006, when rising delinquencies on subprime mortgages and the cooling of the housing market began to affect the financial health of many subprime lenders. Monthly failures of subprime loan originators began to rise at the end of 2006. By August 2007, when the situation reached crisis proportions, more than 100 subprime lenders had shut their doors (see Figure 13.2). After that point, the volume of subprime lending went into a virtual freefall, falling to less than 3 percent of the overall market by the end of 2007.

While the decline in the Alt-A market began somewhat later than it did for subprime loans, August 2007 also proved to be pivotal for this sector of the mortgage market. Alt-A originations fell steadily in the first three quarters of 2007, and dropped by 50 percent in the final quarter of the year. By the beginning of 2008, both the Alt-A and subprime markets had virtually disappeared. The securitization of jumbo mortgages also ground to a halt, leaving the mortgage market almost entirely in the hands of the GSEs and FHA.

EXHIBIT 13.8 Private-Label Securities of Fannie Mae and Freddie Mac ($ millions)

| | | Single Family | | | | | | | |
| | | Subprime | | Alt-A | | Other | | | Total |
Year	Manu-Factured Housing	Fixed Rate	Adjustable Rate	Fixed Rate	Adjustable Rate	Fixed Rate	Adjustable Rate	Multi-Family	Private Label
Freddie Mac									
2008	$0	$8,199	$46	$0	$618	$36	$0	$1,416	$10,315
2007	$127	$843	$42,824	$702	$9,306	$48	$0	$22,284	$76,134
2006	$0	$116	$74,645	$718	$29,828	$48	$0	$16,875	$122,230
Fannie Mae									
2008	$0	$0	$637	$175	$0	$0	$987	$496	$2,295
2007	$0	$343	$15,628	$38	$5,250	$0	$178	$15,998	$37,435
2006	$0	$0	$34,876	$1,504	$10,443	$0	$1,274	$9,690	$57,787
2005	$0	$0	$16,344	$3,091	$12,535	$483	$8,814	$102	$41,369
2004	$0	$176	$34,321	$6,978	$14,826	$221	$34,124	$101	$90,747
2003	$0	$0	$15,881	$7,734	$370	$98	$9,888	$61	$34,032
2002	$56	$0	$2,680	$1,165	$0	$815	$2,664	$36	$7,416

Source: 2008 FHFA Annual Report to Congress, pp. 108, 125

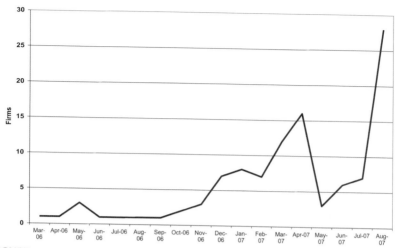

FIGURE 13.2 Monthly failures of subprime mortgage originators. *Source: Rick Green, Lehman Shuts Unit; Toll of Lenders Tops 100: Subprime Scorecard, Bloomberg, August 23, 2007*

Since late 2007, Fannie Mae and Freddie Mac have dominated the mortgage market as never before. The liquidity crisis that began in the subprime and Alt-A sectors subsequently spread to prime jumbo lending, and capital constraints have severely limited the ability of banks to portfolio loans. As a result of these developments, the Agencies' market share has risen to more than 72 percent of originations and 77 percent of all single-family MBS issuances (see Tables 13.1 and 13.7). While mortgage originations are up in 2009 due to record-low interest rates, most lending that occurs today is supported by the GSEs or FHA.

Unfortunately for Fannie Mae and Freddie Mac, the story does not end there. Until recently, the performance of conventional conforming mortgages has remained relatively strong. However, both Fannie Mae and Freddie Mac were exposed to the massive losses from other sectors of the mortgage market. This exposure came from two primary sources. First, both GSEs invested heavily in the triple-A tranches of subprime securities. Indeed, some critics contend that their large investments in such instruments helped to feed the explosive growth of subprime lending. The precipitous decline in the value of these securities, combined with mark-to-market accounting rules, forced both Fannie Mae and Freddie Mac to take massive write-offs at the end of 2007 and again in 2008.

In addition, both companies purchased relatively large volumes of Alt-A mortgages in 2005 and 2006 in an apparent effort to bolster their declining market shares. The poor performance of these loans subsequently led to credit losses on the guarantee sides of the business. In 2008, for example, Alt-A mortgages represented just 9.7 percent of Fannie Mae's book, but accounted for

TABLE 13.9 Net Income Loss of Fannie Mae and Freddie Mac: 1990–2008 ($ millions)

Year	Freddie Mac	Fannie Mae	Total
1990	$414	$1,173	$1,587
1991	$555	$1,363	$1,918
1992	$622	$1,623	$2,245
1993	$786	$1,873	$2,659
1994	$983	$2,132	$3,115
1995	$1,091	$2,144	$3,235
1996	$1,243	$2,725	$3,968
1997	$1,395	$3,056	$4,451
1998	$1,700	$3,418	$5,118
1999	$2,223	$3,912	$6,135
2000	$3,666	$4,448	$8,114
2001	$3,158	$5,894	$9,052
2002	$10,090	$3,914	$14,004
2003	$4,816	$8,081	$12,897
2004	$2,937	$4,967	$7,904
2005	$2,113	$6,347	$8,460
2006	$2,327	$4,059	$6,386
2007	–$3,094	–$2,050	–$5,144
2008	–$50,119	–$58,707	–$108,826

Source: 2008 FHFA Annual Report to Congress, pp. 110, 127

almost 40 percent of the company's credit losses. The experience at Freddie Mac tells a similar story: The serious delinquency rate on Freddie Mac's Alt-A book (which is 8 percent of the portfolio) is more than three times higher than the total portfolio's rate.[13]

As a result of these adverse developments, the net income of both GSEs fell into negative territory in 2007 and then imploded in 2008 (see Table 13.9). Their combined losses in 2008 ($109 billion combined) were higher than the total profits earned by the two GSEs from 1990 through 2007 ($95 billion).

---

13. See Freddie Mac First Quarter 2009 Financial Results Supplement, May 12, 2009.

Mounting financial pressures, along with concerns that the companies might not be able to refinance their maturing debt, ultimately led to their takeover by the federal government on September 7, 2008. Senior management teams were once again replaced. While some believe that the takeovers were at least in part politically motivated, the companies have since required about $60 billion in funding from the US Treasury and the latest OMB estimates now predict that the total could be close to $200 billion. At the same time, the Federal Reserve has had to purchase roughly $500 billion in the GSEs' MBS in order to stabilize the value of their securities.

Ironically, while Fannie Mae and Freddie Mac are now essentially wards of the state, their importance to the mortgage market and overall economy has never been greater. Yet at the same time, most observers believe that their quasi-governmental model is effectively dead, if only because it would be difficult, if not impossible to return to the notion of an "implicit" guarantee. Before turning to some thoughts on alternative models, it is useful to take a critical look at the benefits that the GSEs have brought to the housing and mortgage markets, as well as their underlying weaknesses.

THE BENEFITS OF THE GSE MODEL

In order to understand how we could improve upon the current model, we first need to recognize the benefits that Freddie Mac and Fannie Mae have brought to the mortgage market. The two GSEs have identical charter objectives, namely, to:

- Create a liquid and reliable secondary market for residential mortgages.
- Respond appropriately to the needs of the capital market.
- Improve the distribution of mortgage credit by promoting broader access to affordable mortgage finance.

While opinions differ with respect to the actual accomplishments of Fannie Mae and Freddie Mac, we have organized our discussion around the specific objectives that are embedded in their charters: standardization, liquidity, stability, and access to affordable mortgage finance. For each potential benefit, we discuss both the accomplishments of the GSEs, as well as the specific authorities or functions that were required to produce the results.

Standardization

As noted earlier, one of the first and most important accomplishments of Fannie Mae and Freddie Mac was to standardize the origination, underwriting, and securitization processes. Standardization served to commoditize residential mortgages, which created efficiencies and lowered costs.

For many years, Fannie Mae and Freddie Mac also set the standard for determining an "acceptable" level of credit risk. Their underwriting guidelines and protocols were used throughout the industry in assessing the underlying quality of any loan. While both GSEs abandoned their standards at the height of the subprime boom, they have resumed this role again today, albeit under the watchful eyes of their federal regulator.

Whether or not the benefits of standardization could have been accomplished through other means is a matter for debate. In our view, there is nothing inherent in the GSE model *per se* that makes them particularly suited to play this role, other than their size and market dominance (which were clearly critical). If we abandon the GSE model, this function could presumably be performed by a regulatory agency, the entity (or entities) that take their place, or even an industry consortium. However, in order to be effective and enforceable, standardization requires the entity creating the standards to have sufficient legal, regulatory, or market clout to enforce compliance.

Liquidity

Mortgages, by their very nature, are highly illiquid financial instruments. Not only are they "lumpy"—that is, if you want to invest in a mortgage, you must purchase the entire amount—their performance will differ with the underlying characteristics of the borrower, the property, and the market. The time and expertise required to assess the likely performance of any loan makes them relatively unattractive investments for all but a handful of potential investors. As a result, while there was some interbank trading prior to the development of the secondary market, most institutions held the majority of the loans they originated for the entire life of the loans.

Fannie Mae and Freddie Mac created a liquid mortgage market by purchasing loans from mortgage originators and pooling the loans into mortgage-backed securities. The pooling of loans served to diversify credit risk and enabled investors to purchase shares of the underlying mortgages, as opposed to the mortgages themselves. However, in addition to standardization, the key innovation was the "implicit" guarantee on the credit risk on the underlying loans. While investors continued to hold the interest rate risk, Fannie Mae and Freddie Mac guaranteed the credit losses in the event of mortgage default. Because of their special status as government-sponsored entities, most investors believed that this guarantee was ultimately backed by the full faith and credit of the federal government (despite explicit statements to the contrary that appear on every issuance). As a result, investors had little if any need to conduct an independent assessment of the credit quality of the underlying loans.

Until the recent mortgage meltdown, private label securities were also able to achieve a relatively high degree of liquidity by structuring a security's cash flows into different risk pools, or "tranches," and then using a rating agency to rate the various pieces. In theory, at least, a AAA (or other) rating is supposed to represent the same degree of credit risk regardless of the particular instrument involved. For example, the credit risk on AAA-rated corporate debt and AAA-pieces of subprime securities should in theory be roughly the same. Since investors could presumably rely on rating agencies to take the place of their own due diligence, such ratings played a critical role in fostering the liquidity of private label MBS and, in this sense, achieved the same objective as the implicit guarantees of the GSEs.

However, several other important aspects of the GSE approach contributed to market liquidity in addition to their guarantee. The first is simply their size and market dominance. In general, the larger the volume of securities outstanding, the easier it is to match buyers with potential sellers, thereby enhancing market liquidity. One of the reasons that GSE MBS have traded so well over time is the growing volume of securities outstanding, which totaled about $4.4 trillion at the end of 2008, or about 44 percent of all US Treasuries.

Another important contributor to the liquidity of the mortgage market is the To Be Announced (TBA) market. The TBA market enables mortgage-backed securities to be bought or sold on a forward basis (i.e., prior to the time that the securities are actually formed). While the mortgages that are ultimately used to support the security must have similar characteristics (defined by type, term, and rate), the specific pool (or pools) of loans that will be used to support the securities do not have to be identified at the time of the actual trade. The forward selling of securities in the secondary market enables loan originators to commit to the terms and conditions of loans in advance of their actual funding. As a result, borrowers are able to lock in their mortgage rates well before the mortgage is closed. At the same time, the homogeneity of the underlying pools gives investors the information and confidence they need to invest.

Largely as a result of their assumed or actual guarantees, GSE and Ginnie Mae pass-through securities are traded on a TBA basis, making them the most liquid segment of the mortgage market. In contrast, a TBA market for private label securities has never been developed, in large part due to the complex nature of these instruments, their lack of government backing, and SEC registration requirements. While lock-ins are also available on nonconforming loans, the TBA market is typically used to hedge the interest rate risk. If the TBA market were to disappear, the costs of mortgages would undoubtedly rise, since lenders would have to turn to less suitable instruments to provide the hedge.

Stability

In addition to liquidity, the GSEs were created to ensure a stable and reliable flow of mortgage funding. Although closely linked, liquidity and stability are not synonymous. Although private-label securities were able to provide a relatively high degree of liquidity in recent years, this liquidity rapidly disappeared when the market turned. Indeed, history has consistently shown that in times of crisis, the only way to ensure the continued flow of mortgage funding is to provide some form of government support.

The relative importance of an implicit or explicit government guarantee has never been more evident than it is today. As noted earlier, the GSEs and FHA now account for virtually all lending activity today. While the current crisis began in the subprime and Alt-A markets, it rapidly spread to jumbo mortgages. Despite their relatively strong performance, jumbo originations dropped by about 61 percent between the first quarter of 2007 and the first quarter of 2008. Issuances of securities backed by jumbo mortgages also fell precipitously, from about $120.9 billion in 1Q2007 to just $5.9 billion in 1Q2008. Although some banks continue to originate jumbo loans and hold them in portfolios, their ability to do so has been severely limited by mounting credit losses and increasing demands on their capital.

In response to this situation, loan limits were raised to as high as $729,000 in high cost markets as part of the January 2008 Economic Recovery Act. While the increase was originally scheduled to expire at the end of the year, it was subsequently extended through the end of 2009 with the passage of HERA. Originations of "newly conforming" jumbo loans were at first relatively low. However, once the high cost adjustments were extended[14] the volume began to rise.

Although not as extreme, the patterns observed in the current market have been seen before. Spreads between the rates on jumbo and conventional conforming loans have typically ranged from about 25 to 50 basis points (bps). However, they have consistently widened in times of financial crisis; for example, immediately following the collapse of the Russian Bond Market in 1999 and 911. Spreads today (about 140 bps) are now about three times as high as their historic peak, reflecting the extreme lack of liquidity that continues to characterize the jumbo market. On the other hand, while rates on "newly conforming" jumbo mortgages were initially above those on "traditional" conforming mortgages, the difference has narrowed considerably, suggesting that high cost adjustments to the conforming loan limit have had their intended effect.

Access to Affordable Housing Finance

Finally, the GSEs were also charged with improving the distribution of mortgages and promoting access to affordable mortgage finance. For purposes of this discussion, we have divided this mandate into three components:

- Reducing geographic differences in the availability of mortgage funding
- Making mortgages more affordable to a broader segment of the population, for example, by lowering mortgage rates and reducing down payment requirements
- Serving specific segments of the population considered to be underserved

---

14. Both the GSEs and lenders were initially reluctant to make the system adjustments required to implement the change. In addition, the Securities Industry and Financial Markets Association (SIFMA) opposed including such loans in TBA-eligible pools. (See SIFMA, "Including Jumbos in TBA-Eligible Pools Will Result in Higher Costs for Borrowers," May 2008.) However, SIFMA has since reversed its earlier guidance.

Although the GSEs were generally successful in meeting the first two objectives, their track record on their specific affordable housing goals was mixed.

Reducing Geographic Differences in the Availability of Mortgage Funding

Prior to the development of the secondary market—and the lifting of interstate banking restrictions—local banks and S&Ls were the primary source of mortgage lending. Since they relied on local deposits to fund the majority of their loans, rapidly growing markets—for example, parts of the South and the West—often found it difficult to meet local credit demands. This led to periodic credit rationing and/or spikes in mortgage rates. The opposite pattern occurred in declining markets where there was typically an excess supply of funds.

A Freddie Mac report documented the positive impact of the GSEs on the distribution of mortgage finance by examining regional trends in mortgage rates.[15] During the 1960s and early 1970s, the difference between the highest and lowest regional mortgage rates was generally above one percentage point, rising sharply during periods of disintermediation in 1969–1970 and 1973–1974. By the late 1980s, the regional spread had narrowed to about 0.1 percentage points, a development that was largely attributed to the growth and development of the secondary market.

We could argue that the advent of interstate banking would make this benefit less important today. However, a recent study by Ambrose and Buttimer (2005) found that the GSEs continue to play an important role in reducing regional disparities in mortgage lending. In particular, the study found that prime jumbo lenders tended to avoid rural areas because the small number of transactions in such areas makes it difficult to value collateral. Fannie and Freddie, on the other hand, do as much (relative) business in these areas as anywhere else, because they are required to do so under their charters. The "information" risk arising from rural loans is therefore spread across all conforming lending.

More generally, one of the key benefits of the GSE approach is that it enabled a broad array of institutions to have access to capital markets, ranging from small community banks and mortgage brokers to the nation's largest depositories. This access undoubtedly helps to facilitate a more even and equitable distribution of housing finance than would otherwise be the case. Despite the consolidation that has occurred in the banking sector, geographic coverage remains uneven, particularly in older urban neighborhoods and rural communities. Providing a securitization outlet for smaller, less highly capitalized institutions helps to channel the flow of capital into areas that might not be otherwise served.

---

15. Freddie Mac, "Financing America's Housing: The Vital Role of Freddie Mac," Chapter 4, Exhibit 4.

Lowering Mortgage Rates

Most empirical studies have also concluded that the GSEs have generally lowered mortgage rates by between 25 and 50 basis points (bps). The GSEs have argued that at least some of these savings come from the efficiency and scale of their operations, but most economists attribute the difference to their implicit guarantee. As we discussed in the previous section, the value of this guarantee varies with market conditions, along with the interest rate spread between conforming and jumbo loans. In general, mortgage spreads are relatively high in times of crisis—as they are today—and relatively low when the market has a relatively high tolerance for risk as it did from 2005 through 2007. The same is true for cost of the GSEs' debt.

While most acknowledge that the GSEs have lowered mortgage rates, critics have argued that the GSEs and their shareholders have retained most of the benefits derived from their federal charters. In 1996, a CBO report estimated that less than 60 percent of the GSEs' funding benefits were passed through to consumers in the form of lower mortgage rates, a finding that led it to characterize the GSEs as "leaky" conduits.[16] Even though the GSEs commissioned a number of reports to refute this charge, the evidence remains mixed. Indeed, the extent to which the benefits provided by the GSEs' federal charters are effectively "competed away" undoubtedly varies with the economic environment.

Promoting Access to Low Down Payment, Fixed-Rate Mortgages

The GSEs also actively promoted a market for first-time homeowners by making 30-year fixed-rate mortgages available to borrowers who had relatively little to put down on their loans. By statute, Fannie Mae and Freddie Mac are required to obtain credit enhancement on loans with an LTV of greater than 80 percent. These credit enhancements include mortgage insurance (the most common form), participation, or recourse to the lender. Over the years, both agencies purchased large numbers of loans that fell into this category, thereby providing a cost effective and more efficient alternative to funding previously only available through FHA.

Recently, around 20 percent of Fannie Mae and Freddie Mac's mortgages have been "credit enhanced," meaning that they carry mortgage insurance. Among the mechanisms the institutions used to extend credit to those with small downpayments was the development of increasingly precise underwriting models. These models, along with subsequent review from mortgage insurance companies, had two effects: (1) they made more people eligible for low down payment mortgages; (2) they effectively raised the LTV eligible for prime mortgage funding from 95 percent to 97 percent. Interestingly, Freddie Mac's book of low down payment loans has performed significantly better FHA

---

16. Assessing the Public Costs and Benefits of Fannie Mae and Freddie Mac, Congressional Budget Office, May 1996.

loans: the serious delinquency rate on FHA loans is about twice the rate on credit-enhanced Freddie Mac loans.[17] However, credit enhanced Fannie Mae loans are performing relatively poorly.[18]

Targeted Assistance to Underserved Groups

In addition to lowering mortgage rates for the market at large, the GSEs were given specific Affordable Housing Goals in order to channel a significant portion of their purchase and investment activities to underserved borrowers and neighborhoods. These goals were raised significantly over the years by both Democratic and Republican administrations. For example, FIRREA established an initial goal of 30 percent for mortgages supporting low and moderate income owners and renters. This goal was increased to 40 percent in 1996, 42 percent in 2000, 50 percent in 2001, 52 percent in 2005, 53 percent in 2006, and 55 percent in 2007.[19] In fact, some conservative critics have claimed that the aggressive goals established for the GSEs ultimately led to the subprime crisis and the subsequent collapse of the financial sector (US House of Representatives 2009).

While there is little, if any empirical evidence to support this contention, perhaps a more telling question is whether the GSEs had much of an impact at all on the distribution of mortgage credit flowing to underserved groups. While the GSEs typically met most of their housing goals, most studies have found little if any evidence that their activities have been particularly effective compared to those of portfolio lenders. From the beginning, studies by the Federal Reserve and HUD have concluded that with only a few exceptions, both Fannie Mae and Freddie Mac were consistently "behind the market" in their purchase of so-called affordable loans (i.e., loans to lower income or minority borrowers or underserved neighborhoods). In fact, this persistent finding helped to justify the aggressive increases in the GSEs' Affordable Housing Goals.

Several studies by Stuart Gabriel and Stuart Rosen (2008a, 2008b) have also found little, if any impact of the GSEs on the supply of capital to lower income borrowers and communities. In particular, they

find no evidence of a positive impact of GSE underserved tract status on lending activity in the conforming sector or on local homeownership rates. In addition, underserved status has a negative impact on lending in the non-conforming sector. The absence of a positive GSE impact on conforming mortgage lending activity and homeownership in underserved tracts is striking given extensive loan purchase goals that mandate GSE purchases in such tracts.

---

17. See Mortgage Bankers Association of America, http://www.mbaa.org/NewsandMedia/PressCenter/70050.htm, and Freddie Mac Monthly Volume Summary (2009), http://www.freddiemac.com/investors/volsum/, August.

18. See Fannie Mae Monthly Volume Summary (2009), http://www.fanniemae.com/ir/pdf/monthly/2009/083109.pdf;jsessionid=SOKOIDER5TZABJ2FQSISFGI

19. http://www.huduser.org/Datasets/GSE/gse2007.pdf

Thus, despite claims to the contrary, the body of evidence appears to suggest that the Affordable Housing Goals were not particularly effective in channeling funds to underserved areas. In part, this may reflect the fact that the GSEs were neither required nor inclined to subsidize loans to targeted neighborhoods or borrowers. It may also reflect a genuine disagreement on the underlying purpose of the GSEs. While some maintain that the GSEs should lead the market in terms of their service to targeted groups, others believe that their purpose is to ensure a secondary market outlet for such loans (i.e., to "match" the market). In any event, the wholesale nature of the GSEs' activities has undoubtedly made it difficult for them to support the kind of highly specialized, tailored lending that typically characterizes community loans.

In the end, we believe that the GSEs made credit more accessible and available to the broader mortgage market. They also helped undermine the worst aspects of "relationship lending": blatant preferences for white and male borrowers. One policy purpose of the GSEs—to make mortgages available everywhere—should surely remain intact.

INHERENT WEAKNESSES AND CRITICISMS OF THE GSE APPROACH

Although the GSE approach was highly successful in creating a liquid and stable mortgage market, critics have argued that these were accompanied by a number of inherent weaknesses that ultimately exposed the Federal government to an unnecessary level of risk. Some of these issues have already been described. Others are summarized in the following.

Moral Hazard and Insufficient Oversight

Perhaps the most persistent criticism of the GSE model is associated with the moral hazard that arises from the government's implicit guarantee of their securities and debt. Since the guarantee is provided free of charge, critics have long maintained that Fannie Mae and Freddie Mac are incented to take on excessive risk in order to maximize shareholder profits and executive compensation, with federal taxpayers left holding the bag. This "privatization of profits and socialization of risk" has become a rallying cry for many GSE detractors.

FIRREA established a dedicated federal regulator for the GSEs—the Office of Federal Housing Enterprise Oversight (OFHEO)—to monitor the GSEs' safety and soundness. However, OFHEO's powers were relatively limited, and attempts to increase them over time were consistently overcome by aggressive lobbying on the part of the GSEs. Until the passage of the 2008 Housing and Economic Recovery Act, for example, OFHEO did not have the power to adjust the GSEs' capital requirements, limit their portfolio holdings, or otherwise take them into conservatorship or receivership in the event of impending failure.

Absent strong regulation, GSEs' incentives to manage their overall risk had to come from the market, company shareholders, or the GSEs themselves. Unfortunately, such self-regulation did not produce the desired results. Market discipline was lax as a result of the GSEs' government ties, and management at both GSEs ultimately succumbed to pressures to maintain their market shares in search of profitability. However, although it is tempting to attribute these short-comings to the inherent tensions between the public and private purposes of the GSEs, the same dynamics ultimately led to the demise of "purely private" financial entities. In our view, the events of the past two years demonstrate the importance of strong regulation in addition to an inherent weakness in the GSE model per se.

Systemic Risk/Too Big to Fail

Another related concern was that the GSEs had simply become too big to fail—a concern that ultimately proved to be justified. As noted earlier, GSE debt and securities are now an integral part of global capital markets. Since GSE mortgage-backed securities are given favorable capital treatment,[20] they are a significant part of banks' portfolio holdings. As a result, any significant deterioration in their market value would trigger a wave of secondary effects that would ultimately threaten the banking system. GSE debt is also widely distributed, with much of it held by foreign countries, particularly China. As a result, any devaluation of this debt would have international repercussions that transcended the US housing market. While the charge of "too big to fail" is hardly unique to the GSEs, it is a legitimate concern. The challenge is how to get the volume that is required for liquidity with less concentration and lower risk.

Lack of Competition

Critics have also charged that the lack of competition between the two GSEs (and between the GSEs and the private sector) has led to excess profits and reduced the benefits that otherwise would have been received by consumers. While economic theory suggests that duopolies can be highly competitive, there are strong disagreements on whether this applies to Freddie Mac and Fannie Mae. In our view, the guarantee side of the GSEs' business was in fact highly competitive, as evidenced by the steady erosion of their guarantee fees through much of the period. Average guarantee fees for Fannie Mae fell from around 25 bps in the early 1980s to less than 20 bps in 2001; for Freddie Mac, they fell from a high of 26 bps in 1983 to 16.6 bps in 2005.[21]

---

20. Their risk-based weighted is only 20 percent, meaning that well-capitalized banks need only hold 1.6 percent capital against MBS.
21. See FHFA Annual Report to Congress, 2008, pp. 1, 127. http://www.fhfa.gov/webfiles/2335/FHFA_ReportToCongress2008508.pdf

Nevertheless, the "appropriate" number of GSEs will be an issue going forward. Unless returns are regulated (see the Utility model discussed in the next section), two GSEs are clearly better than one. However, whether or not we should stop at only two is an open question. While additional GSEs would undoubtedly enhance competition, it is important to recognize the trade-off between concerns over excess profits and market liquidity. In general, as long as the securities are issued under the individual GSEs' names, increasing the number of GSEs will reduce the liquidity of their securities and ultimately, increase the cost of mortgages to consumers, thereby offsetting at least some of the potential gains.

Concentration of Risk

Another criticism of the GSE model is that it led to an unnecessary concentration of risk. Ironically, this argument typically focused on the GSEs' growing portfolios and their increased exposure to interest rate risk. Because of their government ties, the GSEs were able to fund their mortgage holdings by issuing massive amounts of debt at favorable rates, and generate returns of 15 percent or more from the resulting spreads. Although the authority to hold a certain amount of mortgages in portfolio can be justified on both operational and policy grounds—for example, it can help to stabilize markets in uncertain times—in our view, the large portfolios developed by the GSEs were primarily driven by the desire to maximize shareholder profits, and take advantage if their debt subsidy, and not their public mission.

At the same time, while it was widely recognized that the GSEs played an important role in the diversification of credit risk by pooling loans across geographic regions, relatively little attention was paid to the fact that as the GSEs increased their market share, credit risk became increasingly concentrated in their hands. To a large extent, this risk was offset by requirements that loans with down payments of less than 20 percent—the riskiest segment of the GSEs' business--carry private mortgage insurance, or PMI. Such insurance not only protected the GSEs from a portion of their losses, it also subjected the loans to another set of eyes in assessing credit risk. Yet, as noted earlier, it was credit, not interest rate risk that ultimately brought the GSEs down.

Inadequate Capital Standards

With the advantages of hindsight, it is also clear that the GSEs' capital standards were insufficient to protect them from the meltdown of the housing market that began in late 2006. Under the guidelines, the GSEs were required to meet a capital ratio of 2.5 percent, or a "risk-based capital" requirement, whichever was higher. In theory, the risk-based capital standards were designed to enable the GSEs to survive two different 10-year scenarios of extreme market stress: one defined by the credit losses that occurred in the so-called "Oil Patch" states in the early 1980s; the other defined by a rising interest rate environment.

Risk-based capital standards were not implemented until 2002. However, in each year thereafter, the minimum capital requirement remained the binding constraint; that is, the amount of capital required under the minimum capital standard was greater than the risk-based capital requirement. This was true for both GSEs, but the differences were particularly large for Freddie Mac. In 2007, for example, Freddie Mac's risk-based capital requirement ($14.1 billion) was only 53 percent of its minimum capital standard ($26,473.)[22] Yet within a year, Freddie Mac had a regulatory capital deficit of $41.3 billion.

Despite the best intentions—and sophisticated analyses that were used to develop the standards and determine capital adequacy—the GSEs' capital requirements ultimately proved to be inadequate. Many papers will undoubtedly be written on exactly what went wrong. However, some potential candidates include:

- Failure to adequately account for the monoline nature of the GSEs' business and their resulting exposure to catastrophic risk
- Mark-to-market accounting requirements in an environment when the market has ceased to function
- The ability to use the value of future tax credits as a form of capital
- The inability to predict the performance of new mortgage products such as Alt-A loans
- The ability to substitute the capital required for the investment and guarantee sides of their businesses, which tended to be offsetting

Once the current crisis passes, regulators will clearly have to go back to the drawing board and determine why seemingly state-of-the-art risked-based capital standards ultimately failed so miserably.

Political Influence

Finally, no discussion of the GSEs could be complete without at least a brief reference to their enormous political influence on Capitol Hill. Until their government takeovers, Fannie Mae and Freddie Mac were among the nation's largest political contributors, and their largess was directed to Democrats and Republicans alike. Both routinely held events in key Congressional districts announcing special affordable lending initiatives or grants to local nonprofits. Both routinely funded national nonprofits and advocacy groups that were useful to their cause. Both routinely hired executives with strong political ties.

---

22. These figures exclude the 30 percent surcharge imposed on Freddie Mac at the end of 2003. Fannie Mae was also subject to a capital surcharge, beginning in 2005. See 2008 Annual Report, Federal Housing Finance Agency, Tables 9 and 18.

Such activities served to protect the GSEs from repeated efforts to reign in their activities by unsympathetic members of Congress and by both the Clinton and Bush Administrations. In the end, it took their financial collapse—and an explicit prohibition to end all lobbying activities—to bring the GSEs' influence to a close. Aggressive lobbying activities are hardly unique to the GSEs; going forward, however, the regulator must be protected from the kind of political influence that made it difficult if not impossible to implement meaningful reform.

PRINCIPLES FOR REFORM

The recent history of the GSEs and the broader mortgage market suggest several guiding principles that might be used in devising an alternative approach. While others could be added to the list, the principles discussed next provide a starting point for assessing the numerous proposals that have posited by advocates of GSE reform. The challenge is to redesign a system that retains most of the benefits that the GSEs have produced to date, while minimizing their major shortcomings.

1. Strong Regulation in Both the Primary and Secondary Markets

Given the experience of the past two years, any proposal for GSE reform must include provisions for strong government oversight. While HERA replaced OFHEO with a new federal regulator—the Federal Housing Finance Agency (FHFA)—and gave it significantly broader authorities and enforcement powers, it did so after most of the major damage had been done. Going forward, HFFA (or its successor) must continue to have the power and independence it needs to provide meaningful oversight. Efforts to strengthen the regulation of the secondary market need to be accompanied with increased oversight of the primary market and stronger consumer protections.

2. Appropriate Capital Standards

Capital standards need to be sufficiently strong to ensure the long-term safety and soundness of the GSEs or their replacement entities. History has clearly shown that sophisticated models can be wrong; in the end, it is simply impossible to predict the future precisely from the past. As a result, the regulator must be given the power and the flexibility that it needs to adjust requirements on an as-needed basis. Issues concerning capital adequacy extend far beyond the GSEs, and will ultimately affect the future structure of the mortgage industry. Such standards should be consistent, meaningful, and designed to reflect the underlying risks that are assumed by any party or associated with any product.

3. Explicit Guarantee

The experience of the past two years has also demonstrated the importance of a government guarantee in ensuring an adequate flow of mortgage funding in good times and bad. It is time to make the guarantee explicit. Even if we wanted to return to an "implicit" guarantee, the market would not believe it. It is better to provide an explicit guarantee—and *be able to charge for it*—than to continue with an approach that is the functional equivalent of "Don't ask, don't tell." Any guarantee should be structured in a way that minimizes moral hazard.

4. Market-Driven Approach

Any efforts for reform should also preserve the market-driven approach that was one of the major strengths of the GSEs. It is difficult to imagine how a government-owned entity—whether independent or part of another agency—could have produced the many socially valuable innovations that were spearheaded by the GSEs, such as state of the art underwriting tools. At the same time, a market-driven approach requires meaningful competition. The current system attempted to achieve this objective by creating two GSEs with identical charters. Any reform proposal needs to assess the extent to which it would encourage or impede a more competitive mortgage market.

5. Risk Sharing

Proposals to reform the current system should also encourage risk sharing. Not only would this help to align incentives among the various parties involved in the transaction, it would also encourage the use of independent analytics and provide another set of eyes in assessing the credit risk.

It is important to recognize that the conventional conforming market already has the principle of risk-sharing embedded in its design. The GSEs are required to obtain private mortgage insurance (or other forms of credit enhancement) for any loan with an LTV above 80 percent. As a result, all high LTV loans have two entities involved in sharing the credit risk.[23] In contrast, investment banks and rating agencies effectively set the underwriting standards in the subprime market and had no skin in the game. As a result, they had little if any incentive to manage the credit risk. While one could argue that the GSEs had insufficient

---

23. In addition, lenders who sell their loans into the secondary market are subject to repurchase requests in the event that the loans do not comply with established underwriting guidelines. Since lenders must hold reserves to cover any future repurchase requests, some consider this a form of risk-sharing, i.e., having "skin in the game." However, since many originators were undercapitalized—and since the lenders were only responsible for *adhering* to established guidelines (as opposed to the guidelines themselves)—this form of risk-sharing was not particularly effective.

skin in the game, their incentives were much closer to being appropriate than institutions who had no capital requirements and whose business was largely driven by fees.

6. More Appropriate Portfolio Authority

The GSEs' authority to hold loans in an investment portfolio should be priced properly and closely regulated. Although it was credit risk that ultimately brought the GSEs into conservatorship, this does not negate the continued interest rate risk that is associated with the $1.6 trillion in mortgages they currently hold. While initially HERA required each GSE to reduce its mortgage assets by at least 10 percent each year until they reach of level of $250 billion, this requirement has been suspended due to the continued turmoil in the market. Going forward, however, it is crucial that GSE portfolios be prevented from growing *in response to a subsidized interest rate bet*. A tax on debt issuance such that the cost of capital for GSEs was similar to the cost of capital for institutions at similar risk would at once allow GSEs to have the portfolios necessary for dealing with times of crisis, while mitigating the problem of subsidizing risk taking. More robust capital standards would also reduce the attractiveness of debt-financed portfolios.

7. Affordable Housing Goals that are Aligned with the Primary Market

The Affordable Housing Goals also need to be reconsidered. Volume-oriented targets clearly did not work, and may have done more harm than good. At a minimum, the goals established for the GSEs should be consistent with the requirements imposed on the primary market to ensure a secondary outlet for such loans. To the extent that subsidies are desired, such subsidies should be made explicit. One approach would be to charge a fee for the government guarantee, and use part of the proceeds to subsidize mortgages to targeted groups, perhaps through a Housing Trust Fund. Another would be to require the GSEs to set aside a certain share of their pretax profits for activities and investments that directly support affordable housing. Presumably, making the subsidies more explicit would improve the allocation of scarce resource, and lead to better public policy.

8. Renewed Focus on Multifamily Rental Housing

Finally, while our discussions have clearly focused on the single-family side of the GSEs' businesses, any reform proposal must ensure the continued availability of mortgage funding for multifamily rental housing. This could be done by establishing a specialized conduit. Like other segments of the private market, the market for commercial mortgage-backed securities (CMBS) has virtually disappeared, and is unlikely to come back any time soon. Although rental housing remains the only viable option for many of the country's lower income families, relatively little is currently being done to support investment in such properties.

ALTERNATIVE MODELS

In this final section of the paper, we examine several alternative structures that have been proposed for the GSEs. While they by no means exhaust the range of proposals that have been or could be made, they represent the some of the major options identified thus far. In considering these different alternatives, we have made a number of key assumptions:

- The federal government should continue to promote a liquid and stable mortgage market. While some will undoubtedly argue that housing already absorbs too much of the nation's capital, we believe that continued support is justified on both social and economic grounds. As history has shown, a liquidity crisis in the mortgage market can quickly spread to other sectors of the economy, leading to widespread declines in consumption and employment. Since any financial reform is unlikely to eliminate future financial crises, the GSEs or their replacements must be built to withstand periodic shocks.
- We have ruled out the possibility of a purely "private" solution. Absent a federal guarantee, a private sector approach cannot produce a consistent, reliable flow of mortgage lending. Although the federal government could conceivably provide a back-stop in times of crisis—for example, the Federal Reserve could be authorized to purchase mortgages on an as-needed basis— this should be a measure of last resort.
- We have assumed that transforming the GSEs into government agencies— perhaps by merging them in whole or in part with FHA and Ginnie Mae—would not produce the innovative, market-driven approach that has characterized the mortgage market for most of the past 30 years. While FHA will undoubtedly continue to play an important role for first-time homeowners, it should not be the source of liquidity for the overall market. However, in the event that a public option is selected, risk-sharing arrangements with the private sector should be encouraged, if not required.[24]
- We have limited our discussion to issues related specifically to Fannie Mae and Freddie Mac. Although we recognize that any solution will have to be achieved in the broader context of financial reform—including the future of

---

24. One such model, which was promoted by the MI industry at the beginning of the decade, would place private mortgage insurers in the first loss position, with FHA assuming the remainder of the risk. See Schnare and Woodward (2001).

FHA, Ginnie Mae, and the Federal Home Loan Banks—such topics simply are beyond this paper's scope.

With these caveats in mind, the following discussion looks at some of the major alternatives that are being considered by policy makers, and one that has yet to reach their radar screen. These models include:

- A "status quo" approach, which would preserve most of Fannie Mae and Freddie Mac, but with stronger oversight, limited portfolio authorities, and an explicit guarantee
- A "public utility" approach, which would limit the rate of return that could be earned by the GSEs
- A "cooperative" approach, which would establish one or more GSEs that are owned by a consortium(s) of lenders
- A "covered bond" approach, which would establish one or more GSEs to issue bonds collateralized by mortgages pledged by banks and carrying an FDIC-like guarantee
- A "guaranteed MBS" approach, which would establish two or more federally chartered entities that would acquire and insure loans like the GSEs do today, but deliver them to a common issuer for securitization and guarantee

While other possibilities are clearly possible—and while the final solution is likely to be different from any of the specific models considered here—we believe that this exercise illustrates the broad advantages and disadvantages of different options for reform.

Reconstituted GSEs

Fannie Mae and Freddie Mac have long been strange hybrid creatures, and are accidents of history. Fannie was created as a public entity in 1938, and then split in two in 1968: the "new" Fannie Mae was to be a private company, while Ginnie Mae would be a public company that securitized government-insured mortgages. Fannie's hybrid nature arose at least in part because its debt was issued as public debt, and then became private. This made the government's treatment of the company ambiguous. According to a former member of the Clinton administration, there was a longstanding debate within the Treasury Department as to what to do in the event that Fannie (or Freddie) blew up—reinforcing the ambiguous nature of how much the government would in fact guarantee Fannie and Freddie debt.

As we have discussed, the GSEs actually worked quite well, and their contribution to systemic risk was quite negligible, until they began to increase rapidly the size of their portfolios in roughly 1997–1998. Before that point, their credit risk was manageable and, because their portfolios were fairly small, the interest rate risk they bore did not create systemic risk for the broader economy. In 1995, for example, the GSEs' total portfolios ($350 billion) was 5 percent of

GDP (\$ 7.5 trillion.) Today, their portfolios (\$ 2 trillion) represent 15 percent of GPD (\$14 trillion).

At the same time, the GSE structure arguably allowed for the existence of 30-year, fixed-rate, self-amortizing mortgages; households could offload their interest rate risk to entities such as insurance companies and pensions funds with long-duration liabilities. At the same time, because of their implicit government backing, the GSEs could raise capital during periods of stress in the financial markets. While other financial conduits shut down during the 1997–1998 financial crises and in the aftermath of the September 11, 2001 attacks, the residential mortgage market kept on cooking along with readily available capital and low spreads.

The clever characteristic of the GSE structure was the hybrid nature that is now under criticism. On the one hand, the fact that they were owned by shareholders and had a valuable franchise meant that they had incentives to cost minimize. On the other hand, when systemic risk outside of the housing market threatened to squeeze mortgage finance, the implied government backstop meant that they could continue to fund mortgages.

As far as we can tell, the only country other than the United States with long-duration, freely prepayable mortgages is Denmark. Denmark, like the United States, uses capital markets, rather than deposits, to fund mortgages, but the structure that it uses is a covered bond structure, and so differs from the GSE structure. Whether a covered bond structure would have performed as well during times of financial stress is an open question. Recent experience suggests that it would not.

But for the GSE structure to work going forward, a couple of genies will need to be returned to their bottles. One genie, of course, never can be returned: implicit guarantees are gone for awhile, if not forever. For the GSE structure to work going forward, however, GSEs must return to being entities whose only mission is to fund prime mortgages. This means mortgages with substantial credit enhancements (either low LTVs or mortgage insurance), lending to borrowers with strong credit histories, and purchasing only well-documented loans.

We also now know that the GSEs used their funding advantage to build large portfolios that were, in the short run, highly profitable. They appeared profitable because of leverage: their capital bases were small, and so the difference between their cost of funds and their returns on mortgages was magnified by as much as 40 times. But this leverage also meant that their businesses were far more volatile than the underlying mortgage market—which has been quite volatile recently even on an unlevered basis. Many of us did not foresee just how volatile the mortgage market could be, but even so, many of us also worried about the rapid growth of the GSE portfolios.

Regulators could take three approaches to limiting the size of GSE portfolios. One—which is currently in place—would place a firm ceiling on portfolio size. While this would limit risk, it could also prevent the GSEs from providing liquidity at times of financial stress. The second approach would raise capital standards on mortgages. The GSEs have been required to hold 2.5 percent capital against their portfolios. If required capital was doubled, it would reduce volatility by

50 percent (this is a standard Modligiani-Miller result; Modigliani and Miller 1958). It would also raise the cost of mortgage funding. If required return on equity is 15 percent above short-term treasuries, and required return on equity was invariant to capital structure (a conservative assumption), then mortgage costs to borrowers would rise by 37 bps. This might simply reflect appropriate pricing.

Alternatively, or in addition, Congress could require GSEs to pay taxes on newly issued debt, so that the cost of debt to GSEs would accurately reflect their risk. Finally, to make it clear that debt holders are on their own, the government could explicitly guarantee mortgage-backed securities not held in Fannie and Freddie's portfolios, while explicitly *not* guaranteeing Fannie and Freddie debt. The combination of higher capital standards and a tax on debt would lead to a natural reduction in portfolio size.

It is worth noting that if the United States is going to continue to have fixed rate prepayable long-term mortgages, someone will have to hold interest rate risk. When depositories held it, as they did in the 1960s and 1970s, the government bailed them out. Were investment banks to hold it, precedent suggests that, in a crisis, the government would bail them out. Whomever holds the risk, the best policy can do is try to get the price and capital structure of it right. But it is difficult to believe that the GSE structure per se creates the risk.

Utility Model

Federal Reserve Chair Ben Bernanke describes a utility model as a potential mechanism for mortgage funding:[25]

A public utility model offers one possibility for incorporating private ownership. In such a model, the GSE remains a corporation with shareholders but is overseen by a public board. Beyond simply monitoring safety and soundness, the regulator would also establish pricing and other rules consistent with a promised rate of return to shareholders. Public utility regulation itself, of course, has numerous challenges and drawbacks, such as reduced incentives to control costs. Nor does this model completely eliminate the private-public conflict of the current GSE structure. But a public utility model might allow the enterprise to retain some of the flexibility and innovation associated with private-sector enterprises in which management is accountable to its shareholders. And, although I have noted the problems associated with private-public conflict, that conflict is not always counterproductive; an entity with private shareholders may be better able to resist political influences, which, under some circumstances, may lead to better market outcomes.

In addition, some believe that having a single mortgage utility could also help to level the playing field for small originators, since guarantee fees would be set by the regulator, and not negotiated as they are today.

---

25. http://www.federalreserve.gov/newsevents/speech/bernanke20081031a.htm, accessed on August 12, 2009.

We could make a case that a conduit for mortgage funding is a natural monopoly since the fixed costs are high and the marginal costs are relatively constant. The fixed costs are the development of the infrastructure to underwrite mortgages and to pass cash flows through to investors in mortgage-backed securities in a timely and accurate manner. Such a setup involves heavy use of technology, and a staff of highly trained statistical and financial analysts. Fannie Mae and Freddie Mac both have hundreds of PhDs on their staffs, and their principal function is the development, calibration, and review of underwriting and capital allocation models. This is expensive.

If the supply of capital for prime mortgage funding is elastic, the average cost curve for mortgage funding will be downward sloping at all relevant points. This means that the most efficient mortgage industry is one that has only one funding firm. But monopolies lead to suboptimal outcomes as well.

If this is an accurate depiction of the mortgage funding industry, it is very similar to a power utility, and therefore might be regulated in a similar manner. Some appealing features of the utility model is that it employs private capital while closely regulating private returns and supports a more "highly focused" use of public benefits by restraining the types and size of mortgages that would be allowed. But there are issues: how does government regulate mortgage pricing such that (1) the mortgage firm engages in cost minimizing practices and (2) earns an acceptable, but not excessive return?

In the context of the guarantee business, the cost of providing the guarantee consists of four components: the expected losses arising from default, overhead costs, float (although this is quite small), and a reasonable rate of return for investors. It would be up to the regulator to determine what constitutes reasonable. This is problem enough. More problematic is the fact that default costs are tied to underwriting policy. Therefore, the regulator of the mortgage utility would have to be a partner in determining underwriting standards. This, again, is a problem.

At the end of the day, a utility model would require reliance on highly standardized mortgages, and might be cumbersome and unresponsive to market conditions. This is one of the reasons so many utilities and utility-like industries, such as airlines, trucking companies, telecommunications companies, and power companies, became deregulated during the 1970s and 1980s. The very pricing structure of utilities, moreover, reduces the incentive to reduce costs via innovation. It may be possible to design a regulatory structure that incorporates incentives for such behavior, but such a model is largely untested, particularly in a financial context.

Cooperative Model

The United States has long had a cooperative model of mortgage finance alongside the more recent GSE model. When Freddie Mac was created in 1970, it was a cooperative owned by savings and loans. One way the government helped the savings and loans recapitalize was by converting Freddie into a publicly traded company and allowing the thrifts to sell their cooperative interests. The Federal Home Loan Bank System is also essentially a cooperative, since the customers of the FHLBs—banks and savings and loans—are also its shareholders.

Spenser, Brown, and Shields (2009) of the Federal Home Loan Bank of Atlanta argue that the FHLB model has provided capital stability. They note:

The first benefit we attribute to the FHLBanks' cooperative structure is capital stability. This feature was cited by FHFA Director Lockhart at the time of Fannie Mae's and Freddie Mac's conservatorship and more recently after some of the FHLBanks suspended excess stock repurchases in order to build capital. Most of the FHLBanks' capital is contributed by members as a result of their use of FHLBank products, such as advances. Because advances are by far the largest asset class owned by the FHLBanks,73 this structure permits the FHLBanks' capital base to grow and shrink with their asset size and has sometimes been referred to as capital "on demand."

They also argue that the FHLBs fulfill their mission better because they are not under pressure to earn a return on capital (although they pay a tax to support affordable housing program, the FHLBs were not subject to affordable housing goals, although this assertion is open to question). Flannery and Wall (2006) are not as sanguine about the safety of the FHLB coop structure. They note that several liability features of the FHLBs create serious moral hazard problems. And recent events have shown that the FHLBs have not been immune from getting into trouble. Recently, the San Francisco and Seattle FHLBs have faced capital shortfalls. And the Chicago FHLB has faced such large losses that it has considered merging with its Dallas counterpart.[26]

The cooperative structure can also lead to self-dealing. Frame, Hancock, and Passmore determined that the banks used FHLB advances for a variety of non-housing purposes. Because money is fungible, banks could use FHLB advances for almost anything—including hiding capital short-falls.

Perhaps the greatest problem with the coop model is the issue of measuring capital. In the case of the FHLBs, it was very opaque: banks were required to purchase equity. Bank holdings were counted as tier-I capital. But the banks, of course, are highly levered. Finally, because the owners of cooperatives are also its customers, we see the possibility that a coop model would be dominated by large banks. We could argue that indeed this has happened in the Federal Home Loan Bank System.

Covered Bonds

Ribakova, Avesani, and Pascual (2007) provide a good description of covered bonds as a funding mechanism for mortgages:[27]

26. http://www.bizjournals.com/atlanta/stories/2008/11/24/story5.html
27. See Ribakova, et al., The Use of Mortgage Covered Bonds, IMF Working Paper No. 07/20.

Covered bonds are debt instruments secured against a pool of mortgages to which the investor has a preferred claim in the event of an issuer default. In EU countries, the issuance of mortgage covered bonds is regulated by laws that define the criteria for eligible assets as well as various other specific requirements. In most cases, assets are earmarked as collateral for the outstanding covered bond and are kept in separate cover pools. In some countries (such as Spain), all mortgages on the balance sheet of the issuer are acting as collateral for the bonds. Following the 'cover principle', the outstanding amount and interest claims on covered bonds must be covered by the amount of eligible cover assets.

In contrast to other mortgage-backed securities (MBS), there is a special legal regime that governs the issuance and provides "special" protection to investors. The law governs the type of eligible assets for the covered pool, the asset/liability management (ALM), credit enhancements and over-collateralization requirements. Additionally, the cover pool remains on the balance sheet of the issuer and eligible assets are substitutable. Individual covered bonds do not face individual claims within the respective pool. Instead, all mortgage loans are facing the total volume of all outstanding mortgage bonds. In fact, mortgage cover pools are dynamic and of unlimited duration (when a loan meets the legal requirements, it is included in the existing pool). At the same time, when a loan is repaid or if, for other reasons, it no longer meets the quality criteria, it is withdrawn immediately. The large number of claims within the mortgage pools should offset the risks of individual claims, which constitutes an important safety criterion for the bondholder.

Covered bonds have worked well as a mechanism for funding loans in Germany, Spain, and Denmark. But despite the features described earlier, only Denmark designs mortgages that have potentially long duration and have an effective mechanism for prepayment (borrowers in Denmark can purchase their mortgages back at par value at any time). It is not entirely clear why this is the case, however it does indicate a limitation with the instrument in a large market.

One point in the description, moreover, is particularly germane: "Additionally, the cover pool remains on the balance sheet of the issuer and eligible assets are substitutable." This creates a regulatory problem for banks. Unlike mortgage-backed securities, which relieve banks of the need to hold capital against mortgage risk (because banks have offloaded the mortgages entirely), covered bonds would require banks to hold capital, which would perhaps make them less able to finance other types of business. If there were a move to a covered bond mechanism, it would be important to think through the implications of the instrument to mortgage borrowing (although perhaps consumers have paid too little for mortgages to this point on a risk-adjusted basis, and requiring banks to hold them—even remotely—on their balance sheet would lead to more appropriate pricing). Once again, we also have some concern that this model would ultimately be dominated by large banks, which would have economies of scale in bond issuance. The recent past suggests to us that maintaining a healthy community bank sector (i.e., a not-too-big-to-fail bank sector) is important.

Guaranteed MBS

The Guaranteed MBS approach would support a securitization model by providing an explicit federal guarantee on mortgage-backed securities.[28] The government guarantee would ensure the liquidity and stability of the MBS market, and support the continuance of the 30-year fixed-rate mortgage. It would also preserve the TBA market, which is critical to that liquidity. However, the federal guarantee would apply only to the MBS. It would not apply to the debt of the entity that issues the bonds.

Although there are many ways to structure a model of this kind, one approach would be to create a relatively small number (e.g., 3 to 5) of federally chartered mortgage conduits that would acquire loans in the primary market and deliver them to a common issuer for pooling and securitization. The resulting securities would be guaranteed by an FDIC-like entity in exchange for an appropriate fee. The federal guarantee would ensure the timely payment of principle and interest to MBS investors in a manner analogous to a Ginnie Mae "wrap." However, the credit risk on the underlying mortgages would be held by the mortgage conduits and other market participants, including mortgage insurers. Since the private sector would be bearing most of the risk, the moral hazard otherwise associated with the guarantee would be reduced.

Mortgages acquired by the mortgage conduits would be delivered to a common issuer for pooling and securitization. Delivering loans into a common security would promote a level of liquidity that would be difficult to achieve if multiple entities issued multiple MBS. In addition, since the mortgage-backed securities would not be issued in the conduit's name, the systemic risk associated with a conduit's failure would be much lower than is the case for Fannie Mae and Freddie Mac.

The debt or other obligations of the federally chartered conduits would not be subject to the federal guarantee. Since the federal guarantee would not apply to the conduits themselves, this will greatly reduce the moral hazard inherent in the current GSE approach. Moreover, due the use of a common issuer, the failure of one conduit will no longer threaten the collapse of the system as a whole. As a result, a conduit can be allowed to fail without jeopardizing the overall economy.

While the conduits could take many forms, competition among multiple conduits with identical missions would help to promote innovation and market efficiencies. This would not be the case if the GSEs were replaced with a single government agency such as FHA, or by an industry-owned utility or cooperative. Since mortgages would be delivered to a common issuer for securitization, the model could accommodate more than two GSEs without jeopardizing the liquidity of the underlying securities. Indeed, we could begin by retaining the

28. This general approach is discussed in Ravi and Mehta (2009).

appropriate parts of Fannie Mae and Freddie Mac, and then adding additional conduits over time.

One of the disadvantages of this approach is that it may be less appropriate for multifamily housing, which is less susceptible to securitization. The CMBS market has all but disappeared and is unlikely to come back anytime soon. Although the GSEs have issued a certain level of multifamily MBS over the years, they retained most of their multifamily purchases in their investment portfolios. Limiting the federal guarantee to securities issued by the mortgage conduit may have the unintended effect of disadvantaging rental housing. As a result, some consideration would have to be given on ways to mitigate such effects, including the creation of a conduit that focused exclusively on multifamily properties, exempting multifamily mortgages from any limitations that are imposed on the conduits' portfolios, or subsidizing the fee for the government wrap.

Another issue that would have to be resolved is the extent to which the conduits should be allowed to hold investment portfolios. At a minimum, limited portfolio authority would be required for operational and pooling purposes, and to ensure that small originators can continue to deliver mortgages on a loan-by-loan basis. In addition, limiting the GSEs' activities to the securitization side of the business could conceivably lead to higher mortgage rates. Since the GSEs will no longer have their investment portfolios as their major source of earnings, guarantee fees could rise even in the face of increased competition.

CONCLUSIONS

The models described in this chapter all have distinct advantages and disadvantages. Even if we accept a given approach, there are numerous variants on each approach, each involving important policy issues. In general, we prefer the structured MBS model, since it combines the liquidity and stability of a government guarantee with the competitive forces of multiple conduits and reliance on private capital. However, like other aspects of the policy development process, the devil will undoubtedly be in the details.

There are also thorny issues related to the restructuring (or dissolution) of Fannie Mae and Freddie Mac and how to handle their outstanding securities. Some have proposed splitting the agencies into a "good bank" and a "bad bank," while others believe that the magnitude of their current losses would preclude a strategy of this kind. Regardless of what happens, parts of Fannie Mae and Freddie Mac are likely to survive, and provide at least some of the basic infrastructure for their replacements.

In the end, whatever approach is selected, it should be driven by the same policy objectives that led to the creation the GSEs, namely, to ensure a stable and liquid secondary mortgage market that meets the needs of investors and promotes access to affordable housing finance. While the solution might differ, these objectives are as relevant today as they were four decades ago, when

Fannie Mae and Freddie Mac were first charged with creating a viable secondary market for conventional mortgages.

REFERENCES

Ambrose, Brent W., Buttimer, Richard Jr, 2005. GSE impact on rural mortgage markets. Regional Science and Urban Economics, Elsevier vol. 35 (4), 417–443.

Gabriel, Stuart A., Rosenthal, Stuart, 2008a. The GSEs, CRA and Homeownership in Targeted Underserved Neighborhoods. http://faculty.maxwell.syr.edu/rosenthal/.

Gabriel, Stuart A., Rosenthal, Stuart, 2008b. Do the GSEs Expand the Supply of Mortgage Credit? New Evidence of Crowd Out in the Secondary Mortgage Market. http://faculty.maxwell.syr.edu/rosenthal/.

Gates, Susan, et al., November 18–19, 2003. "Automated Underwriting: Friend or Foe to Low – Mod Households and Neighborhoods? Building Assets, Building Credit: A Symposium on Improving Financial Services in Low-Income Communities".

Goldberg, Michael, Schnare, Ann B., November 2008. A Financial Analysis of the FHA Insurance Fund. Working paper.

Goldberg, Michael, Schnare, Ann B., January 2009. An Updated Look at the FHA Fund.

HUD, FHA, HUD, Fraud Prevention, June 18, 2009. Statement of Kenneth M. Donohue, Inspector General, US Department of Housing and Urban Development.

Jaffee, Dwight, Quigley, John, 2007. Housing Subsidies and Homeowners: What Role for Government Sponsored Enterprises? University of California-Berkeley working paper. Accessed at http://elsa.berkeley.edu/users/quigley/pdf/JQ_Housing_Subsidies_Proof_053007.pdf (12.08.09.).

McLean, Bethany, January 24, 2005. The Fall of Fannie Mae. Fortune Magazine.

Modigliani, F., Miller, M.H., 1958. The Cost of Capital, Corporate Finance and the Theory of Investment. American Economic Review 48, 261–297.

Ravi, O., Mehta, A., August 7, 2009. Future of the Housing Finance System and the GSEs, The Mortgage Investor. Bank of America Merrill Lynch.

Ribakova, Elina, Renzo Avesani, Garcia Pascual, Antonio I., (2007). The Use of Mortgage Covered Bonds, IMF Working Paper No. 07/20.

Schnare, Ann B., Woodward, Susan E., July 2001. An Analysis of Ginnie Mae Choice.

US House of Representatives, July 7, 2009. The Role of Government Affordable Housing Policy in Creating the Global Financial Crisis of 2008. Staff report, U.S. House of Representatives, Committee on Oversight and Government Reform.

Index